The American Life of Ernestine L. Rose

Writing American Women
Carol A. Kolmerten, *Series Editor*

Ernestine L. Rose.
Courtesy of the Schlesinger Library, Radcliffe College.

The American Life of
Ernestine L. Rose

Carol A. Kolmerten

Syracuse University Press

The paper used in this publication meets the minimum requirements
of American National Standard for Information Sciences—Permanence
of Paper for Printed Library Materials, ANSI Z39.48-1984. ∞™

Library of Congress Cataloging-in-Publication Data
Kolmerten, Carol A., 1946–
The American Life of Ernestine L. Rose / Carol A. Kolmerten. —
1st ed.
p.   cm. — (Writing American women)
Includes bibliographical references and index.
ISBN 0-8156-0528-5 (cloth : alk. paper)
1. Rose, Ernestine L. (Ernestine Louise), 1810–1862.   2. Women
social reformers—United States—Biography.   3. Feminists—United
States—Biography.   4. Women's rights—United States—History—19th
century.   I. Title.   II. Series.
HQ1413.R6K65   1998
305.42'092—dc21   98-10783

Manufactured in the United States of America

To Steve

Carol A. Kolmerten is a professor of English at Hood College in Frederick, Maryland. She is the author of *Women in Utopia: The Ideology of Gender in the American Owenite Communities* and the editor of the Syracuse University Press edition of the 1893 *Unveiling a Parallel* by Alice Ilgenfritz Jones and Ella Merchant. She is also coeditor of *Utopian and Science Fiction by Women: Worlds of Difference* (Syracuse University Press) and *Unflinching Gaze: Morrison and Faulkner Re-Envisioned.*

Contents

Illustrations

Acknowledgments

Almost a quarter of a century ago, I handed a paper I had written for a graduate course to Stephen M. Ross, an English professor I had heard was an excellent editor and critic. Pleased because another professor had commented that the essay might be publishable, I wanted (or thought I wanted) advice on how to transform an essay into my first publication. I was just beginning to write my dissertation—built upon that paper—and hoped that a forthcoming publication would help me in my job search.

So I gave the essay to Professor Ross and waited eagerly for his comments. A week later, as we discussed my essay, I looked at horror at all the red marks on each page. I did not hear him say "has potential"; all I heard was "not publishable as is," "too elliptical," "needs more analysis." I remember trying to keep my composure in his office and then charging out and angrily throwing the essay in a trash can in a melodramatic gesture to the delight of my graduate-student friends, all of us bemoaning how hostile and critical the professors were.

As a reader of nineteenth-century domestic novels might surmise, my attitude did change. I eventually retrieved the discarded essay, rewrote it into my first publication, and fell in love with and married Steve. Steve remains my first and best editor: he is still ruthless and absolutely honest ("this is an information dump," he wrote on the first draft of this manuscript; "it's too elliptical and needs analysis"). But, as I sit on the top of a mountain writing these acknowledgements, and Steve goes through, yet again, another draft of *Ernestine*, I feel incredibly blessed to have a live-in editor willing to spend his vacation critiquing my prose.

I also feel overwhelming gratitude to other scholars who have given so much of their time and energy editing and commenting on drafts of this manuscript. Andrea Kerr, Harriet Alonso, and Edith Gelles offered excellent, extensive commentary on the entire manuscript; Carolyn Karcher, Jeannie Pfaelzer, Greg Claeys, and Molly Best Tinsley provided me with valuable insights and observations on different sections of the manuscript. Bonnie Anderson and Françoise Basch shared ideas and sources with me via e-mail and letters. Glenda McNeill took pictures of Rose's homes in London for me.

The staff at several research libraries aided me throughout the project. At the American Antiquarian Society (surely one of the most utopian of places for scholars in American culture to work), I was helped during my visits and later through E-mail by Nancy Burkett, Georgia Barnhill, and Joanne Chaison and countless other staff members. The staff at the Schlesinger Library offered me specific suggestions on my project. Likewise, the librarians in the Rare Books Room of the Library of Congress brought me countless manuscripts over the past ten years. At Boston University, Charles Niles was particularly helpful when I examined the Yuri Suhl Manuscripts. At Smith College, Amy Hague offered valuable suggestions when I worked in the Sophia Smith Collection.

I am grateful to many of the places I visited for permission to quote from their various collections. Specifically, I would like to thank the American Antiquarian Society; the Trustees of the Boston Public library; Boston Unversity; the Chicago Historical Society; the Kheel Center for Labor-Management Documentation and Archives, M.P. Catherwood Library, Cornell University; Smith College (Sophia Smith Collection); and the Schlesinger Library, Radcliffe College. Mary Anthony Coughlin, Susan B. Anthony's literary heir, allowed me to quote from Anthony's "Diary."

I am also grateful to the friends and relatives of Yuri and Isabelle Suhl for supporting this project and for giving me permission to use the Yuri Suhl Papers at Boston University. Max Rosenfeld, Alice Shugars, and Beverly Spector helped me understand Yuri Suhl's devotion to Ernestine Rose.

At Syracuse University Press, Cynthia Maude-Gembler, Robert Mandel, and John Fruehwirth have encouraged and supported this project from the beginning, and Kenneth Plax supplied the fine copyediting.

This decade-long project was aided by grant support at critical moments. The National Endowment for the Humanities, the American Philosophical Society, and the American Council of Learned Societies all supported the project in its early, formative stages, allowing me to visit historical societies and libraries to gather crucial materials. In 1996 I received an ACLS Fellowship, providing me with a semester's leave to make major revisions in the manuscript.

The people and resources of Hood College, where I have taught for more than twenty years, also supported my research by giving me two sabbaticals and three summer research grants to further the project. Bruce Wilkin, an academic computing specialist, has offered me considerable assistance, including (one weekend from his home phone) helping me "undelete" an entire unbacked-up section of a chapter that I had accidentally erased. Judy Hanson, Rose House, Collete Cooney, and Grace Sheffield have aided me in many tasks as I worked on the manuscript. I am particularly grateful to my excellent students: both Lauren Janney and Beth Patrinicola worked tirelessly for me as research assistants, each for more than a year, reading countless nineteenth-century newspapers and magazines, always on the lookout for Rose's name. To them, and to all the other students who have grown to respect and admire Ernestine Rose as much as I do, I offer this portrait of a courageous woman who spent her life fighting injustice.

Baltimore, Maryland   Carol A. Kolmerten
June 1997

Abbreviations

AACAN	Association of All Classes of All Nations
AFAS	American and Foreign Antislavery Society
AAS	American Antiquarian Society
AASS	American Anti-Slavery Society
BFC	Blackwell Family Collection, Library of Congress
BI	*Boston Investigator*
Diary	Susan B. Anthony's Diary, Schlesinger Library, Radcliffe College
FE	*Free Enquirer*
GFP	Garrison Family Papers, Sophia Smith Collection, Smith College Library
GP	Garrison Papers, Boston Public Library
HWS	*The History of Woman Suffrage*
MASS	Massachusetts Antislavery Society
NAWSA Papers	National American Woman Suffrage Association Papers, Library of Congress
NHG	*New Harmony Gazette*
NMW	*New Moral World*
PWRC	*Proceedings, Woman's Rights Conventions*
Scrapbook	Susan B. Anthony's Scrapbook, Anthony Collection, Library of Congress

Introduction

The editor of a small Maine newspaper wrote "it would be shameful to listen to this woman, *a thousand times below a prostitute.*" A minister in Charleston, South Carolina, forbade his congregation to heed "this female devil."[1] The object of this scorn was Ernestine L. Rose, one of the major intellectual forces behind the American women's rights movement in nineteenth-century America.[2] Rose spent four decades arguing for women's rights and against legal and social restrictions on women. Beginning in the 1830s by gathering petitions for married women's property rights, Rose, by 1837 had begun speaking on American stages for equality for all people. As the women's rights movement grew in the 1850s, she became one of its most important proponents—and the one many newspapers labeled as the "most eloquent."

Despite her importance to the movement, Rose is, perhaps, the most forgotten of the women's rights activists; today virtually no one knows her name. She is, to use Virginia Woolf's words, a "stranded ghost." Though her importance to the movement is clear in the pages of the New York *Tribune*, the *Herald*, the *Times*, the *Liberator*, and the *Boston Investigator* in the 1840s, 1850s, and 1860s, she has been left out of contemporary histories of the woman's rights movement. Many historians mention her

1. The quotes comes from d'Hericourt's essay in the Dec. 8, 1869, *BI*.

2. Even though the term "women's rights" is more common now, I use the term "woman's rights" when quoting or paraphrasing the women involved in the movement, or discussing the movement as it developed in the 1850s, as that was the term the women themselves used.

briefly, if at all, some lamenting, incorrectly, that she did not write anything.[3]

Rose's disappearance from history is telling. Not only was she scorned by newspaper editors and southern ministers, but she also was isolated from and sometimes ignored by the very women and men with whom she shared reform platforms. Rose was an "other" in a movement of others—an outsider in a group of women who banded together against oppression. She was outspoken; she was ironic. Even more important, Rose was a professed freethinker who was born Jewish in Poland. In a movement that drew much of its moral and intellectual energy from appeals to Christian piety, the combination of Rose's atheism, her Jewish and Polish background, her foreign accent, and her outspoken ways made her an

---

3. See, for example, Melder's, "Beginnings," where he writes, "Source material dealing with Mrs. Rose is almost nonexistent, thus it is difficult to estimate her importance" (25). See also one brief reference to Rose as an "exotic . . . beautiful Polish girl" in Smith; six brief references to Rose in Flexner, usually in a list with other women's names; no mention at all in O'Neill; one brief mention in Evans. Rose fares better in specialized histories of Jewish women or radical immigrants. See, for example, Miller, Neidle, and Elinor Lerner.

Only Yuri Suhl has written a full-length biography of Rose (1959), which was reissued with a twelve-page "Revisitation" by Françoise Basch in 1990. Other significant works on Rose include Lewis's pioneering essay in 1927 (based almost entirely on Barnard's 1856 essay); Schappes's two 1949 pieces on Rose, and Basch's excellent work on Rose in *Rebelles Americaines*. See as well Conrad's estimable rhetorical studies "Transformation" and, particularly "Ernestine." In the latter essay (marked by some surprising factual errors—Rose traveled in 1854 to Washington, D.C., with Susan B. Anthony, not Elizabeth Cady Stanton, for example), Conrad cites several obvious reasons for Rose's disappearance from history including her atheism, her confrontational, uncompromising style, and her foreignness. But he also adds a perceptive additional reason for her invisibility in today's history books: from the Civil War on, Rose's belief in the "essential humanness of all persons" became problematic for woman's rights activists (368). Increasingly, nativist sentiment permeated woman's suffrage ideology, he writes, and the more that the moral superiority of white middle- and upper-class women was lauded, the more out of date Rose's emphasis on universal human rights appeared. Conrad's argument is astute, but, as we shall see, Rose's problems with "moral superiority" rationales caused dissention within the ranks long before the Civil War.

obvious target for antagonistic newspaper editors and ministers who wanted to prove how radical and wrong-headed the woman's rights movement was. But the blunt daughter of Eastern European culture also caused discomfort and unease for those within the movement as well. Rose acted as a kind of barometer for the reformers; she registered their anti-Semitism, their anti-immigrationist sentiments, their unconscious racism. Rose's story is thus a story outside of the standard narrative of the struggle for women's rights.

As a contemporary feminist, I begin my story of Ernestine Rose framed by my own story. Like so many women of my generation, I spent my adolescence searching for alternative ways of being, alternative lives to the ones we knew growing up (in my case, middle-class, white, and female) in such places as Northeast, Pennsylvania, or Fern Creek, Kentucky, where our own mothers' domestic intensity stifled and suffocated us as we contemplated our futures as female beings. I certainly needed an alternative way of imagining a life. My Fern Creek of the 1950s and early 1960s was as oppressive and sexually segregated as any "Father Knows Best" episode. The mothers I knew stayed home, washing floors—so clean you could "eat off of them"—and cooking cubed steak and mashed potatoes. Fathers disappeared to that unknown utopia of "work," where life seemed to be, and reappeared promptly at 5:15 P.M. every weekday evening. When I tried to play little league at age nine, I was told it wasn't "ladylike." When I asked to write my eighth-grade "careers" report on becoming a lawyer, I was told "girls don't do that." The only activities open to me in high school were waving pom-poms at male athletic events and acting in the senior play. The only paid activities that seemed to be open to married women in my neighborhood were teaching and secretarial services—but even those were frowned upon as unbecoming to mothers with children at home.

So I searched in high school and college for another way to be. "Official" voices were no help. The church I had been raised in counseled obedience and piety for women; my graduate school advisor labeled me a "terminal master's" student because I was married and a mother; a psychiatrist I saw at the student health center never considered that my problems might stem from thwarted ambitions and instead advised that I drop out of graduate school so that I could be a better wife and "bake more cookies."

Though my search might have gone unrequited in another era, I was fortunate enough to begin my exploration just as the late 1960s women's movement was unfolding. I read everything I could get my hands on—Friedan, Millet, Greer. Through my self-education, I learned other ways of being, and I began to change my life. I didn't have to take my husband's name. I didn't even have to be married. I could be a mother *and* a professional. I could get a Ph.D.—all on my own, with my small daughter in tow. All those things that my daughter, now in her early thirties and a successful environmental lawyer, grew up taking for granted as part of her heritage, I learned through reading about other women's lives. Thus, I am now, indeed, obsessed with providing examples to other women (and men) of women's lives that fit no pattern I ever learned growing up.

Recent biographers of women have recounted their unease as they spent years obsessing about their subjects. Kathryn Kish Sklar, for example, writes of the oppressive physical sensation of her upper body being encased in a pine coffin as she was preoccupied with gathering material on Florence Kelley ("Coming"). Bell Gale Chevigny writes of both the exhilaration in working late at night and of her overidentification with Margaret Fuller. I, too, have felt this projection as I have attempted to recover women's writings. For over a decade in the late 1970s and early 1980s, I searched for and read manuscripts and letters by Frances Wright, one of the nineteenth-century's most undervalued and despised women. Wright, a wealthy Scottish woman who devoted her fortune to a grandiose venture to free America's slaves in the 1820s, developed into a disciplined writer and a radical speaker on the importance of women's rights in the 1820s and 1830s. My simplistic desire to find a perfect female hero with no visible flaws created problems for me as a biographer: I was unable to read how poorly Wright treated her sister, who idolized her. Her sister, Camilla, wrote a series of anguished letters that took me years to be able to decipher, so badly did I want to believe that I had found one woman in the nineteenth century who had it all—a meaningful career and a loving family that made her work easier to do. What I could not recognize at the time was that some of Wright's "ease" came at her sister's expense. The one left at home to serve the others, whether as a wife or as a sister, suffered.

Given my experience interpreting Camilla's letters, I have worried about what blinders I am now wearing that hinder interpretation. My concerns have been reinforced by the hundreds of recent essays, conference talks, roundtables, and scholarly monographs on writing feminist biography.[4] In fact, several years ago, surrounded by such excellent books as *Between Women, The Challenge of Feminist Biography, Revealing Lives, Contesting the Subject*, and the 1993 special issue of *Auto/Biography Studies* on feminist biography, I surrendered to paralysis: I could never find a way to write about Ernestine Rose. Everywhere I read how notions of linear, chronological, unified narratives—to use the words of Sharon O'Brien—to present readers with "an essential self" were passé (126). We live, I read, in an age of deconstruction where our pervasive ideologies act as blinders for our perceptions, where no objectivity or "truth" is possible, and where authors, subjects, and even readers are contested grounds. Exceptional women, rather than being thought of as "exemplary heroines," instead were to be "sites—historical locations or markers—where crucial political and cultural contests are enacted."[5]

Then I remembered those wonderful orange-bound library books I carried home in the fourth grade, those stories of women such

4. See, for example, Bell and Yalom; Ascher, DeSalvo, and Ruddick; Epstein; and the fall 1993 special issue on "Feminist Biography," of *Auto/Biography Studies*. I would note also the many well-attended sessions and workshops on feminist biography at recent conferences of the Modern Language Association, the American Studies Association, the American Literature Association, and the Berkshire Conference on the History of Women.

5. The words are from Joan Wallach Scott, who offers us a compelling deconstruction of "equality" feminism as opposed to "difference" feminism in her study of French feminists (16).

as Clara Barton and Amelia Earhart. Like so many avid readers, I have always loved reading about others' lives, especially lives of famous women. Their experiences helped me escape into a universe I could not have imagined without their concrete examples. Of course Ernestine Rose and other reformers like her were, indeed, "sites," where crucial political and cultural battles were enacted; but women like Rose were also more than a "site" could ever be—and who wants to read about a "site," anyway? We all want to hear about the lives of "real" people, their obstacles and how they overcame them. I thought about all of the people who still needed or wanted to hear about strong, pioneering women and decided that I had to tell the story of Rose's remarkable life, but I also had to consider how I was trying to tell her story, what lenses I was looking through, what shapes I was automatically and unconsciously assuming. I could not discount my own life's experiences, her former biographers' words, or feminist and biographical theory.

I now realize that the more I learn about Rose, whom I discovered when I was working on Frances Wright and whom I have come to admire wholeheartedly, the less I really seem to "know" her. I also question just how informative a series of dates and events can be in understanding a person's life; yet, I am equally worried about interpretative strategies. I wonder how much my zeal to provide some idealized audience of interested readers with a nineteenth-century woman who rebelled against the status quo is influencing my ability to interpret. And, I worry, how much are the accepted literary conventions about how to write biography affecting my ways of knowing? To cite just one small example: in an early draft of this manuscript I found it only too easy to valorize Rose in almost everything she did while demonizing those who opposed her. What this led to, by the end of the eighth chapter, was one "good" character—Rose—surrounded by evil racists (Stanton and Anthony) or foolish compromisers who sold out women's suffrage for black male suffrage (Stone, Kelley Foster, Garrison, Douglass, Phillips). History is just not as simple as the literary structures I was unconsciously adhering to.

I also wonder if I can trust myself? I respond with delight when I find and read for the first time some new speech that Rose delivered. She was witty, caustic, brilliant, and in no way intimidated by her male listeners. Unlike most of the other women on the stage, Rose, with experience speaking on platforms in the 1830s, could think quickly under attack, coming back with the perfect rejoinder that most of us can only wish we would have thought of. Her wit and sarcasm draw me to her—particularly her barbs concerning women's proper spheres according to Christian lore. What does this say about fashions, about preferred ways of speaking and being? Do I like her simply because her sarcasm replicates mine? I know I wish I could have her nerve: I imagine myself speaking in 1853 to a large group of ministers who are hissing and shouting at me—would I have her nerve to tell them exactly what I think? I am afraid I have been schooled too well in cultural acclimation and that I would couch my message in acceptable imagery and muted language and deliver it with diminished fervor. What would it be like, I wonder, to be so hated and scorned? How could one live a life? How thrilling not to care about such things as esteem and respect. The public Ernestine Rose, the one we can "document" through her speeches and letters, seemed not to care that she was scorned or reviled. Yet, the private Ernestine Rose must have cared about such things, mustn't she? Surely her life was much more than I can record. I have recovered her speeches and her public letters, but what of her marriage? What of her friendships? What kind of person was she outside of the public eye? One of my greatest frustrations is that I could find few records of Rose's personal life that I so wanted to uncover, preferably in an old trunk in an attic somewhere. Though it is currently fashionable to scorn the "artificial" division of "public" and "private," I still yearn for more "private." I wanted to find letters written to William, a diary kept during her travels, a note back home to her father, not because I thought it would change my opinion of her life, but because I simply wanted to know more about this extraordinary woman, even if she, alive, might resist that prying.

I try to imagine someone 150 years from now writing a biography of me. No one could get it right; even I can't get it right as I retell the stories that make up my versions of myself. Perhaps the greatest pleasure of meeting a new person is that we can tell whatever version of our life we choose to represent. Nonetheless I forge ahead. We are all full of contradictions; if nothing else, current theory has allowed us to shed the heavy mantle of consistency—for ourselves as writers and for our subjects. Emerson had it right 150 years ago, even if what he said has become a cliché: consistency *is* the hobgoblin of little minds.

Ironically, though, I believe I chose Ernestine Rose as a project because she seems so consistently strong-minded to me, more so even than Frances Wright. A lifetime rebel and advocate for women's rights, Rose battled just the people I would like to take on: bigoted ministers, conservative politicians, sexist male leaders of industry. When I left the church in which I was raised because of its racist policies, I left quietly, without making a fuss. When I interviewed for my first job and was asked what kind of birth control I was using, I tried to deflect the question without losing the job. I imagine Ernestine Rose, then, as my alter ego, acting where I did not; confronting where I appeased. From all of her words that I have read, from all the accounts of her speeches to hissing, booing crowds, she seems to have been able to do things that most mortal women could not. And, unlike most nineteenth-century women, Rose had a husband who worked to support her causes. She was freed by his enterprise as a jeweler and silversmith to travel throughout the United States and Europe preaching her causes. I believe that this part of her story is my favorite: how her husband, who was her closest friend, stayed at home working to cover the costs of her militant causes. From all I can find on their marriage—and it is not much, as Rose, the public person, needed some private space—Ernestine and William were partners, intellectual equals, and lifetime soul mates. He worked in New York City; she lectured to the world.

Like other biographers, I am, of course, also telling Rose's life with the benefits of, and liability of, perspectives provided by lens of others who have recounted her life. During her life, Ernestine

Rose told the story of her childhood to several people, who in turn wrote biographical essays. The stories seem apocryphal to me as a modern reader: the stories of a superhuman who would reach mythical proportion in her lifetime and thus must have had an extraordinary childhood and young adulthood. Several of these people write about how she barely escaped unscathed from howling wolves during a Polish winter when she was 16, how she took on the Polish court system, how she refused her father's choice of a husband, and how she survived a shipwreck off the coast of England. By today's standards, the writing is overblown and sentimentalized; the facts are unverifiable. But the sense of the stories—the background of an extraordinary person—rings true to me, even if the details do not.

Rose's only twentieth-century full-scale biographer was Yuri Suhl, who reported the stories of her childhood by inventing dialogue. As he writes in his "Author's Note" that prefaces the book: "The dialogue is, in the main, genuine. Where direct quotation was lacking it was painstakingly reconstructed from her speeches and newspaper accounts of her utterances. Only in the first sixteen years of her life were liberties taken with the dialogue" (np).

When I first confronted Suhl's manuscript—disappointed, of course, that I would not be the first to tell a version of Rose's life—I was upset at the liberties that Suhl took in making up dialogue or in misquoting her speeches or letters. I noted with some jealousy that at least part of the basic research—writing to countless libraries and historical societies, arranging visits, asking for information—was done by Isabelle Suhl, Yuri's librarian wife, who kept detailed accounts of her letters and the responses to them. But the more I learned about Yuri and Isabelle Suhl from their living relatives and friends, the more impressed I was with their devotion to Ernestine. As a Jewish socialist writing in the 1950s, Suhl was trying, as I would try 40 years later, as a feminist writing in the 1990s, to keep alive the memory of an extraordinary woman. That Rose was Jewish and a socialist were the Suhls' primary concerns. That she was a woman's rights advocate, often outspoken and sarcastic in an era that did not cotton to such fashions, is mine. Our concerns of course overlap. But they also illustrate how I have been able to unearth so much material on and from Rose that Suhl could not. I focused first on Rose as a speaker/worker for women's rights, beginning my search for materials at the Schlesinger Library for Women's History. There, I found literally thousands of documents on the woman's rights movement in the 1850s in which Rose played such a major role. From there, I read every weekly issue of the *Boston Investigator* from 1836 until 1892, searching for every letter, every speech that Rose might have written. But I also read issues of the major woman's rights newspapers, which included speeches and letters that the *Investigator* did not. And, I have been blessed with the suggestions of other scholars in women's history, who have pointed me toward countless sources I might never have thought of myself.

It was not until I read the Suhl manuscripts at Boston University that I finally appreciated this man—this competitor—for *my* subject. Suhl begins his published biography in a traditional, chronological way: "On a cold winter day of January 13, 1810, the most noteworthy event in the ghetto of Piotrkow, Poland, was the birth of a girl" (3). But in his first draft, he began his story of Rose by talking about a dinner party in his New York apartment, where he read to his guests from one of Rose's speeches. The listeners were transfixed, suddenly overwhelmed by the beauty of her language and the power of her argument. It was a revealing introduction to a biography—a powerful, first-person beginning that placed Suhl as the teller of the story, of a story that had to be told because Rose's words were just too important not to hear. His audience reading the biography would be, presumably, as transformed as were his dinner guests. This intimate, confessional opening never appeared in the published biography, however. Perhaps 1950s rhetorical conventions prohibited such a postmodern beginning; perhaps an editor believed it to be too far removed from the data of Rose's life. Perhaps Suhl himself decided it was too personal and removed it. Whatever the reason, it is clear that Yuri Suhl also needs to be appreciated by contemporary readers for launching the work to resurrect Rose's words.

I hope to write about Ernestine Rose's life in both conventional and unconventional ways. Having benefited from the explosion of feminist theory and feminist biographical theory that allows me the freedom to begin where I want to, to tell the story how I want to, to be hypersensitive to issues such as "author" and "subject" and "audience," I am freed in many ways from some of the constrictions Suhl faced. I am able to read material differently than Suhl was able to in the 1950s. I am able, thanks to my predecessors and contemporaries, to ask very different questions of my material.

I am inspired by Lois Banner's words: "those theorists who posit that there is no fixed center in individuals' lives, no structure to self-construction, no predominating ways in which we view ourselves and present ourselves are confusing theory with reality" (166). I am also freed by the notion that biography is inherently a series of contradictions, in the same way that a subject's life and our own lives as the tellers of the story are contradictory. Because I know that I am shaping the story, I know that biography is a type of fiction; yet, at the same time, I search for facts, insights, illuminated moments that will suddenly reveal to readers the "truth" of Ernestine Rose's feisty personality. Like Dee Garrison, I agree that feminist biographers often "illuminate the intersection of public and private . . . [that] they tend to rely upon knowledge of gender-specific social constructs to shape the central pattern in their work" (77). Feminist biographers are also likely to explode the myth that biographers are distanced and objective, and, as Lois Rudnick writes, feminist biographers question the illusion that the life presented equals the life lived (118). Perhaps these differences that feminist biography has staked out derive, at least in part, from the knowledge that women's lives rarely follow a typical pattern of a male biographical hero—a pattern that includes, more than anything else, a rise "up" to riches and power. Ernestine Rose's life, like the lives of so many significant women in nineteenth-century America, differs diametrically from this pattern. She scorned the great nineteenth-century American obsession of getting and keeping money. Rose spent her life dedicated to an idea instead of rising to riches.

I will offer the details of Ernestine Rose's life while placing her in the context of an America over 150 years ago, where the only artifacts I can trust (if I can trust them) are primary documents such as her letters and speeches and essays. Of course, I will also rely on the letters and diaries of others, but I have been disappointed to find that Rose is strangely absent from many of the most famous of the extant letter collections: she is referred to only two times in the voluminous Garrison Papers at the Boston Public Library, for example; yet, she shared the stage with William Lloyd Garrison countless times. It is as if Rose were invisible to many of her colleagues.

I will also examine the accounts of Rose's life as seen through the eyes of her friends (such as Susan B. Anthony and Jenny d'Hericourt) who did leave a record of their perceptions of her and through her enemies (many ministers and newspaper journalists).

I will begin my account of Rose's life in 1836, the year she reinvented herself in mythic American style, by emigrating to North America as a reformer. But unlike any Horatio Alger hero, she did not rise to riches through luck and pluck. Instead, although she had as much pluck as any Alger hero, her "American life" followed a completely different direction. She emigrated to the young republic to be able to start over in this new world where a miraculous document—the Declaration of Independence—promised freedom and equality for all people. She chose to live in America because she took America's promise seriously. Like the religious patriots who settled the Massachusetts Bay Colony two hundred years before she arrived, Rose came to America for an idea, but it was a secular not a religious idea, an idea of the possibility of individual freedom that would have made the Puritans shudder. Yet for Rose, as for many of us today, her example of working to increase freedoms for all human beings reflects, perhaps, the most utopian of all the versions of the American dream.

The American Life of Ernestine L. Rose

······❧❦[1]❦❧······

Cultural and Biographical Contexts

I have not abandoned the trunk to latch onto the branches.

—Ernestine Potowski, Poland, 1817

Ernestine Rose arrived in New York City in May 1836 with her new husband, William Rose, as part of a large influx of immigrants who reached New York in the late spring and early summer of that year. The New York *Herald* reported on May 27, 1836, that within the past two weeks 5,740 passengers had arrived from foreign countries. But William and Ernestine were coming to America with a more specific vision of a better world than drew most immigrants. As devoted reformers, they arrived in New York, appropriately on May 14, Robert Owen's birthday, as part of a small Owenite colony of 36 people who were resolved to realize their ideals through community life.[1]

The New York they arrived in was one of the nation's busiest commercial and cultural centers, populated with a quarter of a million residents. Narratives on shipwrecks and captivity dominated monthly magazines, perhaps, in part at least because ship travel was not safe. Only a few months after the Roses landed in New York, the precariousness of their journey was made clear when an American ship was wrecked and close to 70 people killed in a storm off Far Rockaway. Only a few weeks later, another storm caused the wreck of another ship. Popular writers included Nathaniel Hawthorne, who was writing sentimental schlock in

---

1. For information on the Owenite colony that the Roses were a part of see d'Hericourt, "Madame Rose" 134.

the same vein as the "damned scribbling women" he would later criticize; Sarah J. Hale, the editor of *Godey's Lady's Book*; William Cullen Bryant; and John Greenleaf Whittier. Ralph Waldo Emerson had just published his soon-to-be-famous essay "Nature," and Transcendentalism was waiting to emerge 200 miles to the northeast.

For the rising middle class, new technology such as the steam press allowed daily and weekly newspapers to publish easily and cheaply beginning in 1835. The Roses might have read parts of conservative James Gordon Bennett's *Herald* along with monographs more to their liking such as *Voltaire on Religious Tolerance, Christianity Unveiled,* or *The Philosophical Works of Thomas Cooper, M.D.,* for sale at meetings of the Society for Moral Philanthropists near the Roses' apartment. Streetcars, introduced in the early 1830s, moved people like the Roses quickly across the growing town.

When Ernestine and William Rose landed, Andrew Jackson was president. Like the Jacksonians, who would remain in power only four more years, the Roses were believers in the "little man," the disenfranchised person; they wanted to help create a world where any person would be free to live under a system of laws and representative government based on democracy rather than on privilege. But unlike the Jacksonians, who limited their egalitarian rhetoric to white men, the Roses wanted equality for all people.

The Roses first lived at 484 Grand Street on the Lower East Side, then moved to Frankfort Street, a busy area with shops on street level and furnished rooms for rent above them.[2] As middle-class immigrants, they may have enjoyed some of the fruits of new technology, such as indoor plumbing and piped gas. They probably noticed the devastation of the great fire of 1835 that had raged for more than two days in Manhattan's commercial district.

2. The Roses also lived on Chatham, Chambers, Broadway, Reade, White, Prince, 9th, and East 14th, moving generally uptown with each relocation, but staying in the same general area throughout their more than 30 years in New York. In *Immigrant Life in New York City*, Ernst writes that Broadway, where the Roses lived in the 1850s, had at that time "blossomed into a promenade of beauty and fashion, lined with bookshops, jewelry, upholstery, hat and cap, tailoring, millinery, and large retail dry good stores" (38).

Though they did not continue on with the Owenite colony to establish a community, Ernestine and William nonetheless remained devoted believers in Owenism and set to work to earn enough money to finance their reform ideas. Within a year of their arrival, they had opened a small "Fancy and Perfumery" store at 9 Frankfort Street, where, according to the New York *Beacon*, William repaired jewelry and watches and where Ernestine manufactured "cologne waters" to perfume apartments. They lived above their shop in furnished rooms, with meals provided by their landlady, as did many New York City residents in the early nineteenth century.

Twenty-six the year she arrived, Ernestine Rose was an attractive woman, so attractive that newspapers would comment on her striking beauty for the next forty years. She had long, curling brown hair, which she never covered with a hat. Short and slender, she had clear brown eyes that everyone noticed and a charming half-smile. She was, according to her friends, without affectation, wearing grey or black dresses with a simple gold brooch and ever-present smooth leather gloves.

The story of Ernestine Rose might not be remarkable at all if she and her husband had followed only the path of so many immigrants before them and after them: moving to the Lower East Side, opening a shop, making money, moving uptown, growing comfortable. As followers of the visionary Robert Owen from England, the Roses wanted far more than riches or a comfortable life from the new world: they wanted to follow Owen's path and change their new world into a new moral world, as Owen had tried a decade earlier by establishing the original New Harmony community. Though they possessed none of Robert Owen's fortune, they did possess his idealistic notion that the world could and should be improved, and they came to the young republic to live out the ideals behind the Declaration of Independence.

Information about Ernestine Rose's background before she and William arrived in New York is sketchy at best. Much of what we know of her early life comes from two almost simultaneous accounts published in 1856. One of the accounts comes from Jenny d'Hericourt, a French reformer whom Rose met in France in 1856. D'Hericourt's biography, published in France and never translated into English, provides more details than any other account of Rose's early life. The other account comes from a biographical sketch written by L. E. Barnard in the *Excelsior* and then quickly reprinted in both the *Liberator* (May 16, 1856) and the *Boston Investigator* (July 9, 1856).[3] Given the paucity of firsthand accounts of Rose's early life, we must piece together fragmentary and contexualized information before she arrived in America in 1836, where her documentary history begins.

Early Life

Born on January 13, 1810, in Piotrkow, Poland, Ernestine Louise Sigismund (or Susmond) Potowski (or Potowsky) was Jewish. Her father, a rabbi, taught his only child at home both

3. D'Hericourt also wrote a briefer biographical sketch on Rose that was published in Elizabeth Cady Stanton and Susan B. Anthony's *Revolution* and the *Boston Investigator* in 1869, when d'Hericourt was then living in Chicago. Barnard's sketch was reprinted again, 21 years later in the Feb. 14, 1877, *BI*; it also appeared, with some additional material added at the end, in volume 1 of the *History of Woman Suffrage* (*HWS*) in 1881. The additional material, all concerning matters that Anthony would know well, was probably added by Anthony. Barnard is an enigma—a writer who wrote one book, *The Moral Sayings of Confucius* (1855), the year before writing the biographical essay on Rose. Perhaps Barnard (he? she?) was attracted to Confucius and to Rose because both offered a principled life outside the realm of Christianity.

Other contemporary biographers include Sara Underwood, who included Rose's background in her book *Heroines of Free Thought* (1876). Underwood met Rose in 1868 at the second anniversary of the American Equal Rights Association. Alice Stone Blackwell relates one tall tale about Rose's early life, as told to her by an "old lady" from Indiana, who had known Rose when Rose visited her house when she was 12 years old. See Alice Stone Blackwell's letter to Fanny Goldstein (Dec. 30, 1936) in the NAWSA (the National American Woman Suffrage Association) Papers. Rose tells a bit of her story herself as well. When asked by Susan B. Anthony in 1877 to describe her past labors, for inclusion in Elizabeth Cady Stanton and Anthony's *HWS*, Rose responded that "I could not undertake the task, especially as I have nothing to refer to." But Rose does go on to recount a few of her activities, though she adds, "I did not intend to publish anything about myself, for I had no other ambition except to work for the cause of humanity, irrespective of sex, sect, country, or color, and

Hebrew and the Scriptures. At five she was sent to school, but came home indignant, not wanting to return because she had been punished for something she did not know was against the rules. The intense, bookish father and his only, precocious daughter form a familiar archetype in the history of accomplished women. Ernestine's mother, like the mother of so many nineteenth-century fictional heroines, is absent from her life story. What happened to Ernestine's mother is unclear. D'Hericourt mentions her mother dying when Ernestine was a teenager. Sara Underwood writes that her mother died when she was a child. Alice Stone Blackwell refers only to a father and stepmother. L. E. Barnard says that Rose's mother died when she was 16 and that her father quickly remarried.[4]

Everyone writing about Ernestine's childhood comments on her arguments with her father. When Ernestine questioned her father's idea of religious proof, she was told, according to Underwood, that "a young girl does not want to understand the object of her creed, but to accept and believe it" (260). D'Hericourt relates that from childhood on Ernestine questioned her father's

---

did not expect that a Susan B. Anthony would wish to do it for me" (*HWS* 1: 98).

Unless otherwise noted in the text, when I quote from d'Hericourt, the page numbers refer to her 1856, "Madame Rose"; Barnard quotes comes from the Feb. 14, 1877, *Boston Investigator*. My use of d'Hericourt's "Madame Rose" illustrates some of the wonderful webs of feminist scholarship. I had searched, vainly, for this piece for over five years, having read the 1869 d'Hericourt essay, in which she revealed that she had, indeed, written and published a more extensive version in 1856. I had librarians all over the world attempting to find the 1856 biography, but to no avail. It was only when Harriet Alonso suggested that I talk with Bonnie Anderson about my work on Rose did I find that Bonnie not only knew of the 1856 biography but that she had a copy, which she generously sent me immediately.

4. Suhl also claims that Ernestine was sixteen when her mother died (11); yet in the Potowski family tree that is part of the Suhl Papers, the date for Ernestine's mother's death is given as 1816, when Ernestine would have been only six. The date for the rabbi's remarriage is given as 1817, when Ernestine was seven. See the Yuri Suhl Papers at Boston University Library for Suhl's hand-sketched family tree. He offers no documentary evidence for the date.

Jewish faith. She could not accept a religion that caused him to harm himself by fasting. His response that little girls did not need to understand, they just had to obey, did little to reconcile Ernestine to her father's beliefs. Unable to hide her thoughts, Ernestine became more and more estranged from her religious father. D'Hericourt adds: "Blind faith being not in the intellectual capability of Ernestine, she abandoned her religion and external worship" (*BI* Dec. 8, 1869).

We can imagine the circumstances: young, questioning, Ernestine—who was surely named something else by Jewish parents in Poland in 1810—turning against the teachings and religion of her rabbi father.[5] Given the pattern her life threatened to follow as the faithful daughter of a rabbi in early nineteenth-century Poland, she had to rebel. We need only read *The Memoirs of Glückel of Hameln* to see the preordained course of her female Jewish life: an early arranged marriage, many children, and a constant fear of poverty that could well have led to an emphasis on the getting and keeping of money. But Ernestine was no Glückel, no "loving daughter, devoted wife, the prototypical self-sacrificing Jewish mother."[6]

The stories that all her biographers tell are hagiographical, suggesting Ernestine's legendary status and her concomitant estrangement from the habits and unquestioned mores of the time. Even if Ernestine made up the stories, or exaggerated the events of her life to d'Hericourt, Barnard, and Underwood, the very tales she invented, coupled with the fact that she must have named

5. Although Underwood writes that Rose's full name was "given by her parents," Yuri Suhl astutely suggests that such a name as Ernestine would not have been given a Jewish girl in Poland in 1810. Bonnie Anderson suggests that Ernestine took her new name in Berlin and used both her parents' surnames: Sigismund Potowski. See Anderson's *Joyous Greetings: The First International Women's Movement, 1832–60.*

6. Although Glückel lived 100 years before Ernestine, her domestic life— her arranged marriage, her willingness to live wherever her husband wished, her uncritical acceptance of Jewish laws that relegated her as "unclean" (xvi) and thus unable to embrace her husband as he was dying—gives us a good sense of the patterned female life in a devoutly Jewish community. See also Kaplan.

herself, suggest a power not available to or used by many women in the early nineteenth century.

Ernestine's first betrothal, as related by d'Hericourt, is a good example of her self-creation.[7] By adolescence Ernestine must have realized that she would have to resist her father's stories for her life. When she was only fifteen, writes d'Hericourt, Ernestine discovered that her father had promised her hand in marriage to a man she did not love. Ernestine went to the man and wept at his feet: "I do not love you," said she, "and I feel that I never will. Oh! pray release me" (*BI* Dec. 8, 1869). When he did not release her from her father's promise and sued to retain her dowry (a substantial amount that Ernestine had inherited from her mother), she traveled alone to the Tribune of Calish for a judge to hear her case. On the journey, her sleigh was nearly broken in a snowstorm and she stopped for five hours, frightened by the howling of hungry wolves. At Calish, she herself pleaded her case and won. Worried that a fortune would weigh her down, render her useless, or corrupt her, she left most of the fortune that had been restored to her with her father, keeping only a small part for herself.[8]

D'Hericourt relates, in a similar style, that upon returning from her victory Rose found her father remarried to a young woman close to her own age. Unable to "harmonize" with her new stepmother, according to both d'Hericourt and Underwood, Ernestine left home at 17 for Berlin, where she lived for two years and where she invented a chemical paper to perfume apartments. Although d'Hericourt and Underwood's version of Ernestine's leaving home accords with our romantic notions of evil stepmothers and fathers swayed by younger wives, perhaps she was escaping

7. For more information on "Jewish Marriage Strategies," including arranged marriages and dowries in Germanic countries in the nineteenth century, see Kaplan.

8. D'Hericourt writes in "Madame Rose" that the amount of the dowry was, in French francs, "les cent soixante mille," or 160,000 f.f. (s.c.) (132–33), a considerable fortune given that laborors subsisted on less than 25 francs a month at the time. See page 133 for the three reasons Ernestine returned most of the money to her father.

as much from a religious father with whom she no longer agreed as from a stepmother's temper.[9]

Alice Stone Blackwell's story of Rose's betrothal is even more apocryphal and exaggerated. Blackwell, writing in 1936 that her health was "precarious" and she had better "put on record" the story she had of Ernestine Rose's life, relates that Rose was indeed betrothed against her will by a father who had turned tyrannical after he married a second wife. After Ernestine refused her father's friend, whom she did not like, she was locked in her room, given only buttered bread and water. Soon she became emaciated but plotted an escape. In Blackwell's words:

> Finally she pretended to submit, and gave her consent to the marriage. Then she was carefully nursed back to health. Her father was so delighted by her yielding that he showered her with gifts. She asked that the largest part of her dowry should be in precious stones. These she quilted into her clothing. She had in the city some English friends, who had been associated with Robert Dale Owen. She communicated with them. Whens [sic] she came down stairs, on the day appointed for the wedding, a carriage was standing in front of the house, to take her to the synagogue. But another carriage stood there also, provided by her English friends. She stepped into it, and while the wedding guests were awaiting her in the synagogue, she was carried away to safety. The last thing that she had done before leaving home was to hide a dagger under her clothing. If she did not succeed in escaping, she meant to kill herself."[10]

9. Though the Potowski family trees in the Yuri Suhl papers reflect an 1817 date for Ernestine's father's remarriage (making Ernestine seven at the time), Suhl, nevertheless, writes that Ernestine was sixteen when her father remarried (11). The two women Rose spoke to about her childhood—d'Hericourt and Underwood—disagree as to when Rose's mother died but agree that she was sixteen when her father remarried.

10. See the Dec. 30, 1936 letter from Alice Stone Blackwell to Fanny Goldstein in the NAWSA Papers. Blackwell's story is melodramatic and entirely fictional: Rose would not become involved with Robert Owen (not his son, Robert Dale Owen) until long after she had left Poland. Did the 12-year-old girl who later in life related this story to Blackwell imagine parts of the story or did Rose fictionalize and dramatize her life to entertain the little girl, one wonders?

In Berlin, and in other European cities, Ernestine continued having adventures that suggest a hero in the making. According to Barnard and d'Hericourt, when Ernestine first moved
to Berlin, she had an interview with the king of Prussia about
the right of Polish Jews to remain in that city, an offense unless
the person was a property owner. When told by the king that
she should be baptized in order to escape the edict, Ernestine
purportedly replied that she would not because "I have not
abandoned the trunk to latch onto the branches" (d'Hericourt,
"Madame Rose" 133). In The Hague, Holland, according to
Barnard, Rose became distressed after hearing of a poor sailor
whose wife had been imprisoned unjustly for a crime. Rose
personally presented a petition to the king of Holland and saw
the poor woman released. Such stories of the power of a young
woman still in her teens seem fantastic, unbelievable to many
modern readers.

D'Hericourt and Underwood tell one final story of Rose
moving from the Continent to England, where she would meet
Robert Owen and William Rose and where her life would turn
to Owenite reform. Ernestine left Berlin in June 1829 for London. At some point in her journey to England, she was ship-
wrecked. Given the speed of the disaster, Ernestine could save
only her life and very little money, report her biographers. Thus,
she arrived in England newly "baptized," perhaps taking the
good English name of Ernestine at this time. She had lost in the
shipwreck all Polish remembrances, and she was not to write of
her father and stepmother again.[11] Not speaking a word of English when she arrived, Ernestine bought a dictionary and taught
herself the language.

In England, Ernestine supported herself by selling perfumed
papers and by tutoring four daughters of a duke in Hebrew and
German. She traveled at least once to France, where she participated

---

11. Yet Rose must have maintained contact with her father and his second
wife. When Rose died in 1892 her half-sister's three daughters, her three nieces,
were her primary beneficiaries. See the Yuri Suhl Manuscripts at the Boston
University Library.

in the revolution of July 1830.[12] Through her tutoring, writes d'Hericourt, she found kindred spirits in the burgeoning Owenite movement.

London: Owenite Reform Movements in the 1830s

Owenism in the early 1830s was an interesting pastiche of cooperative ventures, a trade union movement, and a social philosophy that emphasized individual liberty (women's rights, educational rights, religious freedom) and socialistic cooperation. This combination of ideologies and practices originated in Robert Owen's vision to make his world a more perfect place. Leaving his birthplace, Wales, in 1781 at the age of 10, reputedly with only 40 shillings in his pocket, Robert Owen, in a tradition soon to be popularized in nineteenth-century novels glorifying capitalists on the rise, journeyed to London to make his fortune. Success in each of his ensuing apprenticeships led to his eventual management and part ownership of the New Lanark mills in southwestern Scotland. From 1800 on Owen set about transforming New Lanark from a dirty mill town into a showplace of cleanliness and enlightened education.[13]

During his almost 25 years at New Lanark, Owen created a series of plans that he hoped would improve the lot of poor people trapped landless and uneducated in a burgeoning industrial society. Owen unashamedly latched onto the ideas of the Enlightenment thinkers he was familiar with, synthesizing them into his own expanding theory. From Locke he took the idea that the character of man is formed for him, not by him; from Rousseau, that children collectively may be taught sentiments and habits; from the Utilitarians, the importance of happiness, which can be

12. See the Dec. 3, 1856, *Boston Investigator,* where in a letter Rose explains that, in Paris during this exciting time, she saw the glass shattered at the Louvre after the July 1830 demonstrations.

13 Numerous people, including Robert Owen himself, have told the story of his life. See Robert Owen, *The Life of Robert Owen, by Himself;* Frank Podmore, *Robert Owen;* G. D. H. Cole, *The Life of Robert Owen;* Rowland Harvey, *Robert Owen, Social Idealist;* and William Sargant, *Robert Owen and his Social Philosophy.*

attained only by conduct that must promote the happiness of the community; from William Godwin, the notion that private property has to be eliminated in order for equality to exist; and from Adam Smith, the premise that wealth results from labor. Taken together, these ideas appear unrelated, a hodgepodge of the best in late eighteenth-century, male-dominated philosophy. But together they form the nexus from which Owen's ideas for "communities of equality" would spring.

During the early 1820s, Owen's successful efforts to help his workers at New Lanark obtain reasonably priced food and necessities and to educate all of their children with "sensible signs" evolved into a grandiose plan whereby intentional, socialistic communities would allow all people to share an equality and individual liberty lacking in the "old, immoral world." Convinced that his many followers, as well-meaning as they might be, were not serious about effecting a socialism that would, in effect, eliminate private property, Owen turned to the New World to realize his dream of a "new, moral world."

In fall 1824 Owen sailed to America to inspect and then purchase the Rappite community of Harmonie in southwestern Indiana. Arriving in New York City, he was hailed by governors, entertained by presidents, and asked to speak to the House of Representatives. News of Owen's every step was published continually in American newspapers. His theory was relatively simple and appealing in its "Americanist" notions: people are made, not born; with the right environment and a lack of dogma, all people could thrive. But more important to many of his listeners than his theoretical assumptions were the proposed economic and social benefits of his communities: an eight-hour working day, excellent schools for their children, ease of living for the sick or injured. So evangelical was his speaking style, so charismatic was his personality that many people overlooked Owen's revolutionary statements about women and marriage.

"Women," preached Owen, were "enslaved" in traditional marriages (*NHG* July 12, 1826). In his forthcoming New Harmony Community, they would not be economically dependent upon men or mere "domestic drudges," but instead would be educated, rational adults with equal social and political rights with men. Such liberation would be possible because children would be raised communally in dormitories designed for them and housework would be performed "scientifically," with food prepared in public kitchens and all apartments heated, cooled, supplied with gas lights and hot and cold running water at the flick of a switch. All community residents, proclaimed Owen, would live in utmost comfort in a carefully designed parallelogram, which would house the children's dormitory, separate apartments for each adult, a school, a common eating room, and ample recreational areas. The latest technological advances would eliminate the drudgery necessary to maintain an individual home.

Owen's prophecies about life in New Harmony were not to be realized. For a variety of reasons, New Harmony and the dozen or so other Owenite communities that sprang up in the United States in the mid-1820s had all disbanded by the end of the decade.[14] But, despite the lack of functioning Owenite communities in the 1830s, the Owenite movement was far from dead. Robert Owen returned to Great Britain in 1827 and continued to plan his new moral world. In England, Owen became actively involved in the burgeoning cooperative movement that his disciples had begun while he was still at New Lanark. By the beginning of the 1830s, the cooperative movement was emphasizing buying and selling goods efficiently and educating children in common—instead of creating intentional communities.

Although Owen had not given up his communal plan, he did branch out into other areas, including the National Labour Exchange, which he saw as a bridge from the old, immoral world to his new, moral one. Just as the cooperative societies attempted to circumvent the principles of capitalist trading, the labor exchanges, according to J.F.C. Harrison, helped to actualize the labor theory of value—that laborers had the right to their entire labor (201). The labor exchange became a clearing house where individual workers exchanged their products without the use of money.

14. For more information on the reasons why the communities disbanded, see my *Women in Utopia.*

A third facet of Owenite economics in the 1830s, in addition to the cooperative societies and labor exchanges, was the trade union movement. According to R. G. Garnett, the labor exchange brought trade unions into the cooperative movement (141). Although the members of trade unions were suspicious of the communitarian aspects of Owenism, argues Gregory Claeys, Owenite economic ideas formed the basis of the movement. In April 1834 the largest union in the Grand National Consolidated Trades Union struck for higher wages, but the strike was over within a month, effectively ending the burgeoning union movement in Great Britain.

In addition to propounding the underlying theory of women's equality with men, the cooperative societies, the labor exchanges, and the trade unions also sent delegates to "cooperative congresses," 1830s Owenite versions of revivals-cum-academic-conferences. These congresses regularly attracted women and encouraged their speaking in public to promote Owenite economic and social policies. Participants at the congresses attacked organized religion, denounced marriage without the possibility of divorce, advocated equal educational opportunities for all young people, and railed against the isolation and selfishness fostered by capitalism. The nuclear family, one of Owen's favorite targets, came under special attack: Owenites claimed that marriage and individual family life perverted what was "natural" while teaching children to be selfish and hypocritical.

When Ernestine Potowski arrived in London in the early 1830s, her feisty independence must have attracted her to reformers in the Owenite movement and them to her. How and when she became an Owenite and met Robert Owen is not clear. One account relates that Ernestine, a "young girl fresh from Poland," was first introduced to a public audience in London by Robert Owen at the opening of his great hall,[15] whereas L. E. Barnard

15. See Moncure D. Conway in the May 24, 1871, *BI*. Podmore notes that many "halls" opened from the mid-1830s to 1840s. See also Harrison on the building of many halls of science, as places where Owenites could meet, listen to lectures, and exchange ideas; they were, says Harrison, a part-time version of the

claims that Ernestine met Owen in 1832 and then presided at the
formation of the Association of All Classes of All Nations in 1835
(*BI* Feb. 14, 1877).

Certainly Ernestine must have read the Owenite papers for sale
in London during the 1830s: the *Crisis*, the *Pioneer*, and the *New
Moral World*, all of which emphasized the importance of eliminating "selfish" economic systems and increasing the rights of workingmen and, especially, women. In the *Crisis*, for example, Anna
Wheeler, an outspoken Owenite feminist, translated a Saint-Simonian
essay that demanded rights for women, including "equal marriage
laws," and proposed a new world united by love where women of
the privileged class and women "of the people" would no longer
oppose each other (*Crisis* June 15, 1833). Wheeler, as the companion of William Thompson when he was writing his *Distribution
of Wealth* (1824), had convinced Thompson that women everywhere were "domestic slaves" with no access to mental pursuits
and were "tools of male selfishness" (Thompson, *Distribution* 556).

The *Pioneer*, or *Trades' Union Magazine*, began publication
on September 7, 1833, in Birmingham but sold actively in London as well until it ceased publication on July 5, 1834. It stressed
that labor is the source of all wealth, that society can improve with
cooperation, that women of all classes should be educated, and
that all adults should have the right to vote. Although the publication was not sponsored by Owen, it was closely aligned with
Robert Owen's interests.[16] Both the editor of the *Pioneer*, James
Morrison, and his activist spouse, Frances Morrison, demanded

---

New Harmony ideal (222–23). Owen biographer G. D. H. Cole writes in a letter
to Yuri Suhl that the "great hall" could be either one of the buildings occupied
by the Owenite Labour Exchange, one situated first in the Grays Inn Road and
the other subsequently at Charlotte Street or the hall at Cartright Gardens (Yuri
Suhl Papers: Cole to Suhl, Mar. 4, 1957). Perhaps it could also be the "New
Mechanics Hall of Science" on City Road, Finsbury.

16. Owen writes the *Pioneer* on Jan. 11, 1843, that he has been watching
"your progress with deep interest, and with many of the general sentiments
expressed . . . I am much pleased." His quibble is with the *Pioneer*'s sense of
opposition of feelings and interests between employers and employed in the
production of wealth.

rights for all women, including working-class women, rights that included equal educational opportunities, equal employment opportunities, and access to equal wages.

Ernestine may well have been intrigued by the Morrisons' "Woman's Page." On October 26, 1833, James Morrison asks to hear from women readers because "a man cannot feign a woman's feelings;—he does not know her wrongs;—he wrongs her most himself.—He is the tyrant,—she the slave.—How can HE portray HER smothered thought, or write HER anxious wish? Write yourselves." The response was both a "Woman's Page" and a series of occasional columns by "A Bondswoman," the nom de plume of Frances Morrison.

The Morrisons, as socialists, emphasized the importance of the trade unions. In her first Bondswoman column, Frances Morrison urges women to "be slaves no longer, but unite and assert your rights! With the anxious hope that we may soon establish a union that will be a shield from oppression of every kind" (Feb. 8, 1834). Interspersed in the pages of the *Pioneer* are small pieces and notices of trade union meetings for such organizations as "The Grand Lodge of the Women of Great Britain and Ireland" or the "Bonnet Makers of London."

In the "Woman's Page" the Morrisons discussed woman's rights and the limitations to them in often humorous and enlightened ways such that if Ernestine Potowski read them, she would certainly have been delighted with them. Confronted with skeptics who argued that man is stronger than woman, thus superior, they respond: "Then, by a parity of reasoning, a black bear or a wild buffalo is superior to man, for it is much stronger" (Apr. 12, 1834). Facing laws that discriminated against married women, they write that "the very being or existence of a woman is supposed to be extinct during marriage; she is called a 'femme covert'—that is, a woman whose being is not acknowledged—an invisible woman—a species of ghost, who haunts her husband, and only becomes half solidified when he is no more" (Mar. 15, 1834). In part, their solution to woman's problem is unity, a solidarity with other women not available in what Owen called the "old, immoral world." They argue

> divided as men are . . . women are infinitely more so. Men have
> their public meetings, their social meetings, their newspapers,
> their magazines, their male speakers, and their male editors . . . but
> woman knows nothing of woman, except through the medium
> of man—a dense medium, which distorts her native character,
> and bedaubs it with the false colouring of the sex, whose
> feelings . . . must be the very reverse of her own. (Mar. 8, 1834)

Women must, then, "consult with woman on her own affairs;
allow no male to enter her meetings until she has obtained sufficient
skill and experience to act in public, and then let her assembly
rooms be thrown open" (Mar. 8, 1834). The Morrisons also praise
the one woman lecturing in Manchester in 1834—Frances Wright.
They urge their readers to "come, at least, and hear this woman,
to kindle your ambition. Yes, come and see how false the notion
is that woman cannot speak in public with grace and dignity. And
come and see the bonny prospect of woman's freedom" (June 21,
1834).

Four months after the demise of the *Pioneer* in July 1834
Robert Owen's *New Moral World*, the longest-running and most
influential of the Owenite newspapers, began publishing in London. A weekly puff piece for Owen and his activities in its first
several years of publishing, the *New Moral World* offered a series
of essays and a few letters and notices about Owenite activities.
The lead essays in the paper, often written by Owen in his trademark evangelical style, signal a "time for man's regeneration" over
"moral evil" (Nov. 8, 1834). These essays include traditional
Owenite subjects such as "Principles of the Rational System," "What
Is Human Nature," or background pieces on Owen's work from
1816 through the 1820s.

One of the paper's first set of lead essays—Owen's famous
"Lectures on the Marriages of the Priesthood"—ran from December 6, 1834, through mid-February 1835. In these ten essays,
which Owen gave first as lectures on subsequent Sunday evenings
at his "Institution" at 14 Charlotte Street, Owen argues that the
priesthood—and by "priesthood" Owen meant to refer to all religions headed by a leader who interpreted Scriptures for a con-

gregation—is the origin of "all prostitution, endless crimes, evils, and sufferings" (Dec. 6, 1834). As he had argued in the mid-1820s, Owen urged his listeners to adopt an entirely new moral system, because the current system was bankrupt, with the marriage system causing only misery to most men and women and their children.[17] Not only were men and women miserable in these lifelong marriages, living "in a state of the most degrading prostitution, enforced upon them by the human laws of marriage" (Jan. 17, 1835), but traditional single family unions also inflicted "innumerable evils . . . upon the children of both sexes of all ages" because these "artificial unions" generated only single-family interests (Dec. 27, 1834).

As the trade union movement failed in England in 1834, the Owenites became even more convinced that what the world needed was not oppositional strategies but a new order where the "character and condition of mankind" is changed. Thus, Owen established on May 1, 1835, the Association of All Classes of All Nations (AACAN)—an optimistically titled group—to "effect peaceably, and by reason alone, an entire change in the character and condition of mankind, by establishing over the world, in principle and practice, the religion of charity . . . without distinction of sex, class, sect, party, country, or colour" (*NMW* May 23, 1835). The Association was to begin immediately—by establishing an infant school for all ages, by setting up cooperative societies, but its ultimate goal was to create "Communities of United Interests."

AACAN sought to eliminate the piecemeal economic reforms of the 1830s that Robert Owen believed did not go far enough and to establish a community system all over the world, fostered by workers and owners. Unlike the loosely organized cooperative societies and trade union movement, the AACAN would be a formal organization with a branch structure and a national execu-

17. Although Gail Malmgreen writes that these essays express "Owen's fullest and most original statement on women and socialism" (15), they are simply reiterations of Owen's writing and speaking in New Harmony where he was then, as later, far more interested in allowing men to divorce than in creating a real egalitarianism for women.

tive.[18] With its intent to change a world where private interests interfered with all public improvements, the AACAN stressed universal education (for men and women) and association based on harmonies. Thus, regular public meetings to offer "mutual instruction" as well as to hear formal lectures dominated the lives of Owenite followers in London in 1835 and 1836. On Sundays, for example, Ernestine may well have attended both the morning instruction in the principles and practices of the New Moral World as well as hearing Owen lecture at 7:00 P.M. on "Marriages of the Priesthood" or some other subject. Socials and discussions along with "instruction" for newcomers were held on Wednesday and Friday evenings. Every other Monday festivals designed to "improve the habits of the people" (*NMW* Feb. 28, 1835) brought members and potential members together. Every member of the Association paid one penny per week to defray costs.

Although no one can verify that Ernestine presided at the formation of the AACAN as L. E. Barnard claims—and it seems improbable to me that a 25-year-old woman from Poland would have presided at the founding of Owen's enterprise—she was a member and was involved in its myriad activities.[19] Surely Ernestine might have been involved in the Polish Society of Mutual Instruction, a beneficial society of emigrant Owenites established in March 1834 that met at 14 Charlotte Street some Sundays following Robert Owen's lecture.[20] The purpose of the Society, to give mutual instruction to each other and to teach poor children French,

18. For more information about the AACAN, created by a "confederacy of broad-minded capitalists and enlightened workers," see Taylor, 117–18.

19. See the June 1, 1853, *Boston Investigator* where Rose, in a speech celebrating Robert Owen's birthday, told her audience that she had been a member of AACAN: "On the fifth of May, 1834, he [Owen] formed a society (to which I had the pleasure to belong) called the Association of All Classes of All Nations." Rose told Jenny d'Hericourt in 1856 that she was part of the weekly AACAN meetings and that she helped Owen organize the meetings that attracted from 1,500 to 1,800 people. She added that she often washed up and put away, "with my own two hands," all the dishes used to make and serve tea. (134)

20. See the Nov. 28, 1835, *NMW* for an announcement of the meeting of the Polish emigrants to celebrate the Anniversary of the Declaration of Polish Independence.

German, and Polish, seems just like the kind of group that Ernestine would participate in or organize after arriving in England.[21] From the moment she met Owen, she felt she had found someone who understood the world as she did, and she embraced his doctrine completely.[22]

Where and when Ernestine met her future husband, William Rose, three years her junior, is unclear. Perhaps they met at a meeting for Owenites interested in the Socialland Community, whose secretary was H. Rose—possibly a relative from William's family?[23] Perhaps Ernestine and William heard Owen give his lectures on marriage of the priesthood together. Perhaps they knew of the marriage contract that Robert Owen's eldest son, Robert Dale Owen, had drawn up when he married Mary Jane Owen, ensuring that Robert Dale would never suffer from a loveless marriage as his father had. The Roses' own wedding followed Owenite practices: they were married in a civil, nonreligious ceremony in Ernestine's rooms rather than in a church; her belief in the equality of the sexes forbade anything else (d'Hericourt, "Madame Rose" 134).

Devoted reformers, Ernestine and William decided shortly after their marriage to join an Owenite colony formed to create a community in the New World in the spring of 1836. Though they

21. If Rose did participate in this Society, as seems probable, the members' teaching languages to poor children is in keeping with Rose's early biographers' statements that she taught "languages" after she arrived in London.

22. I would like to believe that a letter from "E. L."—Ernestine Louise—published in the Nov. 29, 1834, *New Moral World* was written by Ernestine. Its enthusiasm for discovering Owenite thought reflects an ardor comparable to that expressed by Ernestine in her documented letters. E. L. writes to Robert Owen that she is enthralled with what she has discovered of his ideas: "No words can possibly express the joy and delight I feel in looking over the different plans proposed by you to terminate the irrational existence of moral evil, and to enter upon that of moral good. I have just been perusing the last number of the *New Moral World*, I may add, with great pleasure and a solid satisfaction. Every number that comes out appears to me so big with truth, that almost all the other periodical publications sink into nothingness in comparison with this."

23. See the Feb. 28, 1835, *New Moral World* for the notice of the Socialland Community.

became discouraged with the group's preparation for community life on the long trip across the ocean—they had learned, perhaps from Robert Owen, the importance of being well prepared for community life—they lost none of their dedication to their Owenite ideals. Perhaps they had also read J. B. Matrat's book *Practical Emigration to the United States of North America, Systematized*, which had been well reviewed in the March and April 1836 *New Moral World* immediately before they left for America. According to *The New Moral World*, Matrat advised emigrants to give up the romanticism of the backwoods and move to cities instead where they should associate with people like themselves, speaking the same language, possessing the same habits, customs, and religion. Perhaps following Matrat's advice, Ernestine and William abandoned the ill-prepared colony that was probably on its way to New Harmony, Indiana, and sought out, instead, a group of like-minded reformers in New York City.[24]

New York: Reform Movements in the Mid-1830s

As a utopian reformer with a mission, Ernestine Rose found New York City to be a particularly fertile locale for reformers in the mid-1830s. For many people, city life was still quite primitive and sometimes dangerous: water came from street pumps and refuse was thrown on the streets. Workers' strikes beginning in the early 1830s led to riots in 1834 and ten major turnout strikes in 1836, the year the Roses arrived.[25] Such economic unrest foreshadowed the Panic of 1837, the deepest depression of pre–Civil War America and a disaster for New York City's economy when

24. In the June 17, 1836, *Boston Investigator*, Lewis Masquerier's June 3, 1836, letter gives some background information about the Owenite "colony." Masquerier writes: "I received day before yesterday the packet of letters; one of which was from . . . Mr. Quantrel, an Owenite, informing me of the arrival of the community company at New York on their way to New Harmony. . . . [N]either of the letters [one from Quantrel, the other from Robert Owen] inform me of the number of this community company that has come over."
25. See Wilentz, 255–96, on the strikes and worker unrest.

more than one-third of New York's workers lost their jobs in the aftermath of the panic (Wilentz 294).

Perhaps owing to the worsening economic conditions, the mid-1830s were an era of reform. Some of the movements, such as temperance and moral reform, were religiously based. These movements were given impetus by the preaching of revivalist Charles Grandison Finney in the late 1820s and early 1830s, who, in many of his famous sermons, urged his listeners to become involved in good works. By 1836 the moral reform and temperance movements had spawned dozens of organizations in New York City alone, such as the New York Female Moral Reform Society (founded in 1834), with its journal *The Advocate of Moral Reform*, or the New York City Magdalene Society, founded in 1831 to reclaim prostitutes. They were just two of the many societies working to purify the world by eliminating hard liquor and enforcing chastity. Such groups, sometimes starting as men's societies but increasingly made up of middle- and upper-class women, produced mixed results. Sean Wilentz has argued persuasively, for example, that the temperance movement turned into an anti-union weapon in the 1830s, giving owners and bosses an alternative explanation for workers' economic problems (283).

At the same time, these religiously based moral reform groups indirectly enabled middle-class women to form "bonds of sisterhood," offering a network to women who left their home for "public" work.[26] Although the groups were remarkably ineffective at eliminating drunkenness, prostitution, or gambling, the women who made up the membership of these groups did effectively disseminate images of women as victims of man's lust or violence (Ginzberg 19). Such groups, then, offered middle- and upperclass women opportunities to work together in the public sphere for the "common good"—which, increasingly, was being defined in terms of moral benevolence. These groups, however, offered

---

26. For more information about the "bonds of womanhood" in nineteenth-century America, see the work of Cott, Douglas, Ginzberg, and Ryan, among others.

working-class men and women nothing but further separation as "others"—those who drink or sin—in an increasingly class-bound culture.[27]

Perhaps the most important reform that was deeply influenced by evangelical missionary zeal—and the one that attracted the greatest numbers in New York City and elsewhere—was the abolitionist movement. Hundreds of antislavery societies were established throughout the 1830s.[28] From the eighteenth century, human slavery had presented, in Lewis Perry's words, "an obvious and painful incongruity" in a nation that prided itself on its Declaration of Independence (8). Many of the earliest antislavery societies were established by church groups, responding to the inhumanity of slavery; others were formed by individuals who were eager to have the newly created United States live up to its principles that proclaimed all human beings "free and equal." Yet others formed the American Colonization Society to ensure that freed slaves were expatriated to Africa or the West Indies.

The abolitionist movement accelerated in 1831, when William Lloyd Garrison began printing the *Liberator* and Nat Turner led a rebellion of slaves in the same year. In the 1830s the ideas of expatriation espoused by the American Colonization Society came more and more under attack as Garrison popularized the moral

27. Christine Stansell argues that the bourgeois women who gained some freedom of movement and a wider sphere of influence through these societies had little power to visualize the actual difficulties of laboring women (75).

28. For descriptions of the variety of different types of people involved in antislavery, see the Peases; for the different types of women involved, see Hewitt, *Activism*. Also, as Ginzberg has summarized, women's class and social background corresponded with the causes they espoused: religious middle-class women became involved in the moral reform movements; antireligious or reformist religious women became Garrisonian abolitionists.

Even though a purist might separate the terms "antislavery" and "abolition"—with the former referring to the movement that would use all means (including the political process) to end slavery and the latter to refer to immediate and complete emancipation—I will use them interchangeably. Reformers who were believers in immediate emancipation called themselves "antislavery people" and often called their organizations "antislavery societies." See Friedman, 1, though Friedman does distinguish the terms.

necessity of an "immediate" cessation of slavery. In late 1833 Garrison helped to found the American Anti-Slavery Society (AASS), with Arthur Tappan, a New Yorker, as the first president and Garrison as recording secretary. The AASS helped to unify national abolitionist efforts by bringing together Garrison's powerful New England Anti-Slavery Society (founded in 1832), Tappan's New York Anti-Slavery Society, the Philadelphia Anti-Slavery Society, and a number of other local and regional societies. The Society grew rapidly: by 1838, according to Stanley Elkins, the national organization was made up of 1,350 local and regional groups (quoted in Kraditor, *Means and Ends* 6). Garrison's leadership brought to the national society an emphasis on the importance of education and an atmosphere where women like Garrison's coworker in Boston, Maria Chapman, could speak out and work actively in the public sphere for the antislavery cause. Chapman had, in fact, along with her sisters, established the Boston Female Anti-Slavery Society in 1832 and was responsible for organizing the yearly Massachusetts Anti-Slavery Society Fairs, the most successful of all abolitionist fund-raisers.

The abolitionist and moral reform movements in New York City in the 1830s did, indeed, involve women in public activities such as petition gathering and some, albeit minor, public speaking; but these movements did not, in themselves, lead to the woman's rights movement of the 1850s, as has often been claimed.[29] The women and men involved in abolitionism or in the moral reform groups often differed greatly in their motives for joining such groups: the wealthy Tappans (Arthur, Lewis, Juliana) of New York, for example, were members of the new urban bourgeoisie, who felt it their duty to aid the less fortunate, who might include orphans, destitute women, or slaves (Hewitt, "Own Terms" 27); Lucretia and James Mott, as Hicksite Quakers, joined the antislavery movement because they were responding to the "inner light" of their religion.

29. Nancy Hewitt has astutely pointed out that members of these reform groups did not progress, linearly, from benevolence to reform to radicalism. See "Own Terms," 26.

Ernestine Rose's early reform efforts, though, did lead directly to the woman's rights movement. As a freethinker from an Owenite socialist tradition, Rose, from her first activities, was thinking about reform for all people and specifically about reform for women. As a secular reformer deriving her ideas from Enlightenment philosophy that provided the epistemological framework for the Declaration of Independence, Rose did not have to grow into her woman's rights activism as did Lucretia Mott (who even in the late 1840s still did not believe that women should chair meetings) or the younger Elizabeth Cady Stanton, who needed time, female friends, and the radicalizing events of her own life before she actively joined the Hicksite forces in Seneca Falls in 1848.[30] Rose was remarkably consistent throughout her life: all human beings, regardless of color or sex, should have the same rights and the same freedoms. It was as simple as that.

The Freethinking Tradition

More directly appropriate to Ernestine Rose's interests than the abolitionist or the moral reform movements and leading more directly to the woman's rights movement was America's long-standing freethinking tradition dating from the turn of the eighteenth century. It was the freethinking reformers to whom the Roses first turned. The year 1800 saw the first New York freethinking periodical, *The Temple of Reason*, published by Elihu Palmer, a blind Connecticut lecturer on the merits of deism. After *Temple* ceased publication, Palmer published the *Prospects, or View of the New Moral World* in New York City, while lecturing on Christian "superstition." Palmer, like Owen and Rose after him, celebrated "the unlimited power of human reason" (324); he looked forward to a time when "the empire of reason, of science, and of virtue, will extend over the whole earth, and man, [will be] emancipated from the barbarous despotism of antiquity" (324).

---

30. Keith Melder has pointed out in *Beginnings* that nineteenth-century reform had two basic sources, one secular and the other religious. Secular reformers derived their principles from Enlightenment philosophy and were most active in late-eighteenth-century America. The Roses came from this tradition.

By the mid-to-late 1820s a good number of freethinkers lived in New York. George Houston, a freethinker who had been imprisoned in Newgate for two years for publishing a translation of d'Holbach's *Histoire de Jésus Christ*, emigrated to New York from England. He was the first person to meet Robert Owen on Owen's visit to New York in late 1824 on his way to purchase New Harmony. Houston was so taken with Owen's ideas that he, along with several others, created the first Owenite community in New York state, the Franklin Community in Haverstraw.[31] Publicizing the Franklin community from his pulpit in New York City was Abner Kneeland, another important member of the city's free-thinking community in the 1820s.[32] Kneeland, who had moved to New York City in 1825, preached the glories of freethought first from his pulpit as a Universalist minister and then, after he publicly gave up religion in the late 1820s, as the editor of the *Boston Investigator* during the 1830s.

Joining Houston and Kneeland in New York in the 1820s were numerous freethinkers who were equally vehement about the evils of Christianity, but who were never enamored of Robert Owen's plan to create intentional communities and thus abolish private property. Particularly important to Rose in the 1830s were Benjamin Offen, a shoemaker who came to New York from England in 1824, and Gilbert Vale, a printer who had also emigrated from England in the late 1820s.

These New York freethinkers were, in many ways, out of step with mainstream America. Just as the Second Great Awakening

31. The Franklin Community at Haverstraw was founded on "Mr. Owen's principles" by several New York freethinkers including Houston; Henry Fay, a lawyer known for defending the freethinkers in New York; and Jacob Peterson, who held the deed to the property. Joining these three men at Franklin was New Harmonite Robert Jennings, who left New Harmony in April 1826 to become the president of Franklin. For information on the Franklin Community see my *Women in Utopia*, 62–79; A. J. Macdonald, "Materials from a History of Ideal Communities," (Beinecke Rare Book Manuscript Library); and, for daily life in the community, see James M'Knight, "A Discourse."

32. For information about Abner Kneeland, see a variety of personal comments in Kneeland's *Boston Investigator* from 1837 through 1839. See also Kneeland's "An Appeal to Common Sense" and "A Series of Lectures" in the Boston Public Library, Manuscript Division. Also see Levy and French.

was sweeping across New York State, a group of immigrant and home-grown infidels were preaching reason and individual rights instead of intuition, faith, and obedience. These immigrants had chosen the United States as their new home at least in part because of the promise of individual rights emphasized in the Declaration of Independence. Freethinkers (or "infidels" as they were called) like Offen and Vale feared evangelical religion and its concomitant moral reform movements.

Although George Houston's effort to begin an Owenite community at Haverstraw did not work out, Houston, Kneeland, Offen, and Vale found other ways to spread the word of the infidels. A favored activity was newspaper editing/publishing, a fitting enterprise for people who believed in the power of reason and argument. In 1827, Houston began publishing the *Correspondent*, the first exclusively infidel paper to appear in the United States since a briefly published deist paper in 1811 (Post 45). The *Correspondent*, a weekly newspaper intended to enlarge minds through open, scientific investigation, reprinted the writings of Thomas Paine and published a series of essays on such topics as the "authenticity of the Scriptures." The paper also kept readers informed about Robert Owen's communities. Similarly, Abner Kneeland, after leaving the ministry and heading the New York Society for Moral Philanthropists, moved to Boston where he began publishing the *Boston Investigator* in 1831, the longest-running infidel paper in America, until he left to found an Owenite-like intentional community in Iowa in 1838. The *Investigator* advocated a variety of freethinking platforms and also included ideas of "rational" marriage and the rights of women in addition to freethought. Kneeland, like many of the other freethinking men, believed that the subordination of women was a projection of male self-interest, and he thus advocated equal wages for equal work, separate names for husband and wife, and marriage contracts.

Perhaps the most important paper to the freethinkers in New York in the decade before Ernestine Rose's arrival was an Owenite paper begun in 1825 as the *New Harmony Gazette* and then moved to New York City in 1828 by its coeditors Frances Wright and Robert Dale Owen, Robert Owen's son, when it was renamed the

Free Enquirer. The *Free Enquirer*, published weekly through June 1835, disseminated original and reprinted essays of interest to freethinkers and others across the country. Its colorful coeditor, Frances Wright, a freethinking woman who adopted Owenite communitarian reform and spoke out publicly for woman's rights, is perhaps Ernestine Rose's most influential foremother.

Frances Wright

Frances Wright was arguably the most important Owenite free-thinker among those based in New York City in the late 1820s. Wright, had, in 1825, devoted a portion of her considerable fortune to establishing an Owenite community—Nashoba—in south-western Tennessee. After visiting Robert Owen's New Harmony, Wright attempted to create a model egalitarian community with a special twist: it would provide the means through which slaves could earn enough money to free themselves, thus providing a prototype mechanism for ending slavery in the United States. Wright conceived of a community where equality would be the norm.

Possibly because she herself was a woman, Frances Wright created, on paper at least, a community attuned to the needs of women. Women's rights were spelled out more explicitly at Nashoba than at any other nineteenth-century experimental community. At Nashoba, Wright dictated that "no woman can forfeit her individual rights or independent existence, and no man assert over her any rights or power whatsoever . . . nor, on the other hand, may any woman assert claims to the society or peculiar protection of an individual of the other sex, beyond what mutual inclination dictates and sanctions, while to every individual member of either sex is secured the protection and friendly aid of all" (*NHG* Feb. 6, 1828). All young minds at Nashoba were to learn rational thinking in order to discern the absurdity and ignorance abounding in society's laws and opinions.

Despite Wright's plans, however, Nashoba, like New Harmony and other Owenite experiments, failed in many ways to live up to its hopes during its four-year existence. The most obvious problems were the same ones that plagued New Harmony: too little money, too little food, and too much to do to maintain civilized life in the middle of the "West." Though Wright had proposed that every member build himself or herself a house, after four years Nashoba consisted of only three or four log houses and a few small cabins for the slaves. The proposed school never materialized, though slave children were taught by various members of the community.

In addition, Wright became ill her first summer in Tennessee and her recurring illness (probably malaria) forced her to take a convalescent trip to Europe the following summer. In her absence, one of the members of the community gave a copy of the "Nashoba Book," a journalistic account of life at Nashoba, to Benjamin Lundy to publish in his *Genius of Universal Emancipation* in July 1827. In it one of the white managers of the community revealed that he had begun living with a black woman "the previous night" (*Genius* July 28, 1827). With the publishing of this "proof" of the long-suspected immorality and miscegenation at Nashoba, public outrage against Wright's "free love colony" sprang up all over the country. Former supporters, such as the wealthy and conservative banker Charles Wilkes, wrote to Wright's sister, Camilla, at Nashoba hoping the incident was exaggerated. Camilla, though, responded with vehemence in her sister's absence. Rather than disapproving of the couple's living arrangement, Camilla wrote Wilkes that her disapproval was of "the marriage tie, wh. I regard as not only in the utmost degree irrational, in requiring of two individuals to love each other during life, when they have not the control of their affections for one hour, but in the highest degree pernicious in compelling these individuals to continue united, when the feelings which brought them together have turned to utter aversion."[33]

By the summer of 1828, Wright realized that her plan to provide a model by which America's slaves could all be freed at no cost to slave owners was not going to work. Turning to lecturing and writing instead, she joined forces with Robert Dale Owen and

33. See Camilla's letter in the Theresa Wolfson Papers at Cornell University. Camilla's response, in effect, closed the door of benevolent proper society to Frances Wright.

became a coeditor of the *New Harmony Gazette*. The partnership of Wright and Owen, first in New Harmony and then in New York City after Wright decided to move the *Gazette* to New York and rename it the *Free Enquirer*, created the "first fruits of Owenism," according to Robert Dale Owen's biographer Richard Leopold (62). Similarly, Arthur Bester writes that Wright and Robert Dale Owen effectively translated Owenite radicalism from the language of communitarian experience into the different language of reform in the late 1820s (226–27).

In New York, Wright and the younger Owen became the Free Enquirers, self-appointed crusaders who set about to lobby for the individual rights that were the basis of the American revolution. Wright helped focus the growing freethinking movement, meeting and lecturing with Abner Kneeland (who would remain a lifelong friend), Gilbert Vale, George Houston, and others. Influenced by the elder Owen, but surpassing his reform thinking, particularly when it came to women's rights, the *Free Enquirer* attacked errors in thinking. For both the Free Enquirers, education would be the great equalizer. Wright proposed both in the pages of the *Free Enquirer* and in her lectures a detailed plan for a national educational system which would provide free, public schools for both girls and boys. Like the elder Owen, Wright also condemned the ill effects of marriage, but where Owen was concerned primarily with divorce reform, Wright focused on the effects of marriage on women and advocated increased rights for women within marriage. That a woman at her marriage swore away "at one and the same moment her person and her property, and as it but too often is, her peace, her honor, and her life," that a married woman had no protection under the law horrified Wright. Using rhetoric from the Declaration of Independence, Wright pleaded with "every father not absolutely dead to all human feeling" not to allow his daughters "blindly to immolate all their rights, liberties, and property by the simple utterance of a word, and thus place themselves, in their tender, ignorant, and unsuspecting youth, as completely at the disposal and mercy of an individual, as is the negro slave when bought for gold in the market of Kingston or New Orleans" (*FE* Apr. 29, 1829).

Late in the winter of 1829 or early in 1830, Frances Wright accidentally became pregnant and the direction of her life changed against her will, as has been the experience of many women. Wright quickly traveled to France, had a baby girl (Sylva), married the baby's father, had another baby girl that died in infancy, and spent five years living a domestic life. In 1835, her marriage disintegrating, Wright returned to the United States and began lecturing and writing again. In 1836 she joined her old friend, Abner Kneeland, in Boston, where he was editing the *Boston Investigator.*[34]

The Summer of 1836

By the time Rose landed in America, the freethinking groups based in New York City had helped articulate the importance of woman's rights in a variety of ways. Frances Wright and Robert Dale Owen's *Free Enquirer,* even though they were no longer editing it, circulated considerable information dealing with women's capacities and necessary rights. Such lead essays as "The Mental Capacities of Females" (by G. H.—probably George Houston) printed from an earlier lecture series in Tammany Hall—and an address "Introducing a Bill for Holding and Acquiring Property by Married Women" by Mary Jane Owen, dominated the paper during 1835. The *Free Enquirer* also publicized lecture series on such subjects as "The Social Rights of Women" by Madame Louise D'Auriet, currently being given in Paris.

Similarly, Abner Kneeland, with Frances Wright's help during the summer of 1836, published a variety of essays concerning

---

34. During the final decade of her life, Wright confronted patriarchal power on a personal level as she battled her husband for her property and for the affections of her daughter. Most of her former friends openly condemned her when she tried to resume her lecturing career in America: "Her best friends regret her course," wrote Lucy Sistaire Say in an 1837 letter; "she is more obnoxious now than ever" (Maclure/Fretageot Correspondence: Say to Maclure, Nov. 7, 1837). Even Robert Dale Owen eventually regretted his friendship with her, writing that as a youth he needed to be "restrained, not urged; needed not the spur, but the guiding rein" (323). Wright died in 1851 in Cincinnati, alone and crippled from a fall that broke her hip, a fitting end, most believed, for the first woman's rights activist in the United States.

women's rights in his *Boston Investigator*, including an essay by Mrs. Leman Grimstone on the importance of "Female Education," reprinted from Robert Owen's *New Moral World* (July 1, 1836), along with considerable information about Owen's All Classes of All Nations, the organization that Rose had just left in London. Kneeland also directed readers to Judge Thomas Herttell's speech in the New York legislature on the rights of married women to property.

In 1836, Thomas Herttell was a 65-year-old reformist lawyer and state legislator from New York City. As a rationalist freethinker, he had spent a lifetime arguing for a variety of rights.[35] In 1819 he published a temperance tract and in 1823 an essay on the unconstitutionality of imprisonment for debts. He was also an early believer in universal suffrage. A candidate for Congress in the 1830s on the Workingmen's ticket, Herttell had published several antireligious tracts in the 1820s and 1830s, including "The Demurrer," which argued that the New York Supreme Court erred in requiring religious faith in witnesses.

In 1836, a year ripe for reform, Herttell introduced a married women's property bill into the New York legislature. In New York, as in most states in the union, when a woman married she lost the right to own property. As Thomas Herttell angrily wrote in justification of his bill:

> It is doubtless obvious to those who have paid due attention to the provisions of this *bill* that its primary *principle* is to preserve to *married* women the title, possession, and control of their estate, both real and personal *after as before* marriage; and that no part of it shall inure to their husbands, solely by virtue of their *marriage*. Thus to protect it from injury and waste by means of the unprovident, prodigal, intemperate, and dissolute

---

35. For information on Thomas Herttell, see N. Basch, *In the Eyes*; see also the broadside "Remarks Comprising the Substance of Judge Herttell's Argument," from the House Assembly of 1837 in New York, which was published first in New York in 1839 and republished by the order of the will of Mrs. Barbara Herttell in Boston, by J. P. Mendum, the publisher of the *Boston Investigator*, in 1867.

habits and practices of their husbands; to save it from loss through the husband's misfortunes and crimes, and in short to make each, and the property of each exclusively answerable for his or her own misconduct. . . . It is no sufficient recommendation of that law, that it originated in the *dark* ages; in times of compara- tive intellectual ignorance, debasement and human vassalage, under an absolute and despotic feudal government and the auspices of mercenary men who were interested in its justice. (6–7)

The summer of 1836 also saw the Society of Moral Philan- thropists sponsor a convention of freethinkers. Benjamin Offen had taken Abner Kneeland's place, after Kneeland left New York for Boston to begin the *Boston Investigator*, as the head of the Society for Moral Philanthropists, the freethinking organization that provided Sunday lectures at Tammany Hall and elsewhere in New York City on a variety of freethinking topics. By the fall of 1836, the Society was also sponsoring a weekly radical newspaper, the *Beacon*. The *Beacon* defined itself as a "liberal" paper, a term that did not mean "atheist" or "deist" or any other ism; it meant "extending to others the same liberty of thought and action which we claim for ourselves" (*Beacon* Jan. 14, 1837). Gilbert Vale, one of the freethinking English immigrants of the 1820s, was the editor of the *Beacon*. The paper publicized weekly New York talks and kept people up to date with freethinkers and "rationalists" around the nation, much as Abner Kneeland's *Boston Investigator* was doing in Boston.[36] The *Beacon* also printed the speeches made at the yearly Thomas Paine celebrations that began in New York City but spread to other towns such as Boston, Cincinnati, Cleve- land—all close to disbanded Owenite communities or where former Owenites and freethinkers had moved.

Thus, in May 1836, as young Owenite reformer Ernestine Rose and her husband William stepped off the boat from London,

36. Though Vale's *Beacon* and Kneeland's *Boston Investigator* overlapped ten years of publication—they were often writing about the same people with Robert Owen at the center—the editors spent much editorial time feuding. Vale calls the Boston infidels a "clique" and "the enemy." Rose, closely aligned with the *Boston Investigator*, was often ignored by her local paper, the *Beacon*.

the stage was set for her. Frances Wright, America's first women's rights activist, was back in the states after five years of stultifying domesticity and a disintegrating marriage in France. Thomas Herttell had just introduced a bill to give New York married women their property rights. In this final year before the panic of 1837, with its concomitant depression, everything seemed possible. New York City was the center of the freethought movement and both Vale's *Beacon* in New York and Kneeland's *Boston Investigator* publicized the activities of a variety of freethought reformers bent on changing the world.

First Ventures Out

How Ernestine and William Rose decided who would stay home and work and who would go out into the world as a reformer may have evolved from their first several years in New York City. Less then a year after arriving, it was Ernestine, not William, who began collecting names on a petition urging passage of Thomas Herttell's bill for married women's property rights. Ernestine Rose reminisces in a letter to Susan B. Anthony about her first year in New York: "In the winter of 1836–37, I spoke in New York, and . . . I sent the first petition to the New York Legislature to give a married woman the right to hold real estate in her own name, in the winter of 1836–37, to which after a good deal of trouble, I obtained five signatures" (*HWS* 1: 99).[37] Rose added that when she went door to door some of the women who answered said that their husbands would laugh at them if they should sign such a petition; others told her that they "had rights enough." Some men quipped that women "had too many rights already" (*HWS* 1: 99).

Within their first year in the United States, Ernestine and William began attending weekly lectures held by the Moral and Philosophical Society, with Benjamin Offen presiding. As early as

37. Note that Rose is not alone; see Mary Jane Owen's two-part essay in the *Free Enquirer*, Jan. 4 and 11, 1835, on "Introducing a Bill for Holding and Acquiring Property by Married Women."

June 3, 1837, Gilbert Vale, the editor of the New York *Beacon*, mentions that "a polish lady" spoke of Robert Owen's system in a weekly Tammany Hall gathering of Freethinkers:

> A Polish lady, of great literary attainments and warmly attached to Robert Owen's system, attended, and delivered her opinions, especially in opposition to Mr. Offen: her views were enlightened, and sentiments liberal; her opinions on religion are those benevolent and liberal opinions of Robert Owen's; those of ours, and of every person who has thought on the subject.

By the fall, Ernestine Rose was speaking at least once a month at Tammany Hall, often on socialism and the concomitant evils of capitalism. Rose battled on the stage with just about everyone, as both the freethinkers Gilbert Vale and Benjamin Offen were opposed to Owen's socialistic schemes. Vale's reporting of Rose's speeches reflect his (and Offen's) views:

> The Polish lady gave a most acceptable lecture last Sunday evening at Tammany Hall, on the evils of private property; and notwithstanding the unpopularity of the subject, and the little influence which the lecture apparently made on the audience, many of whom hugged their dollars and looked about with a smile indicating that preaching would not avail; she retained a most attentive audience, who were evidently pleased at the manner of delivery, and number of facts introduced, and the many important isolated truths, which she stated. (*Beacon* Oct. 14, 1837)

These Moral and Philosophical Society lectures at Tammany Hall included all the important New York freethinkers such as Offen, Vale, Thomas Herttell, Abner Kneeland (when he was in New York), and, occasionally, Frances Wright. Wright and Rose shared the same stage several times during the late 1830s, though neither Rose nor Wright wrote of their early meetings.[38] Wright, however,

---

38. Vale writes in the Jan. 26, 1839, *Beacon*, for example, that six people spoke, including Frances Wright, "whose eloquence brought tears to some masculine eyes," and "a Polish lady, now much improved in her English, never read or spoke better."

left a lasting impression on the seventeen-year-younger Rose. As Rose wrote in 1860 thinking back upon Frances Wright and her contribution: "Frances Wright was the first woman in this country who spoke on the equality of the sexes. She had a hard task before her. . . . She had to break up the time-hardened soil of conservatism, and her reward was sure—the same reward that is always bestowed upon those who are in the vanguard of any great movement. She was subjected to public odium, slander, and persecution" (*PWRC, 1860*).

Like Wright, Rose was soon subject herself to odium, slander, and persecution. In December 1837 Rose attended a public lecture on education at the Broadway Tabernacle. When one of the speakers, the Reverend Robert Breckenridge from Kentucky, left the topic of discussion to lambaste freethinking, Rose used a recess in the speeches to direct a question at the Rev. Breckenridge. Vale describes the scene in the December 23, 1837, *Beacon*:

> During a recess in the addresses to the audience, a young, beautiful, and interesting Lady with uncovered head, and fine flowing locks, arose in the gallery opposite the speaker; and saying it is very painful for her, being a woman and foreigner, to intrude upon the audience; and nothing but a sense of duty and regard for truth induced her to rise; and being impressed with desire to propagate knowledge and truth without mystery . . . she humbly begged permission of the Chairman to ask the gentleman (Mr. Breckenridge) . . . a question.

Rose's speech elicited only hisses from the audience and a refusal from the Reverend to let Rose ask her question, saying he had always been taught never to fight with a lady. What does remain noteworthy is that a 27-year-old immigrant from Poland via London could attempt to direct a question at such a figure of authority and that she could conduct herself in such a calm yet forceful manner at a time when few women spoke in public meetings. Vale further reveals that Rose's response to the shouting and hisses that greeted her words was dignified and forceful: "The Lady turned around upon the tumultuous assembly with unbleached brow, and with a look which seemed to pierce the soul, and to say in terms stronger than language can use, 'while I pity your degeneration and ignorance, I am not to be intimidated by your brutality' " (*Beacon* Dec. 23, 1837).[39]

For the hissing audience, Rose's nerve in daring to confront a clergyman in a church was upsetting both because she was a freethinker and because she was a woman. Mainstream religious culture demanded that women be pure, unquestioning follow-ers—following the leadership of their fathers, their husbands, and their clergymen. As Mary Ryan has illustrated, public events in the 1830s in the new republic were male events, marked by "mascu-line signs and often crafted by male hands" (22). In only a few years Ernestine Rose would be called "a female devil" by clergy-men for overstepping the "bounds of decorum and decency" (*BI* Dec. 8, 1869). The young woman who took on clergymen in New York in a little over a year after arriving as a foreign immi-grant was only beginning her role as a "female devil."

39. We assume the "young, beautiful and interesting lady" with the uncov-ered head and flowing locks who called herself a foreigner was Rose. Vale's *Beacon* was not yet naming Rose anything but "the foreign lady," but Barnard cites this example as one of the starting points of Rose's speaking life. See the Feb. 14, 1877, *Boston Investigator*.

···❧[2]❧···

From Petitions to Social Movements in the 1840s

> What rights have women? Are they not the merest slaves on the earth? What of freedom have they? In government they are not known, but to be punished for breaking laws in which they have no voice in making. All avenues to enterprize and honors are closed against them. If poor, they must drudge for a mere pittance—if of the wealthy classes, they must be dressed dolls of fashion—parlor puppets—female things.
>
> —Ernestine Rose, Boston, 1844

As she began her American life, gathering signatures for the New York Married Woman's Property Bill and speaking to a number of different audiences, Ernestine Rose appeared to be an enigma—a sudden female voice, seemingly from out of nowhere. She was without context, without group support, without family ties in her new world. Thus, her early reform activities mostly escaped notice. Once in a while, the *Boston Investigator* or the *Beacon* revealed something slightly personal about Rose—that she was learning English quickly, or that she was looking for donations to help Benjamin Offen when he was ill, or that she had hosted the wedding of Josiah Mendum in her New York City home—but no accounts disclosed intimate details about her personal life that twentieth-century biographers yearn for. And her reticence to talk about herself or to promote herself also kept her out of the public eye. From the beginning of her life as a reformer, Rose dedicated herself to the political realm, seldom recording personal details of any kind. She repeatedly deflected attention from herself when people wanted information about her personal life. Her life, she would tell them, was not important; what mattered were the political acts she was performing, the causes she was fighting for.

A remarkable personal detail that Rose kept guarded from everyone but Jenny d'Hericourt was the fact that she was a mother. According to d'Hericourt, Rose bore two children, both of whom died in infancy.[1] The gaps in Rose's early lecturing from the winter of 1839 until the summer of 1841 and the entire year of 1842 suggest that she might have remained out of the public eye during those periods because of pregnancies and childbirth. Except for talking to Jenny d'Hericourt in Paris in 1856, Rose did not discuss her pregnancies or births in any extant letters or speeches;

---

1. The only record we have of the existence of the children comes from Jenny d'Hericourt's "Madame Rose," where she writes: "Mrs. Rose has a husband whom she loves tenderly and whom she is loved by; she also had two children, whom she cherished, nourished with her milk, and had the sadness to lose in early infancy" (138–39, my translation). Though I distrust some of the hyperbole in d'Hericourt's life of Rose, I find it difficult not to believe this information about the existence of two children, even though it is not repeated anywhere by anyone, including Rose herself.

Trying to verify d'Hericourt's claims has proven frustratingly fruitless. I searched the death records in the New York City Department of Records from 1836 through the early 1850s. No children with the last name of Rose who died in infancy were listed as living on the streets where Ernestine and William lived. In 1839, a newborn, Will Rose, whose parents lived at 3 Walnut, died of convulsions; on March 7, 1840, William Rose, a four-month-old infant also died of convulsions, but his parents resided at 272 on what looks like "Waisby" Street; on April 5, 1841, an infant girl with a last name of Rose was stillborn, but her parents lived on Thomas Street. According to New York City directories, the Roses lived at 9½ Frankfort from 1839 through 1841. In 1844, when the Roses lived at 45 Chatham, a six-month-old baby boy with a last name of Rose died, but his parents lived at 182 20th Street.

Any of these children could have been the Roses' infants. There is no way to authenticate d'Hericourt's claim: the addresses for the deceased children could be wrong or simply illegible, the city directory addresses for the Roses' residences could be incorrect, their infants' deaths could never have been documented by city records, or their children could have been born in England. Despite the impossibility of documenting their existence, though, I find it difficult to imagine why d'Hericourt would fabricate such a fact. Surely Ernestine Rose would not have remained close to d'Hericourt if her friend's account had not been accurate.

thus, Rose has always been assumed to have been childless. That she was not changes nothing except perhaps our speculations as to how her life might have been different had her children lived.[2]

How it evolved that Rose would set out in the mid-1840s to travel throughout the Northeast and Midwest is unclear. On short trips, such as to Boston, William would sometimes accompany her because, in part at least, of their growing friendship with their freethinking colleague Josiah Mendum, the publisher of the *Boston Investigator*, but often William remained in his shop in New York City. Ernestine, the orator, though she enjoyed working in William's shop, nonetheless sought out larger audiences to spread the word of a new moral order where egalitarian community-building would replace competitive hierarchy.

Throughout the decade, the Roses lived in the Lower East Side, a common first residence for European and Jewish immigrants and close to the freethinkers' meeting halls. Although they moved both their shop and their furnished rooms frequently, they never moved far and remained in the same general area for thirty years. Their home base close to other freethinkers and the steady wages that William earned as a skilled craftsman provided Ernestine with a stable base necessary for her travels.[3]

---

2. The one difference I can imagine would be that she might have been more New York–bound during the decade of the 1840s. Instead of traveling so extensively throughout the country, Rose might have concentrated more on speaking and writing close to home. Given the example of Lucy Stone, Antoinette Brown Blackwell, Abby Kelley Foster, and even Elizabeth Cady Stanton, it is clear that the best orators of the 1850s woman's movement managed to speak and travel despite having children. Perhaps Rose would have had to resort to servants, whom she never employed. The other mothers in the movement used a combination of familial support—extended families available to care for small children—and servants to free them for political activity.

3. From their residence on Frankfort Street, where they lived from 1838 until 1841, the Roses moved to Chatham Street, first to number 78½, then to 45, then to 58. In 1846 they moved to 13 Chambers Street, staying for two years, then to 300 Broadway for two more years. In 1850 they moved to 37 Reade Street, where they lived for over six years; in 1856 they took rooms at 72 White Street for another three years. William was consistently listed in the New York City Directories as a "Silversmith," with his shop located below their rooms or close by.

Throughout the 1840s, Rose spoke on a variety of platforms: Paine freethought celebrations, Owenite community-building conferences and social reform conventions, and abolitionist rallies. Rose's activities in the 1840s illustrate how literally and figuratively multilingual she was. Her many activities—their variety plus the fact that she appeared on stages with so many different people, speaking for so many different causes—helped create a political and cultural climate that accepted women as part of a reformist agenda. Rose's experience rousing audiences at conventions during the 1840s provided an invaluable grounding for the woman's rights movement that would fully emerge in the 1850s.

Thomas Paine Birthday Celebrations

One of the earliest stages where Ernestine Rose spoke during the 1840s was also the closest to home—the New York City Thomas Paine birthday celebrations. The Paine celebrations, which unified freethinkers for a half a century, gathered together like-minded reformers once a year to listen to and give speeches and to socialize. In nineteenth-century America a variety of groups affirmed their cohesiveness by celebrating their heroes' birthdays. Conservatives, for example, actively celebrated George Washington's birthday in February. Freethinkers, by contrast, celebrated both May 14 (Robert Owen's birthday) throughout the 1830s and 1840s and January 29 (Thomas Paine's birthday) from the mid-1820s through the 1870s.

New York freethinker Benjamin Offen organized the first Thomas Paine celebration in January 1825 in New York City, shortly after he arrived in this country from England. Offen writes that he was surprised to hear the name of Thomas Paine mentioned in contempt; he gathered that it was "sheer religious bigotry, together with the thousands of falsehoods uttered from pulpits respecting his moral character" (*Beacon* Aug. 10, 1844) that had turned his contemporaries against Paine. Within a few years the Paine celebrations spread up and down the eastern coast and into the Midwest.

Ernestine Rose's evolution from early participation in the Tammany Hall Sunday night lecture series in the late 1830s to later participation in the Thomas Paine celebrations was quite natural, as both had been inspired by her freethinking friend, Benjamin Offen. After the depression in the late 1830s closed the Tammany Hall lecture series, the New York freethinkers under Offen's leadership turned increasingly to the yearly Paine celebrations for unifying speech making. Known for their plentiful food and free-flowing wine, the celebrations often began with music and dancing, followed by speeches, toasts, and singing, and ending with a late supper, music, and more dancing. When the Roses arrived in New York City, the Paine celebrations were an established fact for the city's freethinkers. Both Ernestine and William joined the festivities first as participants and later, always working together, as organizers for the January activities. Both would remain involved for thirty years: Ernestine often as a major speaker, William as a behind-the-scenes organizer and money-raiser.

The celebrations, which when begun had consisted of men doing the speech making and celebrating, changed focus as Ernestine Rose became more and more of a presence. Not content to just listen to the speeches and watch the men eat and drink from the women's second-floor viewing rooms, Rose was soon joining the men during the talks and standing toasts. By the early 1840s, Rose addressed the New York Paine celebration "in a style of argument and eloquence seldom equalled, not easily surpassed, in which she introduced a spice of satire" (*Beacon* Feb. 4, 1843).

These Thomas Paine commemorations celebrated Enlightenment-like values, values that formed the intellectual underpinning of the United States Constitution and the Declaration of Independence. The commemorations extolled freedom, particularly secular freedom relating to life, liberty, and the eighteenth-century notion of the pursuit of happiness, which has little to do with the idea of "pleasure" associated with "happiness" in late-twentieth-century North America. Ernestine Rose's speech to the group in 1848 illustrates her concerns as well as her oratorical style:

My friends—I am happy to have once more met with you, to pay the tribute of respect and gratitude to the memory of Thomas Paine—to the memory of him to whose great mind, strong love of human freedom, unswerving integrity, unbending moral courage, and untiring exertions, we owe to a great extent the national liberty we enjoy. . . .

He has not only labored to throw off political despotism, but also that worst kind of despotism—superstition, under whose oppressive thraldom all other freedom becomes stifled. Yes! he has rung the funeral knell of priestcraft and superstition, the sound of which has been wafted by the genial spirit of freedom to wherever man is to be found It rings on, and wherever the mind of man is open to the voice of reason, it is heard and understood. . . .

I am happy to see so large an assembly here this evening; and particularly so, to see so many ladies present. . . . Superstition keeps women ignorant, dependent, and enslaved beings. Knowledge will make them free. The churches have been built upon their necks; and it is only by throwing them off, that they will be able to stand up in the full majesty of their being, and assert their rights and equality with man. (*BI* Feb. 16, 1848)

The first two paragraphs of this excerpted speech could have been given by any of the Paine celebrants because of the emphasis on freedom from despotism and on religion as "superstition." Rose takes her speech topics from Robert Owen: her subject matter, "The Religion of Charity," or "The Science of Government," were topics Owen had lectured on to the AACAN in London in the mid-1830s. She uses Owenite words such as "superstition" and "priestcraft"—which referred to the errors inherent in all religions except Quakerism and Universalism (neither of which had "priests")—and Owenite concepts, such as women being "enslaved beings." But, in this 1848 talk to freethinkers, the ending is not Owenite at all. Here we see that Rose has clearly incorporated the wording of others as well as her usual Owenite sources because she paraphrases Sarah Grimké when she speaks of churches being "built upon women's necks." Grimké had, in 1838, published a series of "Letters" on the equality of the sexes. In her second letter, dated July 17, 1837, Grimké wrote that she asked no favors for her sex; rather, all she asked of her brethren was "that they will take their feet from off our necks and permit us to stand upright on that ground which God designed us to occupy" (10). It was an image that took hold on the antislavery platform. Rose, tellingly, shifts the image of what is standing on women's necks and keeping women in a subservient position. This change of nouns, from "men" to "churches," was a significant one in antebellum America, where it was safer and easier to criticize "men" than religion. And this small shift may well illustrate why Rose would often receive a particularly hostile reception on American stages.

At the same time, this cross-fertilization of Owenite ideas with an important antislavery image shows one of the benefits of having Rose speak on different platforms throughout the 1840s. With her literal and figurative multilingualism, Rose spread Owenite ideas on abolitionist stages and abolition ideas on freethinking stages. She crossed more platform lines than most public speakers during the 1840s. Because she could absorb others' arguments and reshape them into a logical, persuasive, and passionate lecture, Rose was able to advance both the freethinkers' platforms and the abolitionists' principles. Like Robert Owen before her, she was a silver-tongued orator who could string ideas together in a powerful, persuasive style that remained unmatched in mid-nineteenth-century America. She was an activist, interested in convincing others to listen to voices of reason—whether that voice be Paine's or Owen's or Grimké's, or a combination of all of them.

Community Conventions

Rose's second significant activity in the 1840s consisted of lecturing for and sponsoring an intentional community constructed to create egalitarian living in one fell swoop. According to the Owenite theory that Rose subscribed to when she came to the United States, women could find their rights and assert their equality only with a change of economic systems. The socialism of an intentional community, created so that members could benefit from each other rather than compete with each other, was necessary, the Owenites postulated, for women and men to find a new moral world in communities of equality.

Probably because Ernestine and William Rose had come to the United States in 1836 as part of a colony that may have been on its way to New Harmony, they were drawn to Skaneateles, an Owenite-like community in upstate New York, founded in the early 1840s. In 1843, the first year she gave a major lecture at the Thomas Paine birthday celebration, Rose also took part in a Community Convention at Skaneateles, a convention intended to draw people together to "devise ways and means and to mature plans for giving . . . success to the Community enterprise" (*Beacon* Oct. 7, 1843) and to reorganize the "Social System by a Community of Property and Interest" (*Herald of Freedom* Oct. 6, 1843).

The Skaneateles Community was created in the context of a decade of secular community building in the 1840s in the United States.[4] The economic depression of the late 1830s, coupled with a growing interest in America's new darling of the intellectuals, Charles Fourier and his brand of association, created an explosion of community building. Of course religious communities continued to predominate in the community-building climate of the 1840s. The successful Shakers continued to found new communities throughout the decade and the separatist Oneidans were about to create the most infamous of the religious communities in American history in the 1840s.

The increase in secular community building was energized by two different imported ideologies—Fourierism and Owenism—and by the American reformist impulse that dominated the New England mind and a number of midwestern minds as well. In the most prolific decade of community building in nineteenth-century America, reformers seemed to be able do more than just imagine a perfect world; they could, in the words of one community member

4. For further information on secular communities of the 1840s see my *Women in Utopia*, 142–70. See also C. Clark, Dare, and Spann. The most complete information on Skaneateles is found in Hamm; see also numerous articles in the 1844, *Regenerator*, the *Workingman's Advocate*, the A. J. Macdonald "Manuscript," 100–15; and Leslie.

at Brook Farm, "be actors in the drama" (quoted in C. Clark 2). From the Brook Farm Community, which attempted to unite the head and the hands, to the Northampton Association, with its strong ties to Garrisonian abolitionism, numbers of dedicated community members across the East and Midwest attempted to envision a radically new future based on racial, gender, and economic equality.

Though all the Owenite communities created in the 1820s had disbanded by the end of that decade, by the mid-1840s Owenite communalism was once again spreading across the American landscape. A number of Owenite societies sprang up to support and sustain communities, and in England numerous Emigrating Societies were formed to establish communities in the midwestern United States while several Owenite communities were formed as well. The Owenite communitarians, however, were outnumbered by those interested in establishing Fourieristic communities, called phalanxes. Born less than a year after Robert Owen, Charles Fourier was little known in his lifetime.[5] But as soon as Albert Brisbane translated a selected part of Fourier's writings into English in the 1840s, Fourier's notions of forming "associations" swept through Boston and other cities where people met to talk about his ideas. Brisbane had, cleverly, simplified Fourier's thinking, and had "pruned Fourier's imaginative vagaries," in the words of Bassett (176). Numerous Fourieristic phalanxes sprang up in the early 1840s, particularly in the East and Midwest. For example, Brook Farm, the communal experiment in Roxbury, Massachusetts, began in 1841 as an extension of Transcendentalism and became a phalanx in 1844 after George and Sophia Ripley converted to Fourier's ideas.

Like Robert Owen, Fourier wanted to change the social organization of the world, calling his utopia a "new social world," a term similar to Owen's "new moral world." Like Owen, Fourier criticized a society that allowed and even encouraged great poverty to coexist alongside the great wealth of a small minority. But unlike Owen, Fourier was not a socialist, and his communal plans

---

5. For biographical information on Fourier see Beecher and Guarneri.

did not call for an egalitarian community of property. Perhaps because Fourieristic phalanxes created joint stock corporations instead of attempting to hold all things in common, Fourier's plans received more positive and active press attention in New York City than did Owen's. Popular editors such as Horace Greeley of the New York *Tribune* openly supported establishing Fourieristic phalanxes. Even freethinker Gilbert Vale, the editor of the *Beacon*, wrote that Fourier's system made more sense to him than Owen's, which abandoned private property (*Beacon* July 16, 1842).

The Skaneateles Community that Ernestine Rose supported looked much more like an Owenite community than a trendy Fourieristic phalanx and thus received little publicity outside of the radical weekly newspapers of the time. John Collins, an abolitionist speaker and former general agent of the Massachusetts Anti-Slavery Society, organized the community in upper New York State in late 1843. Like the Northampton Association in nearby Northampton, Massachusetts, Collins's Skaneateles was linked by its leadership to the antislavery movement; but unlike Northampton, Collins's plans for an intentional community called for complete community property and communal housework and cooking.[6]

Despite Rose's obvious interest in Skaneateles, neither she nor William were residential members of the community, as has been claimed by several critics and biographers.[7] Ernestine and William

6. Though Skaneateles was not founded specifically as an Owenite community, both Collins's contemporaries and twentieth-century scholars label the community "Owenite." Skaneateles had the backing of numerous Social Reform Societies that were the purveyors of Owenism in America. When the Philadelphia Social Reform Society addressed all the social reformers in the United States, they advised that "the means for truly reforming society" could "only" be found in the Owenite One Mentian Community and in the Skaneateles Community (*Regenerator* Apr. 15, 1844). Harrison also calls Skaneateles one of the Owenite "lost communities," communities that were either "avowedly Owenite or influenced considerably by Owenite ideas" (163).

7. See Sterling 253, for example. See also Barry, who writes that after Rose "immigrated to the United States and married, she and her husband joined a community in Skaneateles, New York." She then adds, confusing the father Robert Owen with the son Robert Dale Owen, that the community was "modeled after the ideas of utopian socialist Robert Dale Owen" [88].

continued to live in New York City during the years of the
community's existence, with Ernestine aiding the community by
lecturing and both she and William helping by collecting money.
At the originating Community Convention, Rose used typical
Owenite arguments for establishing the community, arguing that
the declaration that man was "born free and equal" was a "dead
letter" until now. She urged her audience to act: "we must remember that our salvation depends upon our exertions." And
association was "the natural relation," argued Rose. She also appealed to women "respecting their degradation and rights." Her
talk was, according to Nathaniel Rogers, the antislavery editor of
the *Herald of Freedom*, "a most effective appeal, and met its response in the tears of the whole audience" (*Herald* Nov. 3, 1843).[8]

Rose also lectured in numerous New England settings on
"Social Reform" in general and about Skaneateles specifically. In
March 1844, for example, she joined a group of well-known
New England reformers in a three-month lecture series at Amory
Hall in Boston. Organized by abolitionist William Lloyd Garrison, who spoke on the first two Sundays on "Worship," "The
Sabbath," "The Church," and "The Priesthood," and on the
final session on women's rights, the Amory lectures included,
besides Rose speaking on social reform, Charles Lane on "Association and Marriage," Adin Ballou on "Non-Resistance" and
"Association," Ralph Waldo Emerson and Henry David Thoreau
on "Reformers," and Charles Dana on "Association." Loosely
tied together by a skepticism toward organized religion and by
a call to explore association (or, in the case of Emerson and
Thoreau, a call to avoid association), the Amory Series placed
Rose in powerful company that spring of her thirty-fourth year,
her eighth year in the United States. The only other relatively

8. Rose's speeches at Skaneateles were paraphrased and sometimes quoted
in the Nov. 3, 1843, *Herald of Freedom*, because its editor, Rogers, was also
giving speeches at the convention. Rogers would be removed as editor from the
Herald of Freedom in 1844 by the New Hampshire Anti-Slavery Association,
which sponsored the paper, after he argued that he did not believe in organizations of any kind—an argument that Rose would take up in the early 1850s. See
Friedman 59.

unknown person on the platform was Thoreau, invited, probably, under Emerson's auspices.[9]

In order to attract more people to the particulars of "social reform" or "socialism," as it was called primarily by Owenites, Rose also took part in a major "Social Reform Convention" in Boston in late May 1844. This convention, attracting both community leaders from Skaneateles and a variety of reformers, began with an invocation of how intentional communities, like the one at Skaneateles, could combat error and reorganize society so that "false relations"—the relations caused by the evils of capitalism that pitted the rich and the poor against each other—might be avoided.

Rose, speaking after Collins welcomed everyone, first addressed the moral character and influence of government officers and governments. She denounced all governmental authority and power, except as "exercised through moral suasion alone." She illustrated her talk with a rare biographical tidbit, explaining that in Poland, when the central government wanted her family's land, it simply took it without much notice or without compensation. Rose continued by lambasting the effects of capitalism:

> There must be a change in our minds in relation to man's nature and its capabilities. We must have more confidence in the integrity of human nature. We all have confidence in our own good intentions—in our own ability. Let us be as charitable to others. We want a society where the goods of life can be equally free to all, without regard to their ability to produce. The poor are in need—they must truckle to the rich, and the rich truckle to each other. Let us unite in communities, where all may labour and produce—where the products of the earth may be as abundant

9. For an excellent discussion of the Amory lectures, see Johnson. For a response from one member of the audience to Rose's lecture on "Social Reform" see Cockrell. Members of the Hutchinson Family Singers, participants in many of the antislavery meetings and, later in the 1850s, in the woman's rights meetings, nonetheless were not overly impressed with Rose, saying "Wednesday evening we were to hear Mrs. Rose lecture on 'Social Reform' [but fell] to sleep and was obliged to go home before the lecture was through" (Cockrell 247).

as the water—where all may enjoy without money and without price. Then, reason will take the place of fanaticism, and love that of violence. (*Communitist* Sept. 18, 1844)

Rose returned to the stage in the evening, quickly getting to the heart of her speech, how "man" is not separate from others and how private property creates hostility among men:

> The great falsehood at the foundation of society is, that man is an individual—that his rights, interests, and immunities, are separate from the rights, interests, and immunities of others. . . . From this great error of man's individuality the earth has been cut up. Separate possessions and hostile interests have been produced. The cunning have got the earth and the powerful live upon the produce of the poor man. (*Communitist* Oct. 2, 1844)

Rose criticized religious leaders for declaring that all the vices in the world originate in innate depravity, not social and economic problems. Then, to the women in the audience, she added:

> [priests] say, that in your appropriate sphere—in the nursery and private circle, you have an all powerful influence—exercise it for their [the clergy's] destruction, and for your own elevation, and for that of the race. What rights have women? Are they not the merest slaves on the earth? What of freedom have they? In government they are not known, but to be punished for breaking laws in which they have no voice in making. All avenues to enterprize and honor are closed against them. If poor, they must drudge for a mere pittance—if of the wealthy classes, they must be dressed dolls of fashion—parlor puppets—female things. When single, they must be dependent upon their parents or brothers, and when married, swallowed up in their husbands. Nothing of nobleness, of dignity and of elevation is allowed to exist in the female. All such traits in her are indelicate and unbecoming. A few are allowed to thrum the keys of a piano—to smatter a little French or Italian,—to do cunning needle-work,—to study the combined colors of the rainbow—but then how masculine, indelicate, and unwoman-like for her to pry into the heavier sciences, into the falsely so-called—sciences of politics and religion.

She may lean upon a gentleman's arm, but to travel alone would be immodest and vulgar. This state of society does not recognize woman's equality. Her living is in the hands of man. My sisters, speak out for yourselves. Tyrants never will willingly relinquish their grasp. All that the lords of creation will yield will be what they are forced to by public sentiment. (*Communitist* Oct. 2, 1844)

Rose ends her speech by urging women to overthrow the property system by spending one tenth of their time in spreading information upon this issue: "I call upon you, then, as you venerate truth and reason, as you love yourselves, your children and the race, never to enter a church again. Countenance them not. They oppress you. They prevent progression. They are opposed to reason" (*Communitist* Oct. 2, 1844).

Much of the rhetoric of Rose's speech derives from traditional Owenite theory, including the notions that private property causes hostility between rich and poor; that the poor must "truckle" to the rich and the rich to each other; that in communities all may enjoy the products of the earth without price; that women are "slaves" with all enterprises closed to them; that if poor, they must drudge for a pittance or if wealthy, be fashion's dolls; that society does not recognize woman's equality. But Rose's actions spoke for a radicalism far beyond any Owen had ever imagined in New Harmony. Here was a woman on the stage speaking with authority. In addition, her subject matter was incendiary: she urged women never to enter a church again and to tithe, not the money they did not have access to, but one-tenth of their time to efforts in opposition to the church.[10] Given Rose's exhortation both to overthrow private property and never to enter a church again, it is not surprising that she electrified and horrified her audience. According to the *Boston Investigator*, Rose's appeal "burst upon a listening throng like a thunderbolt, and [the audience was] instantly lashed into the wildest excitement of fury and applause. The door

10. Rose probably picked up the notion of tithing one-tenth of one's time (instead of one's money) from antislavery stages.

and passage-way were crammed with spectators, most of them the devotees of the church, and the speaker was assailed with a shower of hisses as fierce as though Pandemonium had let loose its metamorphosed angels upon a single woman. Mrs. R. waited calmly until the tumult had subsided, when she again repeated the injunction, and again the tumult rose still higher." (*BI* June 19, 1844).

Ernestine Rose also supported the Skaneateles community by establishing, with William, the New York Universal Reform Society, an organization whose object was "to disseminate, as much as possible, the principles of Social Reform,—to cooperate with and to assist the Skaneateles Community in the solution of the great problem of Social Equality, with such pecuniary assistance as it may possess." Together with William, who served as vice president, Rose raised money to help the community. According to one Skaneateles community member, Rose was an "indefatigable, intrepid and eloquent woman," whose "untiring" efforts helped to establish the flourishing organization (*Communitist* Sept. 4, 1844).

Rose made her final visit to the community in the late summer of 1844. She was welcomed by the weekly paper, which reported that "we are favored with a visit from our able, devoted and worthy coadjutor, Mrs. Rose. . . . We are confident . . . that her visit to Central New York will be of great service to her" (*Communitist* Sept. 4, 1844). Standing on a log, Rose spoke to community members about "dwelling particularly on the advantage of always keeping the great object for which we came together, before us" (*Communitist* Sept. 4, 1844).

At the time of Rose's visit, the community had been established for eight months. After the Community Convention in October 1843 over 75 people joined the venture. Community members began a school, started a weekly newspaper, the *Communitist*, and planted crops. The plans for community life were strikingly similar to those at New Harmony, where "useful" employment and "liberal" schooling were promised. The diet was a modified version of the popular Grahamite diet used at Brook Farm, with most members abstaining from meat, alcohol, tobacco, butter, cheese, and rich pastry. Even Robert Owen, visiting Skaneateles in May 1845, told members that he would find "great pleasure" ending his days at the community (*Communitist* May 21, 1845).

But community life did not go forward without conflict. From the very first, John Collins and Nathaniel Rogers, the editor of the *Herald of Freedom* and a nonresident supporter of the community, quarrelled with Rose, also a nonresident supporter, and with Quincy A. Johnson, a Syracuse lawyer and the community's other important residential leader. They disagreed about how the land should be deeded. As Rogers reports in the November 3, 1843, *Herald of Freedom*, a "spirited discussion" pitted Quincy Johnson and "Mrs. Rose," who both wanted "to take a deed for the farm"— that is, to own it outright—against most of the others.[11] Rose and Johnson's point of view prevailed, and the following month Collins and Johnson took out a deed for the property, despite considerable dissent from Collins and others who opposed founding a socialist community upon the ownership of private property.

In addition to the problems underlying fundamental issues such as whose community it was and under what ground rules it should function, the egalitarian promises of community life were not realized. Even though Rose had spoken at the founding of the community on the importance of woman's rights (she made a "spirited appeal to the women, respecting their degradation and rights," according to the Nov. 3, 1843, *Herald of Freedom*), the women who joined the community were relegated to household affairs. This domestic arrangement directly contradicted John Collins's promises in a printed pamphlet that it should be men doing the household work (*Workingman's Advocate* July 21, 1844). Marenda Randall, a community resident for a short time, was originally enchanted with the promises for egalitarianism but wrote

11. Quincy Johnson has also left a record of his intense disagreement with John Collins, writing that Collins tried to control the community, with the result being "chaos." See Johnson's letter quoted in Hamm 146–47. Hamm adds that Johnson had great intellect but also had a "taste for debate," which makes him sound similar in that sense to Rose.

seven months later that the "communists at Skaneateles have been preaching one thing and trying to practice something else" (*Workingman's Advocate* Nov. 30, 1844). After leaving the community Randall wrote from Vermont that the community had "failed" because the "great and beautiful ideas" that attracted people to Skaneateles could not be realized (*Regenerator* Nov. 1, 1845).[12]

What Rose saw or did in her final visit to Skaneateles in the late summer of 1844 we will never know as she left no journal entry or letter explaining why she, like others, became disillusioned with community life. Perhaps her dispute with Collins over the deeding of the land affected her relationship with him and his leadership, or perhaps she saw the same things Marenda Randall saw. We can infer that something happened because the *Communitist*, which had followed Rose's every word for a year, ceased to mention her or her New York Reform Society after early October 1844. And Rose ceased promoting the community.

12. Marenda Randall would find her "great and beautiful ideas" the following decade in the Spiritualist movement.

One small illustration of how women got relegated to the household tasks is evident in George Taylor's talk at the 1844 Social Reform Convention. Taylor, the first speaker on the platform, began his talk with a story of a woman in the Skaneateles Community who had come to the community without being, in his words, "sufficiently imbued with the true principle of Socialism." She objected to kitchen labor as "servile and degrading" and spent her time with her daughter in the parlor, her accustomed sphere. Taylor relates how her "better nature" prevailed and she left her parlor and sought to fill a post "even lower, in the estimation of a foolish world, than the one she abandoned." Taylor concludes that it is thus that error should be combated—remove the causes and reorganize society, and all humanity will "flourish in the full enjoyment of all the blessings of a life of love and abundance" (*BI* June 12, 1844). What he does not add is that in community life, women, no matter what the community's rhetoric promises, had to assume the housework duties.

Thomas Hamm writes in *God's Government Begun* that women did take positions of leadership in Skaneateles, but he cites as evidence Maria Loomis, Ernestine Rose, and Marenda Randall. Both Loomis and Randall did write for the *Communitist*, but their writings—particularly Randall's complaints—as well as Rose's speeches to convince people to join the community have little to do with taking positions of leadership in the community.

Rose's experience at Skaneateles must have been revelatory because her intensely Owenite-communitarian rhetoric began to change in the mid-1840s. Her observations at Skaneateles must have triggered her discovery of flaws in Owenite communal theory. By the 1850s, Rose came to realize that the implementation of Owenite communal ideology had severe limitations. Most of the early nineteenth-century utopian communal experiments like Skaneateles were not "utopian" at all, because for many of the male leaders (like John Collins), the community itself, as Christopher Clark has explained, was an extension of the domestic sphere, a gendered and sentimentalized place that the male leaders had to order and control. Under this male control, women existed to be the unquestioning servers of the community. Cooperative housework and communal kitchens, then, existed not so much to liberate women as to ensure that daily work got done, efficiently.

When Rose arrived in the United States in 1836 she believed in the common good above all. Doing what was best for the community at large instead of for a single individual was one of her most common themes and one reinforced by her socialist critique of capitalism as selfishness. For her, "individualism" served as the ideological foundation for a destructive capitalism that needed to be supplanted by a cooperative socialism.[13] But after her experience visiting Skaneateles, and seeing how the "common good"— as defined and shaped through the male leaders' vision—relegated women to servile work, Rose, I believe, began to rethink her position. Indeed, without gender equality, working for the common good could become an insidious way to limit women. Although Rose would continue throughout her life to rail against money-seekers as "selfish," she had learned the difference between

13. Even though Rose was a believer in Owenite socialism when she came to the United States in 1836, she was still a practical person above all: she refused to continue on with the "community company" she perceived as unprepared for communal life; she went to work immediately to gather petitions to *gain* property for married women; and she joined with Quincy Johnson at Skaneateles to argue for owning the property on which they wanted to establish the community.

the utopian ideals of the Declaration of Independence, which aimed at enfranchising all individuals, and the dystopian practices of nineteenth-century communities that disenfranchised women in the name of "the common good."

But Rose's problems with Skaneateles did not change her affection and respect for Robert Owen. The following year, in 1845, Ernestine and William Rose organized a convention in New York to honor Robert Owen's visit to the city. The convention was held at 450 Broadway on May 4 through 6, close to the Roses' home on Chambers Street. Thomas Herttell served as president and a variety of other freethinkers attended, including Horace Seaver and Josiah Mendum from Boston, Benjamin Offen and the Roses from New York, John Collins from Skaneateles, and others from New Jersey, Pennsylvania, Ohio, Indiana, Illinois, Kentucky, and South Carolina.

In the first session, Robert Owen addressed the group, hailing their assembly as an index of the future emancipation of the human mind. Rose then spoke on traditional Owenite concerns, arguing that poverty was a construction not a necessity: "How much misery is there in our midst," Rose exclaimed, "not because there is not enough, but owing to the misdirection of it. Those who create the most, get the least" (*BI* May 14, 1845). One conflict at the meeting was the title "Infidel Convention," which the *Boston Investigator* repeated in its May 14, 1845, lead article. The term "infidel" had been given to the freethinkers as a term of derision, and thus many steering committee members opposed using it. Ernestine Rose, one of the few conference attendees and committee members to resist the committee, argued that by taking over the name given to them in derision, the freethinkers could show how nicknames can be lived down or made respectable and fashionable. Though Rose's arguments prevailed, her hope that the term "infidel" could become fashionable was never fulfilled. Her optimistic expectation that reformers could transform the epithet "infidel" into a neutral or positive term in an era dominated by Christian imagery and rhetoric reflects both her naïveté and her idealism.

Trips West and South

When the "infidel" convention was over, Rose, exhausted, decided to travel "west" for "her health," according to the October 8, 1845, *Boston Investigator*. Little is known of Rose's trips throughout what we now call the Midwest in 1845 and 1846 other than what the *Boston Investigator* reported. In the summer of 1845, Rose traveled to Cincinnati, where she lectured on "Social Reform," and to New Harmony, where she was welcomed enthusiastically as a visiting dignitary. "Mrs. Rose of New York has recently made a visit here," wrote a New Harmony resident to the *Boston Investigator* on July 16, 1845. "She is doing . . . service in the cause of mental freedom. Her name will be equally cherished by all philanthropists" (*BI* Aug. 6, 1845). While in New Harmony, Rose stayed with an unnamed family that included an impressionable twelve-year-old, who heard, or thought she heard, the fantastic adventures of Rose's life as a girl—adventures that included hidden daggers and a coach hired by Robert Dale Owen to whisk Rose away from a life worse than death married to a man she did not love.

Rose's western tour—ostensibly for her "health"—was filled with visits and lectures. Ernestine Rose appropriated the one "acceptable" excuse women had to travel, unaccompanied by family, across the United States and its territories: health problems. That Rose as a middle-class woman would be traveling to another climate "for her health" may well have been plausible in an antebellum America that was not yet familiar with or ready for women traveling from town to town to lecture on such subjects as woman's rights or social reform. Ironically, by her return trip Rose found herself seriously ill; the *Boston Investigator* reports on October 8, 1845, that Rose was "lying very dangerously ill at Buffalo" on the way home from her western trip.

Undeterred, Rose traveled west again the following year, lecturing in late March on "The Science of Government," in the hall of the Michigan House of Representatives. She repeated the lecture two nights later, owing to the "great satisfaction" of the members of the Legislature, who invited her to repeat her address.[14] Michigan, with vast unpopulated areas, had become a center of the Underground Railroad in the 1830s when two Quakers, Elizabeth Chandler and Laura Haviland, organized Michigan's first antislavery society in Adrian, Michigan. The area remained through the 1840s and 50s a well-traversed land, with William Lloyd Garrison, Sallie Holley, Abby Kelley Foster, and Stephen Foster visiting in the early 1850s. In Michigan, Rose lectured in Lansing to an audience that had been told she was a "gifted and eloquent Polonaise, whose lectures have been so highly spoken of at the East." The editors of Detroit's *Daily Advertiser* urged people to attend the free lecture because "those who have heard Mrs. Rose speak in the highest terms of her as a lecturer and debater, and all who attend will be gratified to ascertain that talent and genius are not confined to the stronger sex" (Mar. 24, 1846). Rose gave the same lecture in Ann Arbor as well as one on "Antagonisms in Society."

Wherever she traveled, Rose was outspoken. Journeying to the South in 1847, again to help "restore" her health, Rose relates that while in Columbia, South Carolina, she argued with a lawyer who was boarding at the same hotel. The young man expressed his eagerness to be independent of the North, but Rose pointed out to him, "from your head to your feet, you were manufactured at the North" (*Liberator* Aug. 19, 1853). In another encounter, a "gentleman" asked Rose what she thought of South Carolina. She responded: "you are a century, at least, behind, in that the only civilization that you have exists only among your slaves." The so-called gentleman said that Rose should be thankful she was a woman or she would have been tarred and feathered for such sentiments. Rose retorted that she always thanked her stars for being a woman and that because men were so "exceedingly lazy and inactive" in the South, it would be "an act of charity to give you something to do, were it even to give me a coat of tar and

14. The Michigan House of Representatives, in the afternoon session on Monday, March 23, "tendered" the use of the hall to Mrs. Rose so that she could lecture the following evening. See the Mar. 24 and 26, 1846, Detroit *Daily Advertiser*.

feathers." As she left, she said: "I tell you, sir, that if I had never been an Abolitionist before, I would have become one here, and you would have helped to make me one" (*Liberator* Aug. 19, 1853).

The Antislavery Movement

As the episodes in South Carolina would predict, by the mid-1840s Ernestine Rose was speaking on the abolitionist platform. To a cause that had been dominated by religion-inspired reformers she brought a freethinking, libertarian perspective. Like the dominant and uncompromising William Lloyd Garrison, with whom she had shared many stages by the mid-1840s, Rose was outspoken, dedicated to the cause of equal rights for all, and uncompromising. Whereas Garrison's single-minded dedication to his cause of immediate emancipation has been the subject of decades of conflicting interpretations, Rose's equally single-minded dedication to her cause of equal rights has been, by and large, ignored.[15]

The antislavery movement had gained great momentum during the decade since Rose had arrived in New York. Under William Lloyd Garrison's leadership throughout the 1830s and 40s, the abolitionist movement repudiated the idea of gradual emancipation and black expatriation to Africa and argued for immediate emancipation. The movement took a high moral ground—to counter the equally high moral tone assumed by proslavery advocates—with Garrison and his followers declaring a "holy war" on slavery's supporters and on slave-made products.[16] To the Garrisonians, organized religious was complicitous in maintaining

15. Garrison has been historicized and rehistoricized, called everything from a saint to a fanatic; see, for example, Barnes, Dumond, Elkins, Kraditor (*Means and Ends*), Perry, and Lutz (*Crusade*).

16. The idea of boycotting slave products came from Britisher Elizabeth Heyrick's 1824 pamphlet, *Immediate not Gradual Abolition of Slavery.* Heyrick, according to Kathryn Kish Sklar, urged that a "holy war" and a "Christian crusade" replace political discussions. As Sklar writes, Heyrick's ideas spread to women in Great Britain, then to men and women in the United States. See Sklar, "Women Who Speak," in Yellin and Van Horne, 322–23.

slavery and, by the 1840s, they were urging "right-thinking" people to "come out" or abandon organized religion.[17]

Throughout the 1830s, antiabolitionists reacted violently in many cities, with the violence reaching a climax in the November 1837 murder of Elijah Lovejoy, a young antislavery minister-turned-newspaper editor, who was killed defending his printing press from a mob in Alton, Illinois. The escalating violence seemed only to increase the dedication of the many women involved in the anti-slavery movement in the late 1830s, before Ernestine Rose began speaking on antislavery platforms. Following the establishment of the American Anti-Slavery Society in 1830, Lucretia Mott and several other women formed the Philadelphia Female Anti-Slavery Society. The founding of this and other female auxiliary groups in the mid-1830s offered a growing number of women opportunities to speak and organize. Women organized the annual conventions and also established antislavery petition drives throughout the year. By the end of the 1830s, abolitionist women were generating national conventions and some had become members in the larger, male-dominated societies.[18]

The first national women's antislavery convention, held in New York City in May 1837, attracted over 70 women including Lucretia Mott and Sarah Pugh from Philadelphia, Maria Chapman and Lydia Maria Child from Boston, and Abby Kelley from Lynn,

17. Though the abolitionist movement has been accurately labeled a religiously based movement, few of the most radical of the Garrisonian abolitionists were traditionally religious. Many of the Garrisonians criticized organized religion much as Ernestine Rose did, but they never thought of themselves as infidels or freethinkers and, in fact, worked strenuously to defend themselves and others in the movement from the scandalous "infidel" label.

18. For more information on these groups see Yellin and Van Horne. See, especially, Williams's essay, "The Female Antislavery Movement," where she writes that the Philadelphia and the Boston Female Anti-Slavery Society were the two radical societies, with others espousing far more conservative messages and with fewer women moving on into the woman's rights movement. On the petition drives see Van Broekhoven; on the women's organizations and the women who joined the men's groups see Sklar, "Women Who Speak." See also Ginzberg, who writes that the petition campaigns from 1835 through the 1840s were the single most effective tool in grassroots organizing among women (82).

Massachusetts. Much of the business of the meeting was taken up by a discussion of petitioning: Lydia Maria Child proposed that the women organize a network like that used by the American Anti-Slavery Society. In addition to discussing how best to petition, the women also affirmed that it was well within woman's sphere and, in fact, it was her duty to overthrow slavery and to assert some rights for herself: "the time has come," the women argued, "to move in that sphere which Providence has assigned her, and no longer remain satisfied in the circumscribed limits which corrupt custom and a perverted application of Scripture have encircled her" (*Proceedings of the Anti-Slavery Convention of American Women, 1837* 9).

This convention had been organized, in part, by two sisters from South Carolina, Angelina and Sarah Grimké. The Grimké sisters, raised with slaves in Charleston, opposed the numbing effects of slavery and chose as young adults to move north. While accepting, without question, the divine authority of the Scriptures, they interrogated the interpretations of the Bible that claimed it sanctioned both slavery and woman's subordination. Angelina wrote an "Appeal to the Christian Women of the South," an antislavery tract published by the American Anti-Slavery Society in 1836, that declared slavery contrary to the Declaration of Independence and contrary to "that first charter of human rights, which was given by God" (3). "Man," she claimed (and her generic use of "man" was intended to encompass women and men of color), "*never* was put *under the feet of man*" by God (3). Slavery was not sanctioned in the Bible; it was, she claimed, contrary to the example of Jesus Christ.

In her powerful series of letters "on the equality of the sexes" that she wrote in 1837, Sarah Grimké extended the use of Angelina's "foot" imagery to signify unjust domination. She writes in her second letter, from Newburyport on July 17, 1837, that all she asks of men is to "take their feet off our necks and permit us to stand upright on that ground which God designed us to occupy" (10). It is not the Bible, she claims, that has deprived women of their equality with men; rather, it is erroneous interpretation of God's sacred book by mortal men that has created woman's subordination.

Sarah Grimké's letters range from descriptions of the grim conditions for women in Asia, Africa, and Europe to analyses of the conditions that exist for women in the United States. Women, perceived as weak, were also perceived (erroneously to Grimké) as inferior to men. Comparing women's position with that of a slave, Grimké writes that neither woman nor the slave had a "political existence" (74). As Rose would do in the early 1850s, Grimké quotes Blackstone's *Commentaries on the Law* saying, "by marriage, the husband and wife are one person in law; that is, the very being, or legal existence of the woman is suspended during the marriage" (75). Grimké ends most of her letters with the same poignant salutation: "thine in the bonds of womanhood."

Although the Grimké sisters' lectures were met with interest in some quarters, in most arenas they were denigrated, particularly by conservative clergymen. Opposed to antislavery activities anyhow because these activities undermined the authority of the church, conservative clergy took advantage of the "spectacle" of women speaking in public to "promiscuous" audiences to frighten their congregations away from the antislavery heresy and back to orthodoxy. As Carolyn Karcher has written, a pastoral letter, issued by "The General Association of Massachusetts to the Churches Under Their Care" (and authored by a minister who would later defend slavery), pontificated that "deference and subordination are essential to the happiness of society, and peculiarly so in the relation of a people to their pastor" (253). Particularly under attack in the infamous "letter" were practices that "threaten the FEMALE CHARACTER with wide-spread and permanent injury" by violating the Bible's notions of woman's "appropriate duties" (quoted in Karcher 254).

In May 1838 the women convened again, for the second annual antislavery convention in Philadelphia. This time the resistance to their cause turned violent when a mob set fire to the building where the women were meeting. Probably outraged by the women's support of racial cooperation and attempts to eradicate prejudice against Negroes in the North, "hundreds of infuriated men" raced through the streets, and in the words of attendee Sarah Pugh, "none [of us] knew at what minute the howling mob . . . might break in" (Pugh 21). At dusk the rioters broke into the building and in less than an hour had burnt it down.

Indeed, defenders of the status quo had something to fear. As the women gained more experience defending their positions some, like Maria Weston Chapman and Abby Kelley, began speaking to mixed or "promiscuous" groups that included men. In February 1838, for example, Angelina Grimké spoke to the Massachusetts legislature, the first time a woman had ever spoken there.[19]

By the end of the decade, though, the small successes of the women's speaking, petition gathering, and organizing in the antislavery societies faced opposition in a variety of antislavery organizations. Just as mainstream conservative ministers were telling women to remain in their separate, domestic sphere, many voices within the movement were telling women the same thing. One group of antislavery reformers, for example, led by the Tappan brothers of New York believed that women's advocacy hurt the cause of antislavery. Resolutions such as the one introduced by Angelina Grimké at the 1837 convention declaring that "the time has come" for women to move beyond their "circumscribed limits" raised an issue that, according to some, had no connection to the antislavery movement. Another group, however, including among others the Grimké sisters, Abby Kelley, Lucretia Mott, and William Lloyd Garrison, advocated the concepts of justice and liberty for all people and supported women's right to speak out equally with men. The "woman question" dominated regional meetings in 1839 and the 1840 national meeting of the American Anti-Slavery Society when Abby Kelley, who had been encouraged by the Grimké sisters' lecture tour and the women's antislavery conventions, was nominated for the business committee. She refused to withdraw her nomination despite the acrimonious controversy, saying "if the request is made because I am a woman, I will not resign" (quoted in

19. But three months later Grimké married fellow abolitionist Theodore Weld and effectively retired from lecturing, giving it up for domesticity. See Burkett 17.

Burkett 18). Lewis Tappan, who believed that such a nomination was "contrary to the usages of the civilized world" (quoted in Melder, *Beginnings* 109), called for the formation of a new antislavery society, the American and Foreign Anti-Slavery Society, which left Garrison in charge of the AASS. After the conservative group seceded, women such as Lucretia Mott and Maria Chapman accepted appointments to the new executive committee of the AASS.[20]

The woman question continued to haunt the antislavery women. At the World Anti-Slavery Convention in London, held in June 1840 to show the international character of abolitionism, the 500-some delegates debated the appropriateness of seating the women delegates, including some of the most active in the antislavery movement in the United States: Lucretia Mott, Mary Grew, and Sarah Pugh.[21] The organizers of the London conference opposed the recent changes in the AASS, resolving to seat male delegates only. Though the male delegates—Wendell Phillips, James Mott, Henry Stanton among others—were seated, none of the women were. The controversy grew when Garrison and three abolitionist friends arrived late and refused to become official delegates at a convention that would not seat the women; Garrison sat silent in the gallery with the women. The controversy also introduced the newly married Elizabeth Cady Stanton to the antislavery movement and to women's position in it. Stanton had come to London not as an activist or delegate but as the bride of Henry Stanton, a member of the anti-Garrisonian New York Anti-Slavery Society.

Throughout the 1840s the two main antislavery societies carried on their work, along with many other groups devoted to

20. Ruth Bogin and Jean Fagan Yellin write in their introduction to *The Abolitionist Sisterhood* that with the Garrisonian takeover in 1840 of the AASS, the political culture of the antislavery feminists "manifested itself most fully not in single-sex female antislavery societies but in mixed-sex organizations" (Yellin and Van Horne 18).

21. For information about the World Anti-Slavery Convention in London see Sklar, "Women Who Speak" in Yellin and Van Horne; Melder, *Beginnings* 113–18. See also the first chapter of volume 1 of *HWS*.

different forms of antislavery causes.[22] After 1840, women became more and more active in the regular societies instead of the women's auxiliaries. Some took to the lecture circuit, including two of the most important, Abby Kelley and Lucy Stone, with whom Ernestine Rose would share antislavery platforms in the late 1840s and women's rights platforms throughout the 1850s and 1860s.

Like Angelina Grimké before her, Kelley married a fellow abolitionist—Stephen S. Foster—but unlike Grimké, Kelley did not give up her lecturing for domestic duties. She became one of the best known and most effective of the antislavery speakers during the 1840s. In fact, Kelley's ceaseless lecturing on the antislavery platform influenced many women to join the movement. Lucy Stone, for example, heard Kelley speak in 1837 in Massachusetts and corresponded with her while at Oberlin College, shortly before she, too, decided to become an agent for the Massachusetts Anti-Slavery Society (MASS). Upon graduation in 1847, Stone began a productive, lifelong career as a lecturer for abolitionism and woman's rights. Rising quickly to stardom, Stone traveled around the country to speak on antislavery platforms, yet she also determined to "labor for the elevation of my sex" (as quoted in Kerr 43). By the late 1840s her name was appearing along with Garrison's in announcements for abolitionist meetings in numerous broadsides and newspaper advertisements.[23]

The women who joined together throughout the 1840s to work for the antislavery movement were a disparate group. Until quite recently, one of the most glaring of the unexamined assumptions concerning the composition of women antislavery activists was that they were a homogenous group of good, Christian, privileged women who first worked for the slaves, then for themselves. As Nancy Hewitt writes, an erroneous historical image has let us

---

22. Although many historians accepted the dichotomy that Aileen Kraditor set up in her influential *Means and Ends in American Abolitionism*, recent works such as that done by the Peases show that many different types of people were working for abolitionism, not just Tappan-led conservatives and Garrisonian liberals as Kraditor would have us believe.

23. For recent excellent biographies on Stone and Kelley see Kerr and Sterling.

believe in "a relatively homogeneous body of women—white, middle-class, yankee, urban, evangelical—who left their private havens to purify the world under the banner of revivalism" ("Own Terms" 19). Hewitt goes on to deconstruct that image: not only did women not follow a straight or singular path from benevolent work through evangelicalism and abolition to woman's rights, but the women themselves were often anything but middle-class evangelical, urban women (20).[24] The two most important of the women antislavery speakers in the late 1840s—Lucy Stone and Abby Kelley—illustrate Hewitt's point: both were white, but Stone was lower-middle-class at best and neither was evangelical nor urban.

Ernestine Rose is an even better example of the lack of homogeneity in the movement. Like Frances Wright before her, Rose came out of an Owenite, freethought, rationalist background. There is nothing evangelical about her. Rose, unlike most of the women in the antislavery movement, began her public life guided by Owenite freethinking premises. Though some of the women in the antislavery movement were not traditionally religious, none proclaimed themselves "freethinkers"; even the "come-outers" still believed in the authority of the Scriptures or believed that slavery violated God's law. For Rose, slavery violated natural law; thus, the fact of American slavery, lamentable as it was, served as only one living example of what priests and corrupt politicians could and would do to individual liberties. As Rose repeated over and over again, she opposed *all* types of slavery, physical and mental, legal and moral, domestic and public. Her authority was not the Bible but the Declaration of Independence.

Perhaps because Rose refused to single out African slavery for attack, she did not always meet with great enthusiasm from the antislavery speakers who dedicated themselves to that cause above all others. Rose would not let any ideas stand in the way of what she saw as the truth, nor would she permit fallacious assumptions

24. See also Sklar, *Florence Kelley*, where she writes that women's public culture, even that dominated by white middle-class women "was never a homogeneous entity," but that it was always changing, depending upon time, place, class formation, race, and other forms of social identity (xiii).

to go unchallenged, even when used in the abolitionist cause. In the fall of 1849 Rose joined Abby Kelley Foster and Stephen Foster for a series of lectures in eastern New York. Stephen Foster talked about how, in the United States, the people created the law. Rose, who believed that laws created people rather than the commonly held reverse, was unable to resist disagreeing with Foster. Her Owenite background had taught her that character is formed for people not by people, according to how they had been raised and to what beliefs they had been taught to be the "truth." Thus, to Rose, laws helped construct people's perception of the world. To say that people created laws was, to Rose, hopelessly naïve and based upon a complete misunderstanding of how people perceived the world. She thus immediately "repl[ied] to some of Mr. Foster's remarks" (*BI* Sept. 5, 1849), disagreeing with his perception of the origins of law and character, rather than speaking to the gathered audience on antislavery issues. To Abby and her husband, both dedicated antislavery speakers, Rose's intellectual sparring may well have demonstrated a lack of dedication to their life's cause.

Despite criticism, Rose continued to appear on abolitionist stages, often to much abuse both from the general public and from fellow speakers. The political events of the mid-1840s had increased the fervor of the women and men advocating antislavery while concomitantly increasing the zeal of the opposition. In 1845 Texas was admitted to the union, and with that annexation slave territory grew. Similarly the Mexican War in 1846 opened a pandora's box of questions as to whether slavery would be allowed in the lands taken from Mexico, creating a constitutional debate that dominated political discussion throughout the late 1840s and 1850s.

A May 1850 American Anti-Slavery Society meeting reflected the hostilities of the general public to abolitionism and to Rose. Rose was hissed and booed, particularly by a well-known Tammany ruffian, Captain Rynders, who shouted "I have always respected the presence of ladies, but I doubt very much whether white women who cohabit and mix with the woolly-headed negro, are entitled to any respect from a white man" (*Liberator* May 17,

1850).[25] Rose, trying to be heard, urged "worthy Americans" in the audience to read the newspapers about the way freedom of speech had been prohibited in Ireland. While the commotion was going on, Rose, according the New York *Tribune*, was standing in the pulpit, "looking like patience on a monument" (as reported in the *Liberator* May 17, 1850). She continued to repeat with good humor "are you done?" But when no one would let her speak, she left the podium to catcalls such as "Give us a nigger! . . . Mrs. Rose! Where's that sweet rose? Oh, hell! Let's go and drink" (*Liberator* May 17, 1850).

Ernestine Rose's appearance on the antislavery stages is thus a telling one and predicts her status in the woman's rights movement as an "outsider." She was, like all the women who spoke on antislavery issues, hissed and booed by people like Captain Rynders, who equated women's speaking on the same stage as an escaped slave like Frederick Douglass with "cohabiting" and "mixing with woolly-headed negroes"—rhetoric obviously intended to inflame an audience into opposing whatever she said. But, at the same time, Rose, with her combative personality—the personality that allowed her to "look like patience on a monument" while she was being hissed—offended dedicated antislavery speakers when she delighted in arguing with them in public. Devoted to the idea of debate—of getting all ideas out into the open so the "truth" could emerge—Rose's strategies must have seemed contentious to her female colleagues who had been raised under America's cult of True Womanhood—raised to be pious, pure, submissive, and domestic. Although none of the antislavery women argued for submissiveness, many were domestic and most appeared pious. Rose, who happily spent her American life in rented rooms in New York City, from which she came and went with great regularity, never created the gracious home in Philadelphia that all noted about Lucretia Mott; Rose rarely entertained, and when she did, it was for her freethinking friends. To make matters worse,

---

25. William Lloyd Garrison remembers this meeting as a time when the audience got out of hand. He notes that the hissing was particularly directed at Ernestine Rose and Stephen Foster. See Garrison 3: 297.

Rose simply was not pious, and her sarcastic wit made her seem impure, at least by nineteenth-century literary standards where fictional heroines were inevitably religious and naïvely devout. Her atheism and her Jewish background—where she learned to argue with her father—combined to make her appear anything but pious and pure to both her audiences and to the reformers in the antislavery movement. Her lifelong urge to argue—particularly about matters of piety—separated her, irrevocably, from the other women who were to be her colleagues throughout the 1850s and 1860s. As Abby Kelley Foster said about Rose during their series of lectures together in upstate New York in the late 1840s—damning her with faint praise: [Ernestine Rose] "made some acceptable speeches," but she added that "they were not so useful as remarks from a person who sympathizes in full with us would have been" (quoted in Sterling 253). Even though sharing the antislavery stage with the Fosters, Rose was not, and never would be, part of the "us." We will see that in the woman's rights movement, Rose's refusal to adopt pious versions of her rational ideas and her uncompromising vision of truth would keep her from being one of the "us" in that movement as well.

⋯⋙[3]⋘⋯

The Early 1850s and
the Woman's Rights Conventions

We are not crusading here for the rights of the women
of New England or of England but of the world.

—Ernestine Rose, Worcester, 1850

The early 1850s marked a turning point in Ernestine Rose's life and, in many ways, in the life of the nation. The New York City that Rose lived in was growing steadily more crowded; while the middle and upper classes enjoyed ever enhancing creature comforts, the gap between the rich and the poor widened. The opening of the science and art exhibits at Crystal Palace in 1853 seemed to promise a utopian tomorrowland possible through technology. Yet, the Compromise of 1850 reflected increasing divisions over territory gained in the Mexican War. Although the majority of people in the North opposed slavery, most either remained aloof from abolitionism or were openly hostile to it. The passage of the Fugitive Slave Act in 1850, however, forever changed the shape and intensity of the antislavery movement, as it interjected more of the reality of slavery into the lives of northerners. The federal law gave commissioners authority to force northerners to help capture escaped slaves. Accused runaways were denied a jury trial and the right to testify on their own behalf. In 1852 the publication of Harriet Beecher Stowe's *Uncle Tom's Cabin* exacerbated the tensions that the Fugitive Slave Act aroused. Many feared the passage of the Kansas-Nebraska Act in the spring of 1854 would mean that slavery would spread across the newly developing states and even perhaps into the North.

In 1850, concerned as ever with the enslavement of all people—women as well as men, white as well as black—Ernestine Rose helped create the woman's rights movement, a movement that would change the course of her adopted nation.[1] The structure that would turn Rose's advocacy of woman's rights into organized social action was built by the national woman's rights conventions that were held every year but one from 1850 until the Civil War. Rose, schooled in the importance of conventions from her early Owenite experience in London and practiced in participating in and leading a variety of freethought and social reform conventions during the 1840s, brought fifteen years of practical experience in organizing and speechmaking to the first national woman's rights meeting in 1850. Rose's background helped her assume a leadership position from the beginning.

Until 1850, Rose's arguments for increased women's rights were relatively isolated. In her speeches at the annual Paine celebration, for example, she was often the only voice urging increased rights for women. At other Owenite functions, such as "community conferences," "world conferences," or Robert Owen birthday celebrations, Rose, like Frances Wright before her, spoke earnestly and eloquently on extending the rights inherent in the Declaration of Independence to all citizens. Yet, Rose's references to women, as Wright's had been, were addressed to audiences whose first priorities had little to do with women's rights. Thus Rose was in the position of being heard and, perhaps, respected—certainly important in the 1840s when few women appeared on "promiscuous," or mixed sex, platforms—but she remained without a community of listeners who felt passionately about her prime concern.

Some others with whom Rose had shared antislavery platforms had spoken and written for woman's rights by the late 1840s as well.[2] Rev. Samuel J. May, for example, wrote of the "unjust" disenfranchisement of "females" in his 1845 sermon, "The Rights

1. Rose would become a citizen of the United States in May 1869, less than three weeks before she left New York permanently for retirement in Europe. William had become a citizen in 1845, nine years after arriving. Perhaps Ernestine's desire to take out citizenship immediately before leaving reflected her desire to be able to return easily if she so wanted.

2. Others not connected with the antislavery movement had written for women's rights in the 1840s. Margaret Fuller, for example, wrote "The Great

and Conditions of Women." May, born in Boston in 1797, was a Unitarian minister who advocated temperance then antislavery in the 1830s. Though he initially questioned the propriety of the Grimké sisters addressing public forums, he quickly understood his attitude to be "a miserable prejudice" (*Memoir* 165). Shortly after moving to Syracuse in 1845, where he would remain for 22 years until his retirement, May gave his first woman's rights sermon. The sermon, which when printed had a larger circulation than any other of his writings, posited that women, as human beings, deserved basic political rights: "This entire disfranchisement of females is as unjust as the disfranchisement of the males would be; for there is nothing in their moral, mental or physical nature, that disqualifies them to understand correctly the true interests of the community, or to act wisely in reference to them" ("Rights" 2). Certainly, he says, women are inferior in stature, but why should being smaller "consign them to mental, moral or social dependence?" ("Rights" 3). Woman is not the dependent of man, but of God. May, like so many of the antislavery reformers, believed that Christianity had elevated women, but, he argues, "much is yet to be done," ("Rights" 9) including giving women access to more education, "that grand leveller," ("Rights" 12) as well as combating the current literature of the day that prescribed marriage for all women. May would continue to advocate woman's rights until his death in 1871.

Lucretia Mott, who had been moved by Sarah Grimké's *Letters on the Equality of the Sexes* in the late 1830s, also lectured for woman's rights in the late 1840s. At the Rochester Woman's Rights Convention in August 1848, for example, Mott spoke on how people received their ideas of woman from the clergy instead of from the Bible. The Bible, according to the religious Mott, contained none of the prohibitions in regard to women that many of the clergy were promulgating (*PWRC, Rochester, 1848* 5). In her "Discourse on Woman," delivered on December 17, 1849, at

---

Lawsuit" in 1843, an essay (later expanded into *Woman in the Nineteenth Century*) that cites literary and historical women's liberated actions as an incentive for her contemporaries to change their way of thinking about Woman.

the Assembly Buildings in Philadelphia, Mott says "far be it from me to encourage women to vote, or to take an active part in politics, in the present state of government," reflecting her Garrisonian beliefs that participation in civic government indicates collusion with governmental laws and regulations. Woman's right to the elective franchise, Mott adds, is the same and should be yielded to her, whether she exercise that right or not (15). She continues: "Let woman then go on—not asking as favor, but claiming as right, the removal of all the hindrances to her elevation in the scale of being" (19).

Frederick Douglass and Lucy Stone both spoke out for woman's rights as well as for rights for African Americans. At the Rochester Woman's Rights Convention in 1848, Douglass argued that the true basis of rights was the capacity of individuals and that he would not dare claim a right that he would not concede to woman (*PWRC, Rochester, 1848* 6). Later in the 1850s, he would appear on many stages with Ernestine Rose, seeking, as she did, rights for all people. Lucy Stone, who had read Sarah Grimké's *Letters* in 1838, wrote that Grimké's words were "first rate" and that they helped her confirm that she would "call no man master" (quoted in Kerr 26). By 1840 she was using the Grimké sisters' bondage imagery in a letter to describe the American and Foreign Anti-Slavery Society's split from the Garrison-led AASS: "it [the AFAS] is *actually* summoning all its energies to rivet more and more firmly the chains that have always been fastened upon the neck of woman" (quoted in Kerr 27). As an agent for the Massachusetts Anti-Slavery Society in the late 1840s, Stone blended discussions of woman's disabilities into her antislavery speeches; she was admonished by Samuel May, Jr. not to dilute the antislavery message with another cause, but Stone, undeterred, lectured for the MASS on weekends and for woman's rights during the week, including set speeches on women's social disabilities, legal and political disabilities, and moral and religious disabilities.[3]

3. The admonishing Samuel May should not be confused with his cousin, the Rev. Samuel J. May, the author of the 1845 sermon, "The Rights and Conditions of Woman." This Samuel May was younger (born in 1820) but was

The national woman's rights conventions that began in 1850 created a unifying space for women and men interested in promoting women's enfranchisement and increased political and social rights.[4] They provided a yearly respite from an often hostile press that reacted in horror and disbelief to the women's demands. The conferences offered a brief moment when women like Ernestine Rose could be surrounded by women and men dedicated to causes she shared instead of by voices of authority such as ministers, educators, and editors of newspapers who constantly told such women that they were wrong-headed or immoral for even suggesting that woman's sphere of influence be enlarged. From the 1850 Worcester convention on, as Keith Melder has written, the woman's rights movement looked more and more like an organized reform crusade (*Beginnings* 153).

The national conventions also spawned many state conventions where women, particularly married women with children, could meet closer to their homes. These local conventions generated enthusiasm comparable to the many revivalist camp meetings of the Second Great Awakening, where individuals came together for both social and spiritual uplift. The "equal rights" women and men, likewise, gathered for social and spiritual inspiration, though their notion of the spiritual was not always a conventionally Christian one. The conventions served a social function quite similar to

---

also a Unitarian minister (in Massachusetts) until his involvement in the antislavery movement led to his resignation. Both men advocated woman's rights.

See Lasser and Merrill 11–13 and the December 1848 letter from Antoinette Brown to Lucy Stone in Lasser and Merrill where Brown writes to Stone "How glad I am that you are going to lecture for the Womans [sic] Rights Convention or Soc. rather" (46–47). See also Kerr 52.

Other public voices, though, were already speaking out against woman's rights. Several "ladies" published poems and essays like "The Ins and Outs," an anti–woman's rights poem. See the Broadside Collection for 1849 at the American Antiquarian Society.

4. Although Flexner writes that the early women's rights movement "showed little interest in getting the vote" (82), from the Seneca Falls convention and the early Worcester conventions the majority of women did, indeed, include women's suffrage as an important part of their demands.

that of evangelical revivals, bringing together isolated people for conversion and reinforcement, uplifted by the energy and excitement of shared belief.

The Seneca Falls State Convention, 1848

The first national convention in Worcester in 1850 was preceded by several local women's rights conventions in Salem, Ohio, and in Rochester and Seneca Falls, New York. The Seneca Falls convention, popularized by many historians as the birthplace of the woman's rights movement, was, as Eleanor Flexner astutely points out, only one small moment in the movement's birth. The movement itself, she writes, had begun much earlier (77).

The Seneca Falls convention was organized by Lucretia Mott and Elizabeth Cady Stanton, who had met in London in the summer of 1840 at the World Anti-Slavery Convention. During the eight years that passed before the women called for the Seneca Falls convention, a confluence of events, both personal and public, laid the groundwork for the woman's rights movement. The reform movements that swept the 1840s both in North America and in Europe helped create the cultural atmosphere that made questioning women's "sacred and domestic" sphere possible. The rise of numerous women's periodicals such as *Godey's Lady's Book*, created in their essays and short stories a women's culture that criticized prevailing "male" values while promoting such reforms as education for women. The economic recovery from the depression of 1837 and the rising factory system helped create more middle-class families who emphasized the importance of education for all their children.

Accidentally meeting Elizabeth Cady Stanton when she traveled to upstate New York to visit her sister and attend the yearly meeting of Friends, Lucretia Mott gathered her sister, Martha Wright, and her sister's friend, Mary Ann McClintock, and Stanton to talk. Piqued that neither the antislavery movement nor the temperance movement took women seriously enough, they decided to announce a woman's rights convention the next week in

Seneca Falls.[5] The two-day meeting attracted over 300 people who agreed with the Declaration of Principles that included the radical phrase: "We hold these truths to be self-evident: that all men *and women* are created equal" (my emphasis). By adding only two simple words to the Declaration of Independence, the members of the convention wisely based their demands—including property rights for women and the franchise—on the ideological foundation for American independence and freedom.

The Seneca Falls convention was Elizabeth Cady Stanton's first opportunity to speak in public on the subject of woman's rights, and she argued, as had Rose since the early 1840s, that woman's current position was like that of a slave: "So long as your women are slaves you may throw your colleges and churches to the winds. You can't have scholars and saints so long as your mothers are ground to powder between the upper and nether millstone of tyranny and lust" ("Address" 19). Stanton's rhetoric, unlike Rose's, was tinctured by the Temperance movement, where men were lustful beasts and women were victims to be "ground to powder." Both Stanton and her ally, Frederick Douglass, who lived in nearby Rochester, resolved to give women the franchise, a resolution that was adopted but not unanimously.

The First National Convention in Worcester, 1850

A little more than two years later reformers gathered for the first national woman's rights convention in Worcester, Massachusetts.[6] The 1850 convention had been organized by Lucy Stone

5. The short time between the Call and the meeting suggests the local nature of the convention and also suggests why the New York City–based Ernestine Rose did not attend. Many have written on the Seneca Falls convention; for just a few see Gurko; Lutz, *Crusade*; and *HWS* 1: 67–73.

6. For further information on this convention see the *PWRC, Worcester, 1850*; see also *HWS* 1: 215–26; and 820–25, for a list of the people who signed the "Call" and who were "Members" of the convention and for the "Resolutions" and letters of support. For this convention, as for all conventions, I cite the *Proceedings* when they are available and use a shortened Abbreviation in the text to refer to that year's *Proceedings*. I also cite the year the convention took place rather

and Paulina Wright Davis, who had drafted the call for the convention. Stone and Davis, part of a group of disaffected women attending the May 30, 1850, antislavery Society meeting in Boston, decided that they needed to plan their own convention instead of trying to tack woman's rights issues onto antislavery meetings. Spurred on by letters of support from such public figures as Ralph Waldo Emerson, William Lloyd Garrison, and popular writer Catharine Sedgwick, they called the meeting for October in Massachusetts. Convention participants included orators like Ernestine Rose, who had been active in freethought reform, as well as a core group of antislavery reformers such as William Lloyd Garrison, Frederick Douglass, Stephen Foster, Abby Kelley Foster, Lucretia Mott, Sojourner Truth, and newcomer Antoinette Brown.

It was difficult for many of the participants to even get to the convention. The women traveled to Worcester from 11 states in sooty, uncomfortable railroad cars or on stagecoaches that jolted them over muddy roads for hundreds of miles. On their way to Worcester, they ate sporadically at best, often in small roadside inns where they shared any available food with other travelers. They all wore many layers of long skirts and petticoats along with corsets that increased their discomfort while traveling.

The convention was called to order at Brinley Hall by Sarah Earle of Worcester, with Paulina Davis elected president. In Davis's opening address, she proposed a "radical and universal" reform (*PWRC, Worcester, 1850* 7). Lucretia Mott, the oldest woman on the stage, followed Davis, speaking on the condition of women and the need for improvements to that condition. That afternoon,

---

than the year the *Proceedings* were published. When the *Proceedings* are not extant, I cite the speeches and summarized proceedings that are available in national and local newspapers. I turn to *The History of Woman Suffrage* to quote speeches as a last resort. *HWS* does not always accurately reflect everything that went on in the meetings, emphasizing as it does Stanton's speeches and Anthony's issues sometimes to the exclusion of other voices, particularly when those other voices might disagree with them. The *Proceedings* occasionally include audience commentary, as was the custom for reporting meetings in mid-nineteenth-century America. When audience comments are available, I include them.

Abby Price of the nearby antislavery/utopian community of Hopedale, Massachusetts, spoke on the importance of women having equal opportunities with men for well-compensated employment, for financial security, and for legal and political rights. Quoting Blackstone, Price reminded her audience that women's legal disabilities "are too well known to render it necessary to quote many of the laws respecting them" (31). She countered current law with her own example of being able to vote in the Hopedale community: "I have never, in the small State of Hopedale, heard of one home being neglected, or one duty less thoroughly attended to by allowing women an equal voice" (34).

During the two days of the conference, participants often argued from their own fields of interest. Harriot K. Hunt, a Boston physician, lectured on the medical education of women; Sarah Tyndale, a merchant in Philadelphia, spoke on the business capacity of women. Antoinette Brown, recently graduated from Oberlin, interpreted the Bible as mandating complete equality for women with men; Lucy Stone called for circulating petitions demanding female suffrage.

Advocates who could not attend wrote letters of support. Helene Marie Weber, a Belgian woman who often wore a dress with pantaloons, wrote a letter to the convention concerning woman's enfeebled condition as a consequence of the clothes she was supposed to wear. Elizabeth Cady Stanton asked participants to look behind the curtain of people's private marriages to see how few harmonious households really existed, because, she argued, no true happiness can exist where there is subordination. Rev. Samuel J. May of Syracuse, unable to afford the expenses of travel because he was funneling his funds to help withstand the despotism of the recently enacted Fugitive Slave Law, wrote that without women's participation in government, the state is only half human.

Rose was an outsider at this convention from the beginning, albeit one who was appreciated for her wealth of organizational and speaking skills. Many of the other women knew each other well from various familial, religious, or educational networks. Lucretia Mott and Martha Wright were sisters; Antoinette Brown and Lucy Stone had been students together at Oberlin and later were sisters-in-law, but Rose was a loner.[7]

As would become increasingly clear as the decade proceeded, Rose, as a freethinker, an atheist, and perceived as Jewish—though she did not consider herself religious—was surrounded by what Anna Speicher has called "sets of concentric circles" of religious women (225). Many of these women had joined together to form bonds of friendship based not on geographic proximity but on dedication to an abolitionist cause that reinforced their religious convictions. Although few of the antislavery women who would turn to the woman's rights platforms in the 1850s were conventionally religious, most believed in the importance of their actions as "Christian" acts.

From the beginning Rose was "Mrs. Rose" to all the mostly younger women, but even to Lucretia Mott, who was 17 years her senior. Rose looked and sounded different from the other women. Her dark hair (in long curls), her gloved hands, her European manners and mannerisms, her Jewish intellectual heritage that celebrated argument—all combined to signify her as someone foreign, someone strange. Despite Rose's activity in both woman's rights and on antislavery platforms throughout the 1840s, Rose remained semantically and spatially isolated from the other women, who were, often, "friends and sisters" with each other but not with her.[8]

But Rose, even though an outsider to the antislavery core of women who organized the convention, was one of its most active participants, serving on the important "Central Committee" and also chairing the "Committee on Civil and Political Functions."

7. Antoinette Brown Blackwell's biographer Elizabeth Cazden writes that Brown and Stone may have been more than friends at Oberlin: "they may have become lovers," she posits (30). Stone's biographer, Andrea Kerr, demurs, interpreting the young women's passionate letters to each other as demonstrating "preternaturally innocent intensity" rather than sexual passion (36).

8. Antoinette Brown, for example, writes to Lucy Stone on December 19, 1850, shortly after the first Worcester convention, from New York City that "if I knew where Mrs. Rose was I would call on her." (Lasser and Merrill 98); but she did not know where Rose lived, so did not call upon her.

On her committee were Lucy Stone, as secretary, Wendell Phillips, William Lloyd Garrison, and the absent Elizabeth Cady Stanton, who would not participate in any of the national conventions until 1859. The convention was, to Rose, a perfect forum to air different sides of an argument; ever the optimist, Rose believed that once people heard and understood "the truth" then they would accept it and change their lives.

In her first speech to the 500 or so convention participants and audience in the afternoon of the first day, Rose spoke to two resolutions she had prepared for the convention: she argued that woman's "very constricted" sphere of action, based on an unjust view of woman's nature, was injurious to her health and to her mental and moral development.[9] Therefore, Rose articulated the benefits of eliminating the distinctions between the rights of the sexes. Using her Owenite background that emphasized the importance of education, Rose asserted that both men and women needed to be trained as human beings, without regard to sex. She related that when parents have a son, they consult about his education; when they have a daughter, they do nothing because "girls are educated with one single aim . . . to catch a husband." If woman were educated equally with man, though, then woman would not be "transferred" from the parent to the husband at her marriage and marriage would become a union of equals who have real affection for each other rather than, as is too frequently the case, "an artificial bond producing often more misery than happiness" (*Tribune* Oct. 25, 1850).

Later in the evening, Rose spoke again, adding that man is as much the victim of his despotism as woman. Unwilling to cast men as villains, Rose relied on her Owenite background to explain the cultural construction of "character": people could not form their own character, rather character was formed *for* them (by the lucky or unlucky combination of cultural forces acting upon them)

9. The most complete summary of Rose's three speeches at the Worcester convention is found in the Oct. 25 and 26, 1850, New York *Tribune*. The incomplete *Proceedings* include only a few speeches, summarizing Rose's in one line. The Oct. 25, 1850, *Herald* also summarizes Rose's talks.

not *by* them. Thus, Rose differed in her remarks from many of the other women. Unlike temperance speakers, who were used to portraying men as evil drunkards, and antislavery reformers who were accustomed to demonizing slave owners, Rose understood all people—men and women, slave owners and abolitionists, clergy and freethinkers—to be products of their cultural constructions. Thus, no one was to blame for his or her current belief systems.

Others on the stage were not as sanguine about Rose's refusal to demonize the opposition and to excuse men from responsibility for woman's condition. As Sarah Grimké's striking image of men's feet on women's necks had demonstrated, a vivid portrayal of concrete villains, flesh-and-blood men who physically kept women subordinate, appealed to audiences. At this meeting, Lucretia Mott stood to speak after Rose to say that "it strikes me . . . that Mrs. Rose has made a better apology for man than he could make for himself (laughter). Woman is crushed, but nobody is to blame; it is circumstances that have crushed her . . . it is an abstract evil, that's all" (*Herald* Oct. 25, 1850). To Mott, and to many of the other speakers, "evil" needed a human face to move crowds; to Rose simple "truth" was all that was needed: do away with prejudices that relegated women to a specific role and both men and women could be brought to a better state of existence, without blaming either sex for the state of current affairs.

In the course of the two-day convention, Rose would speak formally three times and briefly many more. Besides arguing for woman's equal education with man, Rose spoke to other concerns, such as making women and their contributions visible to history: "We have heard a great deal of our Pilgrim Fathers; but who ever told us anything of our Pilgrim mothers? And were not their trials, and is not their glory equally great?" (*Herald* Oct. 25, 1850). Or she offered a rationale why women were not inventive: "the reason they have not produced high inventions is that they have been continually employed with trifling duties, as drudges in the kitchen, or a puppet-show in the parlor" (*Herald* Oct. 25, 1850). This effective imagery suggests why Paulina Wright Davis and the New York *Tribune* labeled Rose as the most "eloquent" speaker of the convention.

An activist in thought and deed, Rose followed up on the conference's demands for suffrage by circulating a petition for signatures to present to the state legislature of New York. Her petition read:

> The laws of this State in relation to Woman do violence to her natural and inalienable rights, and are contrary to the spirit and principles of a republic which is based on the declaration that taxation without representation is tyranny. . . . We therefore pray your honorable body to enact such laws as will give all women the elective franchise, with the privileges of holding office, etc., the same as man; and to married women, in case of separation or death, the right to fold, bestow or bequeath an equal share of all the property her husband and herself may possess. (*Liberator* Jan. 21, 1851)

The first national woman's rights convention drew comments from sources as disparate as the New York *Herald* and the *Westminster Review*. The *Herald*, berating the convention's "awful combination" of "socialism, abolitionism, and infidelity," announced the meeting with sensational headings: "Bible and Constitution Repudiated" (Oct. 25, 1850). The convention was, according to the *Herald*, "calculated to strike terror into the heart of the stoutest man." The *Herald*'s writers, in their summary of the proceedings, paraphrased the speakers and, in Rose's case, added their disparaging perception of her accent, attempting to ridicule her ideas. About Rose's first appearance on the platform in the afternoon of the first day, the *Herald* relates:

> Mrs. Rose rose upon the platform.—Madame President and ma dear sisters and bredren, I do regret no one rises better dan myself to speak; but I shall offer you but a few remarks on de subject before us. Mrs. Rose spoke at length, saying among other things, dat woman is in de quality of de slave . . . and dat

> when de distinction of rights between de sexes ceases, then, and
> not till then, will woman get her just deserts.

Note the use of what sounds like a direct quote: "I do regret
no one rises better dan myself" coupled in the same paragraph
with summary: "Mrs. Rose spoke at length." The "direct" quotes
also include the nonstandard "bredren," "dan," "de," and "dat,"
intentionally making Rose sound both uneducated and foreign
(or black).

"Enfranchisement of Women" in the London *Westminster
Review*, by contrast, celebrated the women's call for practical
political action and rejoiced that this movement was not merely
for women but *by* them. Although the question of woman's rights
was not a new one to "thinkers nor to any one by whom the
principles of free and popular government are felt," (289) Harriet
Taylor Mill, the author of the essay,[10] summarized the principal
demands of the convention as being for equal educational opportunities, for partnership in business, and for a coequal share in
forming and administering laws (291). Closer to home, the New
York *Tribune*, perhaps the most influential national paper in 1850,
sent reporter J. G. Forman to cover the entire convention and
then printed summaries of most of the speeches for two days in
late October 1850. Rose was treated better by the *Tribune* than
by the *Herald*, though Forman misconstrued Rose's nationality,
writing that "Mrs. Ernestine Rose of New York spoke with great
eloquence on the subject . . . [and] "her French accent and extemporaneous manner added quite a charm to her animated and forcible style" (Oct. 25, 1850).

---

10. Authorship was first attributed to John Stewart [sic] Mill by Harriet
Martineau in a letter of support sent to the second annual woman's rights
convention (*PWRC, Worcester, 1851* 16). Then Emma Coe of Ohio reported that
Martineau was wrong; she understood the author to be Mill's mother (*PWRC,
Worcester, 1851* 16). Later, Stanton and Anthony explain that Harriet Taylor,
soon to be the wife of John Stuart Mill, read the *Tribune's* account of the
convention and then wrote an essay for the *Westminster and Foreign Quarterly
Review* (see *HWS* 1:225). When the essay appeared, the married Harriet Taylor
had taken her husband's name.

The Second National Convention, Worcester, 1851

In October 1851 Rose again met her colleagues, at the second annual woman's rights convention, also held at Worcester.[11] At this convention, several of the women had begun wearing the practical new "costume," soon to be known as "Bloomers" because of Amelia Bloomer's advocacy of them in the *Lily*. Dress reform had long been a subject of interest to earlier reformers such as Frances Wright, who had adopted a type of culotted skirt during the 1820s. Some of the utopian communities that sprang up in the 1840s also instituted dress reform for women. Helene Maria Weber, a year earlier in her letter to the 1850 convention, had also championed the new, practical split skirt that allowed women to move more easily. Some of the younger women had adopted the new dress, "a sort of Turkish costume" with "full drawers and tunic," with culotte pants that came mid-calf instead of to the floor.[12] Rose, one of the oldest in the movement—she was in her early 40s by the time of the Worcester conventions— never adopted it.

The first day of the convention began with the Paulina Wright Davis's introductory speech lauding the publicity of the previous year's convention and describing other hopeful signs that more occupations and schools were becoming available to women. Letters were read from supportive reform-minded men and women such as Ralph Waldo Emerson, Horace Mann, Henry Ward Beecher,

11. For information on the second national convention, see *PWRC*, Worcester, 1851. See also *HWS* 1: 226–46 and the Feb. 12, 1852, *Boston Investigator* for Rose's toast at the Worcester convention. *HWS* 1: 825–26 lists the Resolutions for this convention, including, the first—"the Right of Suffrage for Women, is, in our opinion, the corner-stone of this enterprise" (825).

12. See Martha Wright's letter of Mar. 14, 1851, to Lucretia Mott, GFP. By 1852 the Bloomer costume had become a political statement of several of the most radical of the woman's rights advocates including Susan B. Anthony, Elizabeth Cady Stanton, and Lucy Stone. But because of the hostility the women received in public meetings when wearing the new costume, Stanton dropped the costume by early 1854 and urged Anthony to do so also because Anthony was, according to Martha Wright, "the least graceful of anyone who has adopted the dress" (Wright to Lucretia Mott, Mar. 8, 1854, GFP).

Angelina Grimké Weld, Harriet Martineau, and Elizabeth Cady Stanton. Abby Price and Lucy Stone both addressed the assembly.

In the evening of the first day's proceedings, Ernestine Rose addressed the gathering in a major speech that Paulina Wright Davis argued "has never been surpassed" in all the women's rights speeches and conventions.[13] Following William Henry Channing, who read a letter from Jeanne Deroin and Pauline Roland, two French women imprisoned for demanding their rights following the 1848 revolution,[14] Rose began her speech by alluding to the French women, probably much on the minds of her audience, arguing that such lack of rights might well be understood because France was ruled by Russian and Austrian despots. But even in America, "this far-famed land of freedom," woman has still to beg for her rights.

Paraphrasing Frances Wright, Rose argues eloquently that woman should have the same rights as man, in that "humanity recognizes no sex—mind recognizes no sex—life and death, pleasure and pain, happiness and misery recognize no sex" (37). She urges men in power to fulfill the principle of universal suffrage or substitute the following on American banners: "Freedom and Power to one half of society, and submission and slavery to the other"

13. See Davis's *History of the National Woman's Rights Movement* 19. Davis adds that Rose, at her own expense, had her essay printed and circulated it widely. Stanton and Anthony included part of Rose's speech in *HWS* 1: 237–42 and 245–46. Another version of this speech was published separately in 1851 by Josiah Mendum, Rose's friend and the publisher of the *Boston Investigator*, under the title "An Address on Woman's Rights." Rose gave this version of her speech at Cochituate Hall in Boston on October 19, 1851, following the convention in Worcester. This version is similar to the convention speech, only adding information on girls' education at the end.

My in-text page numbers refer to the speech as it is reported in the 1851 *PWRC*.

14. Roland in 1848 nominated herself as mayor of her city; later that year she claimed the right to vote for the Constituent Assembly. Deroin claimed she could be a candidate for the Legislative Assembly. Both were elected members of the Central Committee of the Associative Unions, upon which they were thrown in jail "for their liberal opinions." See *HWS* 1: 234–37. For more information about Jeanne Deroin's activities in the Revolution of 1848, see Scott, chapter 3.

(39). Rose goes on to illustrate the rights woman lacks—she has no voice in her government; she is taxed without representation. She is, says Rose, subject to man's power from the cradle to the grave: "Father, guardian, or husband, one conveys her like some piece of merchandise over to the other" (37). At marriage, particularly, she loses her entire legal identity, though she still has to pay taxes and is taxed without representation. Her very property may be consumed by taxes to defray the expenses of "that unholy, unrighteous custom called war," yet she has no power to veto it (37).

Then Rose switches to a technique her hero Thomas Paine often employed in his argumentative writing: she takes up her opposition's arguments and refutes them one at a time. To the argument that the husband provides for the wife, Rose counters with how degrading that idea is—to be "kept," as one would "a favorite horse"(38). She illustrates her point by giving as an example two men whom she saw brought before a Justice of New York. One man had stolen boots and another had assaulted his wife: the first man was sent to prison and the second dismissed—his crime was not a crime as his wife was his property. "You must remember," Rose argues, that "the boots were taken by a stranger, while the wife was insulted by her legal owner!" (39).

Unequal laws, continues Rose, allow woman to be degraded by man. To illustrate her point, she uses the example of that "detestable law, which was written in human blood . . . the Fugitive Slave Law" (39). Rose asks her audience whether even a year ago any states would have been "base enough" to desire such a law. Yet, as soon as it was passed, "law-loving, law-abiding" people began obeying it. "Such is the magic power of law," Rose says; "hence also the reason why we call on the nation to remove the legal shackles from women," as it will benefit all of society (39). Just as the Fugitive Slave Law allowed whites to degrade blacks, so current laws permit, even encourage, men to degrade women.

Having dismissed her opposition, Rose argues that irrationalities about woman's nature and proper sphere must be overcome by reason. Women need to be able to develop robustly in mind and body. With scorn, Rose relates how the Rev. Henry Bellows of New York opposed woman's taking part in public life: "place woman unbonneted and unshawled before the public gaze and what becomes of her modesty and her virtue." Rose responds by saying that in Bellows's mind "the modesty and virtue of woman is of so fragile a nature, that when it is in contact with the atmosphere, it evaporates like chloroform" (45).

Rose concludes her talk by alluding to the words of the Apostle Paul in his letter to the Ephesians (6:13–17). Well aware of the Christian leanings of her audience, Rose appropriates—and alters—biblical images of the armor of God, the belt of truth, and the breastplate of righteousness: "We must remember that we have a crusade before us, far holier and more righteous than led warriors to Palestine—a crusade, not to deprive any one of his rights, but to claim our own. . . . We therefore must put on the armor of charity, carry before us the banner of truth, and defend ourselves with the shield of right against the invaders of our liberty" (47).[15]

Rose's speech combines her wit and sarcasm with an Enlightenment-like rhetorical strategy that diffuses the opponents' arguments while illustrating how reasonable her own logic is. Always using common cultural myths, particularly reverence for the Declaration of Independence, Rose aligns herself with speakers such as Thomas Paine, who incorporated many of the same strategies to illustrate how inconsistent Americans were about religious principles; or, even closer to her own experiences, she aligns herself with Frances Wright, who also spoke in the same impassioned ways about the reasonableness of woman's rights. But Rose manages to add her own unmistakable sarcasm, such as her reference to woman's fragile nature "evaporating like chloroform" if it were exposed to "the atmosphere." This fearless rationality—speaking straight, acting as if errors in thinking could be eradicated if only

15. Rose changes the armor of God to the armor of charity, the belt of truth to the banner of truth, and the breastplate of righteousness to the shield of right. My thanks to Vickie Johnson for pointing out the passage from Ephesians 6:13–17.

reasonable people would put their minds to it—is one of Rose's greatest legacies to us.

Rose's effective oratorical style combines a passion for her beliefs with an intellectual conviction in the promise of America as a place where people could, indeed should, live a life of liberty and be free to pursue ideas that might not be popular. Rose's passion comes from her righteousness, her own antinomianism in interpreting and extending to all the "holy" word of the secular founding fathers, whose promises were made for people like themselves (white, male, and propertied). The audacity of an unpropertied Jewish female immigrant demanding the authority to say what she wanted in the manner she wanted was an unspeakable outrage to many people in the United States, including mainstream newspaper editors and ministers who would interpret her speeches for their readers and congregations throughout the 1850s and 1860s.

Perhaps her greatest victory of the conference, though, comes from the pages of the *Christian Inquirer*, edited by none other than the same Rev. Henry Bellows whom Rose had lambasted in her speech. Bellows writes following the convention:

> We have read the report of the proceedings of this Convention with lively interest and general satisfaction. We confess ourselves to be much surprised at the prevailing good sense, propriety, and moral elevation of the meeting. . . . We confess our surprise at the weight of the reasoning brought forward by the recent Convention, and shall endeavor henceforth to keep our masculine mind,—full, doubtless, of conventional prejudices,—open to the light which is shed upon the theme. . . . But woman insists upon being respected, as a kindred intellect, a free competitor, and a political equal. And we have suspicions that she may surprise the conservative world by making her pretensions good. (*HWS* 1: 243–45)

This second national convention also brought out conflicts and disagreements, though one might never know it from reading Stanton and Anthony's carefully edited *History of Woman Suffrage*, rather than the complete *Proceedings*. Abby Kelley Foster, after hearing Elizabeth Oakes Smith speak, rose to argue that the cause of women's inequality lay in their own laps, not necessarily in men's. Why, questioned Kelley Foster, did woman not occupy that place she was qualified to fill? Because, she argued, she does not have the will:

> We complain on the platform, in the forum, in the pulpit, in the office of teacher, and so on to the end of the list, she does not hold that place which she is qualified to fill; and what is the deep difficulty? I cannot, I will not charge it all upon man. I respond to . . . an old, homely maxim . . . 'Where there's a will, there's a way,' and the reason why woman is not found in the highest position which she is qualified to fill, is because she has not more than half the will. (99)

Abby Kelley Foster goes on to introduce a resolution that begins: "Resolved, that in regard to most points, Woman lacks her rights because she does not feel the full weight of her responsibilities" (100). She then paraphrases Mary Wollstonecraft's "Thoughts on the Education of Daughters, with Reflections on Female Conduct in the More Important Duties of Life," which urges women (particularly mothers) to cultivate their daughters' minds to avoid indolence and foster rational employment. She adds her own twist to Wollstonecraft's advisory guidebook to women: "when woman shall feel her duty, she will get her rights. We, who are young on this question of Woman's Rights, should entitle our next book 'Woman's Duties.' Impress on your daughters their duties . . . and we shall have our rights" (101).[16] Women, she resolved, should take more responsibility for their lives; some

---

16. This small volume by Wollstonecraft is an interesting one, as it lauds rational development and simplicity in dress and urges women to avoid early marriage and card playing—"the universal refuge to which the idle and ignorant resort" (145). It also reveals Wollstonecraft's attitude toward servants that places her firmly within her class's system of thinking about domestics: servants are "ignorant and cunning" she writes and young women must learn to treat them "properly" (118).

were too "lazy." She added that "there are thousands of women in these United States working for a starving pittance, who know . . . they are fitted for something better, and who tell me, when I talk to them, and urge them to open shops, and do business for themselves 'I do not want the responsibility of business—it is too much.' Well, then starve in your laziness!" She concludes by referring to her own life: "for fourteen years I have advocated this cause by my daily life. Bloody feet, sisters, have worn smooth the path by which you have come hither" (102). Kelley Foster's contempt for working women who do not "better themselves" is palpable.

Abby Kelley Foster's speech startled her audience and it particularly offended Ernestine Rose. Immediately Rose, whose Owenite background helped her to understand industrial slavery better than Kelley Foster did, contradicted her: "rights," argued Rose, had to come before duties and "he who enjoys the most rights [man], owes in return the most duties" (104). And, she added, "as it is, while man enjoys all the rights, he preaches all the duties to woman . . . instead of writing and preaching so much about the duties of woman, it is high time," said Rose, that man set an example and give woman her rights. Blaming women for "laziness" without educating them as men are educated and with no power to decide what duties they were supposed to perform seemed to Rose to be looking at the problem backwards. From Abby's privileged viewpoint (relatives stayed with her child when she traveled), women who were not willing to "assume responsibilities" were "complainers" (102).

The stark conflict between Rose and Kelley Foster—foreshadowed in the late 1840s when they appeared on the abolition stage together and Kelley Foster complained that Rose's talks were not "so useful as remarks from a person who sympathized in full with us"—helps explain why Abby Kelley Foster was only sporadically involved in the woman's rights movement until long after the Civil War. The conflict was unfortunate because Kelley Foster, one of the most experienced woman speakers on the antislavery stage, devoted herself more and more to abolitionist causes while

retreating from the woman's rights movement.[17] Locked into thinking that complaining women caused their own problems—"Do not
go home to complain of the men, but go and make greater exertions than ever to discharge your every-day duties. Oh! it is easy to
be lazy" (102)—Foster did not understand Rose's point, which
was simple: when a woman had her rights, she would perform her
duties, "not only as a wife and mother, but also as a free, enlightened, rational member of the great family of man, highly conducive
to the elevation and happiness of all" (104). To blame women for
complaining or to order them to "discharge their duties" before
giving them rights was, to Rose, utter folly.

Horace Mann and the Westchester Convention, 1852

The following February, Ernestine Rose directed her energies
to fighting, in print, another so-called friend of woman's rights
who seemed to Rose to be sabotaging all that the women were
working for. In 1852 Horace Mann was known as a reformer who
had expanded public school education in Massachusetts, when he
was the state's first secretary of the Board of Education. Elected
to the House of Representatives as an antislavery Whig in 1848,
Mann was involved in a number of reform movements in the early
1850s including temperance and abolitionism. In 1853 he became
the president of Antioch College, which, like Oberlin before it,
was established to provide educational opportunities to all without
regard to race or sex.

17. Kelley Foster feuded with more than just Rose. She had public disagreements with both Frederick Douglass and William Lloyd Garrison and, in fact, did
not speak or write to Garrison from 1859 until after 1867. Although Dorothy
Sterling cites Abby's feud with Garrison as stemming from his accusing her of
fraud, recent scholars such as Anna Speicher suggest that Sterling is being overly
charitable to her subject and that Kelley Foster did much to isolate herself; see
Speicher 207. See also Kelley Foster to Wendell Phillips and William Lloyd
Garrison for July through September 1859 in the Abby Kelley Foster Papers,
AAS.
    Abby Kelley Foster's attitude changed eventually. In 1873, she refused to pay
taxes on her farm because she was not allowed to vote.

Fresh from another successful speech at the 1852 Paine Birthday celebration, Rose responded angrily to Mann's public lectures, "Hints to a Young Woman," delivered in New York City in February 1852, only four short months after writing a letter of support to the Worcester convention. Rose had gone to Mann's lecture optimistic, knowing the reputation of the man as a reformer. Though she did not necessarily expect him to advocate woman's political rights, she felt that the topic itself, when exposed to the "fiery ordeal of reason and justice" would help the truth shine brighter. Her outrage stemmed, at least in part, from Mann's lack of reason, his pandering to an "already prejudiced public opinion." The day after she heard Mann speak Rose shot off a letter to him, refuting his most grievous errors of thinking: that the sexes were now and forever separate and distinct and should therefore be educated differently and have different political rights; that God created the human soul as distinctly "male" and "female"; that woman was created a religious being whereas man was made to command; that despite being oppressed and degraded by man, woman "unsexes" herself when she calls conventions that might improve her conditions.[18]

Rose begins her letter to Mann with an "apology" that sets the tone for her angry letter: "pardon the liberty of a woman, from a foreign land, in troubling you with a few lines." From the first line on, Rose systematically refutes Mann's assumptions. First she questions him for beginning his talk by referring to Helen Maria Weber of Belgium as a leader of a "sect" that "adopted man's attire and behaves like a man." This behavior, according to Mann, offended "the design and works of God," who has "forbidden" this "commingling." Rose responds by asking what "acting like a man" means? She points out that Weber, who had written

18. Rose's letters—one to the *Boston Investigator* and one to Horace Mann— were published in the Apr. 21, 1852, *Boston Investigator*, from which I quote all passages. Rose's responses to Mann were published separately in a pamphlet entitled "Review of Horace Mann's Two Lectures, delivered in New York, February 17th and 29th, 1852," now part of the NAWSA Collection in the Library of Congress.

a letter of support to the first Worcester woman's rights convention in 1850, was a practical agriculturalist who although young, managed a large estate quite successfully. If "acting like a man" meant deeper reflection, clearer reasoning, better judgment, and wiser actions, then, says Rose, perhaps we shall all soon act "like a man."

To Mann's statement that women could not be equal with men because woman's bodies were structured differently from man's, Rose questions the causal analysis. Even should men and women have different internal organs—"the heart, lungs, liver, stomach, or any other of the organs requisite in the human economy are larger, smaller, situated a sixteenth of an inch higher, or lower, more to the right or the left, in man or woman"—Rose queries "what then?" What difference does this make and what possible relevance to social and political rights? What does the size of a limb have to do with rights? Does not woman's mind, her faculties, her powers require cultivation and development? To Mann's ridiculous comment that one might as well have knives and forks, hooks and eyes, buttons and buttonholes claim equality, Rose sarcastically responds that she cannot possibly comment on this "philosophical simile, it being the product of the 'higher intellect of the sterner sex.' "

After hearing Mann admit that woman was, indeed, oppressed and degraded by man, Rose responds with outrage to his claim that women would only "unsex" themselves if they tried to claim their rights: "and will [woman] not always remain in this degraded state as long as man arrogates to himself the right to command and force her to obey?—make laws and compel her to observe them? And if she revolts against that tyranny and degradation, and claims her rights as a human being, who, whatever the differences in her organic structure, has the same aims and objects in life as man has, does she not 'unsex herself' "? Rose adds, speaking directly to Mann: "think of these questions and answer them, not according to the popular notions on the subject, but according to reason and truth before you give the next 'hints' to man or woman." Rose's sense of affront was clearly fueled by a sense of betrayal: Mann was a reformer, an enlightened educator and antislavery speaker who, for reasons Rose could not fathom, had turned away from the clear light of reason.

So appalled was Rose at Mann's bigotry that she incorporated her own "hints to young ladies" into her talk at the Westchester Woman's Rights Convention, held near Philadelphia in early June of 1852.[19] Lucretia Mott, a longtime resident of Philadelphia, called the meeting to order; Rose served on the business committee along with James Mott, Lucretia Mott, Dr. Harriot K. Hunt, and Frances Gage. Writing about the convention on June 9, 1852, the *Boston Investigator*, quoting the *Philadelphia Ledger*, summarized that the women demanded an equality before the law; that the property of the husband should descend to the wife, as his only heir; that woman should be permitted to hold offices of trust and profit; and so trained to unfold her nature that every path should be regarded as her appropriate sphere, wherever duty pointed. These views, the *Ledger* pointed out, were ably maintained by Mrs. Gage, Mrs. Rose, and Lucretia Mott.

Rose spent much of her speech time responding to Mann's essentialism that relegated women to the home as "religious" beings and men to the world. Her arguments led her to propose a tongue-in-cheek resolution: "if it be true, that it is woman's province to soothe the angry passions and calm the belligerent feelings of man, we know of no place where she would find a riper harvest awaiting her labor, than in the Halls of our National and State Legislatures" (16). Frustrated with Mann's rigid delegation of different duties to men and women, Rose added:

> The idea of a female doctor is ridiculed. But what is she worth as a nurse of the sick without a knowledge of the art of healing? Why am I in the prime of life in such feeble health? In my country, the laws of life are, comparatively speaking, kept in a nut shell. The girl must not exercise herself; it is not fashionable! She must not be seen in active life; it is not feminine. The boy may run, the girl must creep. (18)

19. For information on the Westchester convention, see *PWRC, West Chester [sic], Pa., 1852*; and *HWS* 1: 350–75; 829–34.

Rose added that the intent of the convention was to discuss these "grave inequalities." In addition, she concluded that women need all honest means of support and self-development open to them and they need all legal shackles removed that blocked their pathway through life.[20]

Syracuse Convention, September 1852

The third national convention for woman's rights was held at Syracuse, New York, on September 8, 9, and 10, 1852.[21] Ernestine Rose was, according to the *Proceedings*, the first person listed on the nominations committee that selected Lucretia Mott president, with Paulina Wright Davis, Gerrit Smith, and Susan B. Anthony among the other officers. Mott's presidency was, according to Stanton and Anthony looking back on the convention, evidence of the "progress of liberal ideas," as Lucretia Mott had only four years earlier at the Seneca Falls convention strenuously opposed a woman presiding over a "promiscuous" audience. Rose was also on the business committee and spoke often in numerous sessions throughout the three-day meeting. It was Susan B. Anthony's first national woman's rights convention; she attended the Syracuse convention, located close to her Rochester home, only as an agent of the Woman's Temperance Society.

Rose's agenda and her type of arguments continued to be different from those of the other speakers. Lucy Stone, for example, urged the franchise for women by employing what sounds like anti-immigrant arguments: if foreigners, "who cannot even speak [the] mother tongue correctly," free blacks, and drunkards are "all entrusted with the ballot," why not women? (20). Stone's

20. Forty years later a young Charlotte Perkins Stetson (later Gilman) would adopt the same creeping imagery in her now-famous short story "The Yellow Wallpaper" and be acclaimed by twentieth-century critics for her innovative use of such imagery.

21. For information on the convention, see *PWRC, Syracuse*, 1852; see also *HWS* 1: 517–46 and 848–54 and the New York *Tribune*, Sept. 11, 1852. Rose's major speech is reprinted in the Oct. 13, 1852, *BI* and was also printed separately. Quotes in the text come from the *Proceedings* unless otherwise noted.

comments on immigrants who spoke poorly may have offended Rose, an immigrant who spoke with an accent. Even though Rose continued to appear on platforms with Stone throughout the 1850s and 1860s, the two women were never friends and Rose would, in 1854, express her pain to Anthony over what she perceived as Stone's anti-immigration beliefs.[22] Immigration had become an increasingly sensitive topic to reformers. In part, this sensitivity was based on sheer numbers: in the 1830s, there were 600,000 immigrants; in the 1840s, 1.7 million; and in the 1850s, more than 2.5 million (Walters 4). But the immigrants who came to the United States as a result of the potato famine from the mid-1840s on were often desperate, hungry, and unskilled (Stansell 44). And they were Catholic. From the 1830s on, anti-Catholic sentiment spread even among some reformers who perceived Catholic immigrants to be superstitious and dominated by priests. The popular backlash against immigrants was reflected in the meteoric ascension of the Know-Nothing party, which attracted over one million members by the mid-1850s. Rose, who vigorously opposed the Know-Nothings, was distraught when she perceived—perhaps wrongly, since Stone also vigorously opposed the Know-Nothings—the tone of their prejudices taken up by a fellow reformer on the woman's rights platform.[23]

Antoinette Brown's argument also bothered Rose, though not for anti-immigrant reasons. The Christian Brown incorporated the popular ideology of appropriate separate spheres for men and

22. See Susan B. Anthony's Diary for Apr. 9, 1854. Lucy Stone's biographer, Andrea Kerr, argues that Stone was never "anti-immigrant," that she steadfastly opposed legislation that would have curbed immigration, and that she was not trying to take the vote away from these groups nor suggesting that they should not have the vote.

23. Just as Lucy Stone's arguments appeared anti-immigrant to Rose, so Rose's scathing comments on the "priestcraft" and on "superstition" might seem anti-Catholic (another Know-Nothing tenet) to any reader from the 1840s on. But Rose, whose English was learned as an Owenite in England, used the terms "priest" and "priestcraft" and "superstition" not to refer to Catholics, as would become common from the mid-1840s on, but rather as general terms that referred to all religions that employed theologically trained ministers.

women into her speech, arguing that women, having such different natures from men, could not be adequately represented by men and needed the vote in order to represent themselves in a democracy. Although Brown's "separate spheres" argument was a common one that seemed to sway some people, Rose opposed it. As soon as Brown completed her speech, Rose countered that whether men and women differed mentally or not, women were entitled to equal rights. Rose was joined by Gerrit Smith in her refusal to appeal to woman's soft and domestic nature: Smith objected to another's characterization of woman as an angel: "She is not an angel! (Cheers.) She is a woman. I do not believe in getting her to heaven before her time" (29).

In her main speech at the Syracuse convention, Rose, for the first time before a large audience, referred to herself as a "foreigner" and a "Jew," probably because she was introduced as being from Poland and educated in the Jewish faith (63). Perhaps feeling epistemologically and socially isolated, she pleaded on a personal level for the equal rights of her sex, not as an American woman, or as a Christian, but as a daughter of poor Poland and a "down-trodden and persecuted people called the Jews" (63). It was an unusual beginning for her—one that not only called attention to herself but also one that called attention to her Jewish heritage, a heritage that could arouse hostile feeling even on abolitionist and suffrage stages.

Speaking immediately after Antoinette Brown, who argued that the Christian Bible was truly democratic, Rose disagreed, insisting that she saw no need to appeal to any written authority. Where Antoinette Brown claimed "some right interpretation of the Bible," Ernestine Rose responded: "Miss Brown has . . . as good a right to her interpretation of the Bible, as any other Minister; but if we accept it, it is after all only her definition, and not the meaning of the text" (91).[24] In an era when spiritual authority had to be dealt

---

24. Rose was joined in her opinion of the Bible by Elizabeth Cady Stanton, who, though not present at this or any other of the national conventions in the 1850s, sent a letter that lambasted the "priestcraft" and argued that woman, like the poor slave "Uncle Tom," instead of being made noble and free by religion,

with, Rose refused to recognize that authority. She resisted any authority save the authority of "reason" and "common sense." She was forever separated from most of the other women on the woman's rights platform and from most of her audience because of her refusal to acknowledge biblical authority. This resistance caused her to disagree even with earnest, sincere women like Antoinette Brown.

Rose turned to the only authorities she believed worth citing, freethinkers. Beginning her speech by using the language of free-thinking Owenites William Thompson and Anna Wheeler, Rose argues, "woman is a slave, from the cradle to the grave. Father, guardian, husband—master still. One conveys her, like a piece of property, over to the other. She is said to have been created only for man's benefit, not for her own. This falsehood is the main cause of her inferior education and position" (64). Rose calls for an end to such irrationalities, because "the whole race suffers by it." The interests of the sexes, she argues, cannot be separated (64).

Rose structures her main speech of the conference by refuting the ideas of an English member of Parliament, a Mr. Roebuck, who, though advocating an extension of the franchise to more male voters, argued that women should not have an equal right because their "gentle influences" might be lost and because he "cannot rob myself of that inexpressible benefit" (70). Rose's response is sarcastic: "Well, this is certainly a nice, little romantic bit of parliamentary declamation. What a pity that he should give up all these enjoyments, to give women a vote. Poor man! His happiness must be balanced on the very verge of a precipice, when the simple act of depositing a vote by the hand of a woman, would overthrow and destroy it forever" (70).

Rose continues by pointing out how dangerous the "happiness of society" is for women, upon whose backs that happiness is laid.

---

was enslaved by it. Religion, wrote Stanton, has "made [woman's] bondage but more certain and lasting, her degradation more helpless and complete" (*HWS* 1: 851).

As Rose argues, Roebuck's blind self-interest took over his reason; if women were independent, they might not be willing to be "the obedient, servile tool, implicitly to obey and minister to the passions and follies of man" (71). Drawing on a cross-cultural perspective, Rose points out that the Turk deems it inexpedient, for the happiness of society, to give women any personal freedom; thus, he encloses her in a harem. Even in "this glorious land of freedom," a land that has written on its banners universal suffrage, even here half the population is "deprived of her natural and inalienable rights," her sphere is prescribed, her education restricted, and her physical, mental, and moral energies are crippled so that man may have "a docile, obedient slave to do his bidding" (73). Thus, Rose shows how notions of "the common good" can often be used to keep women servile and without rights because the so-called common good benefits only one-half the human race.[25]

Rose concludes her speech by turning the ideology of woman's gentle, special nature back on her opponents. Since she perceives that one objection to woman's voting is men's fear that women would be corrupted by the present state of party politics, she argues that women should be allowed to vote in order to change the atmosphere of party politics, an argument many women put forth in convention speeches. "Leave forever our legislative halls, the Stygian pools, as the honorable Horace Mann calls them . . . For what rational hope have we that they will ever become purified unless woman takes them in hand, seeing that man has had the exclusive possession of them so long and they only seem to have grown worse." What must be done, according to Rose, is only

25. This speech is the first, full example of Rose's changing attitudes toward the "common good." Though Rose was a remarkably consistent thinker, she changed her mind about the implications of sacrificing for the common good. Given her experiences supporting the Skaneateles Community, Rose discovered that, without gender equality, evoking the "common good" instead of emphasizing individual rights could become an insidious way to limit women. Though she would always associate capitalism with selfishness, Rose had by 1852 differentiated between the theoretical importance of political and social equality for all people that the United States legal system all but ignored and the popular ideology of individualistic economic opportunity.

"expedient": use the "purifying influence" of women—and Rose uses quotation marks around this term—to cleanse the legislative halls.

In addition to giving speeches, the women and men at the Syracuse convention also discussed policies, such as forming a permanent organization instead of having a separate central committee each year to organize the conference. Although a permanent central committee would have been efficient, the women feared the potential lack of freedom more than they worried about the inefficiency of a new committee organizing the convention each year. Angelina Grimké Weld wrote to the conference that having a national organization would be a mistake because organizations are "too narrow for humanity," tending not to protect the sacredness of the individual (80). She added that the women were already "bound together by the natural ties of a spiritual affinity" (81). Although uninterested in the *spiritual* nature of any organization, Rose nonetheless agreed with Grimké Weld that with a permanent organization "you cannot be free" (86); organizations were like "Chinese bandages"—they hindered the growth of humans (85). Even though she admits that "men must sometimes combine to effect great purposes" (the subject of much of her speech making of the 1840s), she is now "decidedly opposed to organization . . . [because having been] born into a sect, [she] had cut herself loose from it, and [she] knew what it cost [her]" (85).

The irony of Rose's arguments against a national, permanent organization cannot be missed today. Only when reformers such as Ernestine Rose joined together with other activists to hold yearly national conventions and numerous state and local meetings did public opinion begin to change about woman's right to hold property and vote. And only when the women's rights groups, splintered by controversy over the Fourteenth and Fifteenth Amendments in 1869, joined together again at the end of the century did woman's suffrage move forward. Fearing the "Chinese bandages" of a tightly knit organization may have cost Rose and her colleagues a half a century of voter's rights.

The conference ended with the Doxology, sung to the tune of "Old Hundred" and one final resolution from Rose, showing perhaps the depth of her feeling of betrayal from a fellow reformer: "Resolved, that the young women of our land be warned against the fallacies contained in Horace Mann's lectures" (97).

Numerous papers in Syracuse and all over the country commented on the woman's rights convention. The Syracuse *Daily Star* reported on September 11 that for the past three days, "these bad women have vomited forth" a "mass of corruption, heresies, ridiculous nonsense, and reeking vulgarities" (quoted in *HWS* 1: 852). The New York *Herald* asked a typical question: "Who are these women? What do they want? What are the motives that impel them to this course of action? . . . Some of them are old maids, whose personal charms were never very attractive, and who have been sadly slighted by the masculine gender in general; some of them . . . have been badly mated . . . and they are therefore down upon the whole of the opposite sex. . . . Some [are] mannish women, like hens that crow." Others, the paper continues, want to consign man to "his proper sphere—nursing the babies, washing the dishes, mending stockings, and sweeping the house. This is 'the good time coming.' Besides the classes we have enumerated, there is a class of wild enthusiasts and visionaries—very sincere, but very mad—having the same vein as the fanatical Abolitionists." The paper goes on, however, to note that one particular speaker, despite her repellent beliefs, was particularly effective: "In point of ability, the majority of the women are flimsy, flippant, and superficial. Mrs. Rose alone indicates much argumentative power" (quoted in *HWS* 1: 853–54).

As they gathered for this third year, what "these women" wanted was a government that acted out its promises in the Declaration of Independence. The "vulgarities" that the women were "vomiting forth" were simple demands for the equal rights promised by the founding fathers. Few were "old maids"; even fewer were "down upon the whole of the opposite sex." Yet the *Herald* demonized the women—to make them appear like man-hating fanatics—because their message was threatening to the status quo of American society.[26]

26. Bonnie Anderson, in her work on the international woman's movement, has found that the core group of women activists that she has studied "shatter

In spite of his attitude toward the movement, the editor of the *Herald* admitted that Ernestine Rose's arguments, above all others, had "power." Part of what separated Rose's talks from the other women's was her rhetorical force. Unlike many of the speakers, who might talk in generalities about laws hindering woman's rights, Rose knew how to be specific. She attacked specific people and specific arguments, demolishing what she perceived to be inadequate thinking in careful, logical steps with words often tinged with sarcasm. And she knew how to give a talk; she was a natural orator, comfortable enough on the stage to speak extemporaneously, without notes. She looked directly at her audience, compelling them to listen to her. But Rose's talks were also distinct in their content. Although many of the women believed in the "natural" ties of a spiritual affinity, Rose refused to affirm woman's special, spiritual sphere or her special female "nature." It is this refusal to buy into masculine and feminine essences that sets Rose apart from many of her contemporaries and seems to make her a denizen of the 1990s.

---

these stereotypes." In her group of 20 women, which includes Rose and Lucretia Mott among others, 75 percent were married, some, like Rose, quite happily. Anderson adds, "the only demographic way in which these feminists differed from other women was that they had fewer children" (22). The women were also, unlike the *Herald*'s stereotyping, quite attractive.

···❊❊❈[4]❈❊❊···

A Year in the Life of Ernestine Rose

> Human rights include the rights of all, not only man,
> but woman, not only white, but black; wherever there
> is a being called human, his rights are as full and expan-
> sive as his existence, and ought to be without limits or
> distinction of sex, country, or color... and only igno-
> rance, superstition, and tyranny—both the basis and
> influence of the Bible—deprive him of it.
>
> —Ernestine Rose, Hartford, 1853

The year 1853 was a crucial one for Rose: she was the first woman selected to become president of the New York Paine celebration; she was a star performer at what would become an infamous "Bible" convention, and she became known as the "strong-minded woman" who was, according to the Cleveland *Plain Dealer*, the "master-spirit" of the woman's rights conventions. Rose's activities during 1853 give us glimpses as to how Rose's life as a public persona was taking shape.

Rose's growing success, and the growing success of the woman's rights movement, was reflected in the broader culture. The Pennsylvania Medical College, for example, issued a broadside in 1853 urging "ladies" to attend their sixteen-week course to become a physician. The college stressed that the men and women, though they would attend in separate terms, would have "equal privileges."[1] But for every advance, it seemed that other groups responded in reactionary ways to women's increased demands for equal rights. For example, the American Party, popularly known as

---

1. See the advertisement for the Pennsylvania Medical College in the 1853 Broadside Collection at the AAS.

the Know-Nothing party, issued an anti–woman's rights platform in 1853 that was staunchly conservative. Their platform included proposals to prohibit immigrants from voting for 21 years, while proclaiming that the Bible "is the source and fountain of all true and rational liberty and should be made the basis of all popular education." They encouraged penalties against those who "shut out" the Bible from the public schools. The Know-Nothing party also affirmed that states rights were more important than freeing America's slaves: "freedom is national, slavery sectional," their Broadside proclaimed.[2]

Freethought Platforms, 1853

In January 1853 Rose was selected president of the New York Paine celebration, a first-ever accomplishment for a woman in any Paine society. On a Monday evening, January 31, over 700 people celebrated the 116th anniversary of the birthday of Thomas Paine in the City Assembly Rooms, at 450 Broadway. The celebrants joined together to dance and then feast while Ernestine Rose spoke to them. Rose acknowledged the honor, saying "I have never been so conscious of a marked progress towards the rights of man as to-night, for not until to-night has woman ever been sufficiently recognized as the equal with man, to be honored with the presiding office on a festive occasion" (*BI* Feb. 16, 1853). Rose noted that it had been only a few years since women had been admitted to any part of the celebration except the dance but added that it was her New York Paine Society that first "changed the barbarous custom of exclusiveness to a more rational and consistent practice of combining the physical, intellectual, and social branches of an entertainment for the equal enjoyment of both sexes." She ended her speech praising liberals as "the salt of the earth, that keeps the world from entire corruption—the little leaven that enables society to rise higher and higher in the scale of human progress" (*BI* Feb. 16, 1853).

2. See the "Platform of the American Party of Massachusetts of 1853" in the 1853 Broadside Collection at the AAS. The Know-Nothing party would go on to win control of the Massachusetts legislature in the mid-1850s, owing, at least in part, to the collapse of the Whig party and the Democratic disagreement over the Kansas-Nebraska Act in 1854.

Rose was also selected president of another freethought function a few months later, the anniversary celebration of Robert
Owen's May 14 birthday, held at 600 Broadway. The evening, like
the Paine celebrations, consisted of dancing (to the music of a
harp, violin, and a few other instruments), supper, toasts, and
speeches. In her presidential address to an audience that included
Gilbert Vale and Lucy Stone, Rose described Owen's life, adding
that on the fifth of May, 1834, Owen formed a society, the Association of All Classes of All Nations, "to which I had the pleasure
to belong." Rose astutely pointed out that Owen's belief in the
power of the environment to shape a personality was the root of
moral reform in the United States and elsewhere—that the influences
of education and position operate upon human beings throughout
their lives and form their characters. The old, erroneous idea—that
human nature is depraved—is, she says "daily giving way." When
Lucy Stone rose to speak, she first offered a toast to woman's "co-
equality with man," then commented that she was glad to see the
group had practically illustrated the truth of her sentiment by
electing Ernestine Rose as their president (*BI* June 1, 1853).

Rose also was invited to participate in the Robert Owen birthday celebration in Philadelphia by a group of "Progressive Friends."
Well paid for her efforts, Rose writes from New York City on June
21 that she was pleased the "seed of an enlightened liberality has
been thoroughly sown" but was somewhat disappointed that the
group was not ready, yet, to adopt a platform that would encompass "a grand union on the broad basis of Human Rights, with a
platform wide enough for Humanity to stand upon, where no
creed . . . should be adopted and no 'test' enforced—where every
one should have a right to advocate his or her own views . . . where
progress should be the motto, and the law of mutual charity and
kindness the only law to govern all the proceedings."[3]

3. The "Progressive Friends" consisted of a group even more liberal than
the Hicksite Quakers; they had formed a faction of their own, which, Rose
explained, advocated human rights without distinction of sex, country, or color;
yet, as Rose found by speaking to them, their rhetoric outmatched their practices
and she was disappointed. See the July 6, 1853, *BI*.

In early June Rose traveled to Hartford, Connecticut, for a convention, at which, ostensibly, Rose and other freethinkers such as Joseph Barker, a former Methodist minister who was the president of the convention, along with reformers such as William Lloyd Garrison would address the question: was the Bible an inspiration of God? During the two-day meeting, the aim was to discuss the origin, influence, and authority of the Scriptures.

The freethinkers' plans to question the authority of the Bible were immediately challenged by several local ministers who were not pleased with what they perceived as the freethinkers' attempts to demonstrate the "falsity, inconsistency, and corruption of the Bible" (*BI* June 29, 1853). Both times Rose spoke to the 1,600 people who filled the hall her talk was interrupted by lights being turned off and many people shouting and hissing at her. In 1853 few women lectured publicly; even fewer questioned the tenets of Christianity. That the Bible was being interrogated was bad enough to many of the members of the audience; that it was being interrogated in public by a woman—a professed atheist, who was also of foreign birth and Jewish ancestry—only made the inquiry even more scandalous. The New York *Tribune* reported that although the "mob" would listen to other speakers such as William Lloyd Garrison, when Rose spoke the noise increased to deafening proportions; trying both pleasantry and sarcasm, Rose attempted to speak but was repeatedly drowned out (June 14, 1853). As one member of the audience wrote to the *Boston Investigator*, "such was the confusion and uproar that it was impossible for the reporter to hear or understand many of [Rose's] arguments . . . for the yells, laughter, hisses and applause were so liberally bestowed upon." When Joseph Barker appealed to the sense of self-respect that Christians were supposed to entertain, it was to no avail. As the member of the audience wrote, "their zeal for religion entirely destroyed their good manners (if they ever had any!) and so instead of acting like gentlemen they conducted themselves like rowdies, blackguards, and fools. It was a most disgraceful exhibition, and I hope that no 'Infidel' will ever be found base enough to imitate it. Free speech must be preserved" (July 20, 1853).

Undaunted, Rose characterized her opponents as simpletons whose main rhetoric consisted of "oft repeated exclamations—'I go for the Bible!' 'I defend the Bible!' without any shadow of the ghost of any argument as to the why and wherefore" (*BI* June 29, 1853). Despite the constant interruptions, or, perhaps, because of them, Rose's two speeches were among her most forceful, full of sarcastic rage.[4] In her first speech, Rose quickly dismisses the Bible's authority because of what she considered its inconsistencies and absurdities. The Bible's account of creation, says Rose, is contrary to accepted scientific fact. Similarly, the creation story makes the biblical God appear rather "stupid"—creating man and then, as an afterthought, creating woman. Rose argues: "This might be sublime if it were not ridiculous. And yet, do you know, my sisters, that most of the subjugation of woman, the tyranny and insult heaped upon her, sprung directly or indirectly from that absurd and false assumption. It is an insult to the suposed [sic] creator to say he created one-half of the race for the mere purpose of subjecting it to the other" (8). The Bible also inculcates war, slavery, incest, murder, and blind selfishness. That many people believe the Bible to be the word of God, Rose insists, has resulted in man persecuting others and woman having yet another millstone tied to her neck to keep her down. The Bible is not the word of God but more simply "the work of different minds, existing in different ages, possessing different degrees of knowledge and principle; and in accordance with their state of progress, their knowledge, and feelings, so did they write—they could do no better" (9–10). But, as it is, because the writers were, indeed, men of their time, the Bible is a "concoction of incongruities, absurdities, and falsehoods almost impossible to conceive" (10).

4. Rose's two speeches were reprinted by J. P. Mendum in Boston in 1888 and are found in the Rare Books Room of the Boston Public Library as "Two Addresses by Ernestine L. Rose at the Bible Convention, Hartford, Connecticut, June, 1854." All page numbers refer to this copy. Note that the stenographer has included audience comments in parenthesis; thus, a quote of Rose's speech might well include a parenthetical comment such as "applause" or "hisses and boos" that was obviously not part of Rose's delivered speech. I include these parenthetical indicators of audience response.

In the middle of this speech Rose argues that the proclamations of "he that believeth shall be saved" and "he that believeth not shall be damned" have caused considerable mischief to man, as they ignore the nature and formation of belief. To Rose, belief does not derive from divine inspiration or inner light, but from experience: one believes according to what one had learned, consciously or not, from one's environment. She illustrates her idea of the importance of cultural construction with an example:

> a child may [easily] be made to believe a falsehood and die in support of it, and therefore there can be no merit in a belief. We find in the various sects in Christendom, among the Jews, Mohammedans, Hindoos, in fact, throughout the entire world, that children are made to believe in the creed in which they are brought up. [For example,] the children of the sect called Thugs are made to believe in their creed, their Bible—for they, too, have a Bible, and priests to interpret it, and Bibles are always written so obscure as to require priestly interpreters (Applause.)—[that] their means of salvation is to strangle every one they come in contact with who does not believe as they do; and the more Infidels and heretics they strangle the surer their reward in heaven, and the most pious and conscientious among them try to bring the most human sacrifices; and as humanity is not quite dead even among them, so they have quite a refined way to dispatch their victims; they have a silken cord made into a lasso, and when they come in contact with an unbeliever, they throw it adroitly over his head, and by a quick pull strangle him without the shedding of blood, and almost without a struggle. (Applause)

Rose ends her speech with her own incorporation of the familiar "subjugated necks" imagery that she and many of the other women have used before. But in Rose's version, she urges women to "trample the Bible, the church, and the priests under your feet" because "the Bible," not man has "enslaved you, the churches have been built upon your subjugated necks" (18).

Rose was constantly interrupted during her first speech, but she adroitly dispatched her antagonists. Referring to some loafer in the gallery, with his boots hanging over the railing, Rose quipped:

"I do not know but exhibiting the boots over the railing may be a part of the defence of the Bible, but whether it is so or not, we live in an enlightened age, in the free United States of America where every one may do as he pleases, so long as he does not interfere with the rights of others, even to exhibit his boots or discourse in favor of the Bible" (14–15). Rose's ability to give a clever comeback or to weave a critique of an impolite man's actions into the fabric of her speech illustrates both her quickness of mind and one of the reasons she infuriated her detractors.

The following day, Rose was back on the stage to even more hisses and catcalls. In this second speech, Rose extemporaneously employs one of her favorite strategies, refuting, one by one, the arguments of the Rev. Turner who had spoken before her. To Turner's comment that women are "well protected" by Christian men, Rose answers that women are anything but well protected by the Bible. Citing Blackstone, who must have "taken his ideas of right from the Bible" (28), Rose points out that the English common law treats the husband and wife as one and that "one" is the husband, unless "the wife violates a law of the land, then they become two again, for instead of hanging the husband, they hang the wife" (27).

Using irony to full advantage, Rose tells her audience that she is not ridiculing the Bible, for it is "utterly impossible to ridicule a thing so sublimely ridiculous as the whole account of the flood in the Bible." Rose argues, as had Thomas Paine before her, that the Bible places God in an impossible position: He "created man, pronounced him good, found him bad, repented for having created him, resolved to destroy, not only him, but the whole animal and vegetable creation, then repented again of having done it, and resolved never to do it again. Would any of you like to be placed in so ridiculous a position? (Cries of no, and laughter). Yet this God, this same book tells us, possesses all wisdom, all knowledge, and all goodness. It is almost an insult to common sense to talk about believing in such stuff and nonsense" (32–33).

But Perhaps Rose's angriest tirade comes when she refutes Turner's assumption that Christianity has "freed" woman. Rose replies that freedom coming from the Bible is a "fallacy," because the priests "have done enough to keep us down . . . my very appearing here to raise my voice in behalf of freedom and humanity is contrary to the Bible; but the desire nature has implanted in me for knowledge and freedom is more powerful than the injunctions of a superstitious book" (38–39). Rose then claims equal rights for women, not as a charity but as "our birthright," because humanity did not come into existence

> with chains and shackles, but free as the breath of heaven (applause) to develop human nature as it ought to be—free to think, feel, and act. . . . Human rights include the rights of all, not only man, but woman, not only white, but black; wherever there is a being called human, his rights are as full and expansive as his existence, and ought to be without limits or distinction of sex, country, or color . . . and only ignorance, superstition, and tyranny—both the basis and influence of the Bible—deprive him of it. (39)

Rose ends her speech by saying that as long as man is deluded into the belief of a Christian heaven "we [will] be prevented from forming a real heaven here" (45).

Papers all over the United States wrote of the "Anti-Bible" convention as being a "piebald assemblage of Atheists and Abolitionists and misguided fanatics" (Hartford *Courant* June 7, 1853), overlooking the fact that it was the freethinkers and reformers who organized the convention in order to interrogate the authority of the Scriptures. The person who received the most hostile criticism was, of course, Rose. The Boston *Bee* reported that Garrison, the prince of blasphemers, was at the Bible convention, but also there, and "worse and more melancholy than all, was Mrs. Ernestine Rose of New York, her heart saturated with the fiery liquid of infidelity, and her tongue uttering sentiments too shockingly wicked to repeat" (quoted in the *Liberator* June 17, 1853). A local reporter for the Hartford *Courant* agreed with such sentiments:

> The most revolting scene was when a specimen of "the fair sex" pronounced her tirades against the Deity and the Scriptures—

said to be the most blasphemous stuff uttered in the Convention. Nothing but Christianity has rescued woman from the degradation to which the tyranny of brute force had subjected her, in all savage nations—nothing but Christianity has bestowed upon her all that ennobles and purifies her character and softens and dignifies her condition—Shame then to the woman, who will so far unsex herself as to be engaged amid an assembly of male Infidels and scoffers in attacking that institution which has rescued her from bondage. (June 7, 1853)

Antislavery and Women's Rights Conventions

On August 4, 1853, Rose again joined William Lloyd Garrison on the stage, this time at the nineteenth anniversary of British West Indian Emancipation in Flushing, Long Island.[5] Sponsored by the New York Anti-Slavery Society, the day drew five to six hundred people to celebrate the August 1, 1834, freeing of 30,000 British slaves in Antigua.

Rose's speech that day, following Garrison's opening talk, was ostensibly an antislavery talk, even though here, as throughout the 1850s, Rose turned abolitionist stages into woman's rights platforms. Her speech was a model of a short, effective crowd-pleaser. Rose admits at the outset that she is not a member of any abolition society. Instead, she tells the crowd: "I go for emancipation of all kinds—white and black, man and woman." The crux of Rose's talk is that Americans, despite their republican Declaration of Independence, have not lived up to their promises: "Ah, were only that great, noble truth of the Declaration of Independence carried out, as it ought to be, there would be no need of our meeting here to-day." Great Britain, she adds, even without a "Declaration" has managed to show a noble example to the

5. For information on the occasion, see Schappes, "Address." Schappes explains that the merchant class in New York that had once opposed the extension of slavery had, in 1850, been intimidated by southern threats of secession into supporting the Fugitive Slave Act. The newly reinvigorated New York Anti-Slavery Society organized the West India Emancipation Day as its first major activity. See also Suhl 139; the Aug. 19, 1853, *Liberator*, reprinted Rose's August 4 speech, from which all quotes in the text come.

world in emancipating all her chattel slaves. Rose urges sympathizers of the antislavery movement to refuse to purchase slave products, an idea she had gleaned from women in the antislavery movement, who had adopted the tactic from women in Great Britain the 1830s.

One of the most striking moments in Rose's speech comes when she talks about how slavery feels. "What is it like to be a slave?" she asks her audience, some of whom knew directly what it felt like. "Slavery is," she responds, "not to belong to yourself—to be robbed of yourself. There is nothing I abhor as that single thing—to be robbed of one's self."

Rose ends her speech by bringing women's rights directly into her talk, concluding that the slaves of the South are not the only people in bondage: "All women are excluded from the enjoyment of that liberty which your Declaration of Independence asserts to be the inalienable right of all. The same right to life, liberty, and the pursuit of happiness, that pertains to man, pertains to woman also. For what is life without liberty . . . Emancipation from every kind of bondage is my principle. I go for the recognition of human rights, without distinction of sect, party, sex, or color."

In early September, New York City was the site of antislavery meetings, a temperance convention, and a woman's rights convention. Both the antislavery meetings and the woman's rights convention were disrupted by "rowdies," who were "bent on a disturbance" (William Lloyd Garrison to Helen Eliza Garrison, Sept. 5, 1853, GP). Garrison, in New York for the antislavery meetings, labeled the men who disturbed both meetings as "southerners," but the woman's rights meeting was disrupted more than the antislavery meetings and by residents of New York.[6] The very successes of both movements—the current production, for

---

6. See Garrison's Sept. 5, 1853, letter to his wife (GP). Rose would remember this convention as one of the most threatening and violent she ever attended. See the May 7, 1856, *Boston Investigator*.

example of "Uncle Tom's Cabin" in New York and Boston, or Antoinette Brown's recent moving sermon to over 4,000 people— antagonized people who felt threatened by such portentous changes.

Ernestine Rose was the first vice president for the woman's rights convention, the third of the reform conventions taking place in New York City in September. The women's convention was held in the Broadway Tabernacle, a grand structure, built for Charles G. Finney in 1836, that could hold up to 3,000 people.[7] This regional woman's rights meeting was held only one month before the national meeting in Cleveland, possibly as a compromise to placate Rose, who had urged in Syracuse bringing a woman's rights convention to New York because New Yorkers were most in need of such a meeting.

Beginning before and then running concurrently with the woman's rights convention was the "Whole World's Temperance Convention," a gathering fraught with tension about the role women would play.[8] A planning meeting in May foreshadowed trouble when a conservative minister objected to having Susan B. Anthony admitted as a member of the Business Committee. Supporting Anthony's right to be on the committee, the Reverend Thomas Wentworth Higginson requested that his name be stricken from the business committee, believing that in a World's Convention women should be represented, "otherwise it would be only a Semi-World's Convention"(4). Yet the meeting itself in September was full of compromises, with even Higginson and Abby Kelley Foster agreeing that the temperance meeting "would have no Woman's Rights questions brought into the convention" (71). Antoinette Brown, perhaps remembering why women in 1850 decided that they needed their own forum to talk about their rights, told convention goers: "I am reminded that in this Temperance gathering teetotalism is to be discussed in its length and

7. For information on the history of the Broadway Tabernacle Church, see Ward.

8. For information about the Whole World's Temperance Convention see *The Proceedings of the Whole World's Temperance Convention*. All quotes from this convention in the text come from these *Proceedings*.

breadth—nothing else and nothing more; not a word about Woman and her rights. This may be well, but there's a good time coming, friends; wait a little longer" (16).[9]

The most immediate "good time coming"—the woman's rights convention nearby at the Broadway Tabernacle—was anything but. Most of the sessions of the meetings were interrupted by the "mob," a group of anti–woman's rights and antiabolitionist men. Rose, chairing an evening session, found herself calling on police to bring order, though the police were slow to respond. The *Boston Investigator* commented that it was "brave business" for New Yorkers "to mob a meeting of women" and to deny them free discussion (Sept. 14, 1853).[10]

Other papers also reported the disturbances, though from an unsympathetic position: according to the New York *Express*, "Bedlam broke loose—Uproarious scenes at the Tabernacle—The Bloomer Women, Abolitionists—Police on the ground; arrests." The paper continued, reporting that Rose shouted: "I invoke the intervention of the Police. Is the Chief of Police present? Where

9. Many of the speakers at the woman's rights conventions used the imagery from the song, "There's a Good Time Coming," popularized by the Hutchinson Family and sung at antislavery rallies in the late 1840s and woman's rights conventions in the 1850s. Rose began using the phrase at the Paine Birthday Celebrations in 1847, a year after it was arranged from a poem by Charles Mackay and put to music both by Stephen Foster and by the Hutchinson Family. The utopian lyrics appealed to Rose and then to the pacifist Garrison: "There's a good time coming boys,/ a good time coming. . . . / We may not live to see the day,/ but earth shall glisten in the ray,/ of the good time coming. . . . / War in all men's eyes shall be/ a monster of iniquity/ in the good time coming./ Nations shall not quarrel then,/ to prove which is the stronger,/ nor slaughter men for glory's sake,/ Wait a little longer." See the words and music in the Broadsides Collection at the AAS.

10. The *Una*, a recently established woman's rights paper published monthly in Providence, Rhode Island, by Paulina Wright Davis as "Editor and Proprietor," reported on the "riotous misconduct": "On Tuesday September 6th, the Women's Rights Convention assembled at the Tabernacle. When the call was made for the police it was already too late, they had the excuse of not hearing, though made by Mrs. Rose, whose voice, clear as a clarion, would have been heard, if any one's could, amid the din and uproar" (Sept. 1853). The convention was also reported in the New York *Tribune*.

are the police? Will they come up here?" (quoted in the *Libera-tor*, Sept. 16, 1853). The New York *Herald* added its familiar disparagement of the women's attractiveness as a way of dimin-ishing the movement's importance: "It is needless for us to say that these women are entirely devoid of personal attractions. They are generally thin maiden ladies or women who perhaps have been disappointed in their endeavors to appropriate the breeches and the rights of their unlucky lords" (quoted in the *Liberator*, Sept. 16, 1853).

The very fact of the woman's rights meeting, despite its inter-ruptions, helped some of the women like Susan B. Anthony—even though she did not attend the meeting—begin to understand that it was in woman's rights, not in temperance, where reform for women should be centered. Looking back at the World's Temper-ance meeting, Stanton and Anthony write that it was because of this meeting that "liberal men and women now withdrew from all temperance organizations." That left the movement, they add, "in the hands of the time-serving priests and politicians, who, being in the majority, effectually blocked the progress of the reform for the time—destroying, as they did, the enthusiasm of the women" (*HWS* 1:512). Although in retrospect their history is a bit too pat, nonetheless women like Anthony and Stanton did increasingly devote their time to woman's rights instead of temperance after the splinter in the World's Temperance meeting of 1853 demon-strated clearly that their rights were secondary or unimportant or even a threat to the many religious men who dominated the tem-perance movement.

The constantly interrupted woman's rights meeting that was excoriated by the tabloids and that contrasted so dramatically to the World's Temperance convention was chaired by Lucretia Mott, with Rose as first vice president.[11] As was the custom at woman's rights conventions, the ticket price for admission—in this case twenty-five cents for the entire convention or twelve and a half

11. For information on this convention see the *PWRC, New York City, 1853*. See also *HWS* 1: 546–76 and the September 28, 1853, *BI* for a list of the Resolutions. Page numbers refer to these *Proceedings*.

cents to each of the six individual sessions—was kept as low as possible so that "the poorest sewing-girl in New York" would be able to afford hearing the speakers (19). The convention at the Broadway Tabernacle brought together United States women with women such as Mathilda Franziska Anneke, a recent immigrant from Germany, who had been active in the German revolution and had fled with her family to Milwaukee. With Rose translating her German, Anneke accused the mob of not being republicans. On her side of the Atlantic, Anneke said, where there was no freedom of speech, she could understand such disruption, but "here, too, there are tyrants who violate individual right to express our opinions on any subject. And do you call yourselves republicans? no; there is no republic without freedom of speech!" (88)[12]

The speakers covered a wide range of subjects, sometimes supporting one of the ten convention resolutions. Lucretia Mott, with her polite, Quaker manner, admitted that the women had obstacles to encounter, but she hoped the women would not be dismayed by these obstacles on their way to "co-equality" with men. Antoinette Brown, about to be ordained as a minister the following month, spoke of her morning's experience at the World's Temperance meeting at Metropolitan Hall where, even though she was a temperance delegate, she was not listened to by the "gentlemen" who preferred that only men occupy the speaking platform. William Lloyd Garrison talked about being called derisively a "Woman's Rights Man," though he argued that he knew no such distinction, as he claimed to be a "Human Rights Man, and wherever there is a human being, I see God-given rights

12. See the *Una*, September 1853, which responds to the women's terrible treatment and to Rose's lack of interest in talking about herself: "Mrs. Rose, while by Mrs. Anneke's side to translate her words, might have contrasted, with good effect, the difference of Mrs. A's reception before this audience, and her's [sic] in London, when her own English was but imperfectly spoken. But Mrs. R. rarely alludes to herself, or her own works." See Anderson for more information about Anneke, who first lectured in the United States in 1850, after reading about the efforts of Frances Wright, Lucretia Mott, and Ernestine Rose. In 1852 she began to publish a *German Woman's Newspaper* (primarily in German) and was invited as a delegate to the New York woman's rights convention.

inherent in that being, whatever may be the sex or complexion" (22). Paulina Wright Davis spoke briefly about how her new journal, the *Una*, would help chronicle the progress of the woman's rights movement. She then gave a long speech on how to redress the wrongs done unto women, including the loss of woman's fortunes and functions. She argued that women should reclaim the right to make a profit at the power loom or in the healing arts or in the press—all arts now lost to women.

In her first formal speech of the convention, Rose spoke with wit and force, playing off Davis's notions of wrongs done unto women, which Rose believed to be "sanctified by superstition" (45). Constantly interrupted, Rose argued that one of the causes for woman's lack of rights was the biased legal system. Interested from the late 1830s in women's lack of legal rights, Rose turns in her speech to the legal system's slavish following of Blackstone. Rose says, in her lively style using some of the same imagery she had used at the Bible Convention in Hartford earlier in the year, "According to Blackstone, the husband and wife are one; and that one is the husband, except, indeed, when SHE violates some law, the penalty of which is imprisonment, or death; then the one-ness falls asunder. Blackstone's husband is not the one to suffer; the elements separate,—'Richard is himself again,' and the wife, the woman, has to bare her neck to the stroke of the man-made law" (47).

Rose acknowledges that the Married Woman's Property Rights Act, for which she worked so hard, was still imperfect. Even with the Act recently enacted in New York, married women were still bound by irrational and immoral laws. For example, Rose points out with much humor that when a husband dies without a will,

the law very magnanimously allows the widow to remain in [his house] forty days without paying rent. In addition, the law allows the widow during her life, an interest in one-third the real estate. . . . As to the personal property, after all debts and liabilities are discharged, the widow receives one-half of it; and, in addition, the law allows her, her own wearing apparel, her own ornaments, proper to her station, one bed, with appurtenances for the same, a stove, the Bible, family pictures, and all the schoolbooks; also all spinning wheels and weaving looms, one table, six chairs, ten cups and saucers, one tea-pot, one sugar dish, and six spoons. (Much laughter). But the law does not inform us whether they are to be tea or table spoons; nor does the law make any provision for kettles, sauce-pans, and all such necessary things. But, the presumptions seems to be that the spoons meant are, tea-spoons; for, as ladies are generally considered very delicate, the law presumed that a widow might live on tea only. (49)

Rose continues sarcastically highlighting how outdated current laws were: "but spinning wheels and weaving looms are very necessary articles for ladies now a days." She adds, "these great lawmakers, who seem to have lived somewhere about the time of the flood, did not dream of spinning and weaving by steam power" (49). Many in the audience may have attended the current Crystal Palace exhibit that featured a woman showing visitors how a modern sewing machine could, in effect, perform the work of forty women using an old-fashioned spinning wheel.

This convention's *Proceedings* also gives us a brief insight into Rose's relationships with other woman's rights leaders. More confident on the stage than most of the other women, Rose was also not as demure. Her experience speaking to many different kinds of audiences and her Jewish heritage that emphasized argument combined to give her a force of personality that few of the other women possessed. Often in the early years of the conventions, the women speakers had to be asked to "speak up." Rose never had to be asked to raise her voice. When heckled, she fought back, making fun of her hecklers. Rose could think quickly on her feet and she never hesitated to respond, often sarcastically, to interruptions. That Rose was outspoken, quick, and often sarcastic made her a frequent target for attack. Where Lucretia Mott's Quaker simplicity and gentle demeanor and Antoinette Brown's obvious piety rendered them more palatable to the public, Rose's outspokenness often doomed her to opprobrium.

Even within the movement Rose could not keep from disagreeing with others on the platform with her. Just as she could not keep from challenging Stephen Foster in the late 1840s when she shared an abolitionist stage with him, so Rose felt equally compelled to correct her fellow woman's rights activists on the woman's rights platform. Toward the end of this conference Frances Gage spoke about the Law of Wills, which allowed a husband to control his wife's property even after he is dead. To bring home her point, Gage imagined a will made out by a husband as if it had been made by his wife, by interchanging the names, thus the wife left to her son some horses and carriages, her daughter some property, and her husband 40 acres of wild land in Illinois and their bed, as long as he remained a widower. After some laughter, Rose continued the satire by adding that according to the Revised Statutes of the State of New York—statutes that Rose made sure she read herself and understood—"a married women has not a right to make a will." She gave a specific example: "the law says, that wills may be made by all persons, *except* idiots, persons of unsound mind, married women, and infants. Mark well, all but idiots, lunatics, married women, and infants. Male infants ought to consider it quite an insult to be placed in the same category with married women" (64). Lucy Stone then broke in: "Just one word. I think Mrs. Rose is a little mistaken; I wish to correct her by saying that of some states in . . ." Rose quickly interrupted saying: "I did not say this was the universal law; I said it was the law in the State of New York." Lucy Stone, ever the diplomat, responded: "I was not paying close attention, and must have been mistaken" (64).

It is interesting to see the forcefulness of Rose's speech, her rudeness even, directed at a colleague working on the same cause. Stone backs off verbally, using qualifiers "I think," "a little mistaken," and then apologizes for being wrong. Rose is forever and absolutely "right" and never hedges her subject with qualifications. Perhaps this absolutism, which seems both ennobling and maddeningly inflexible, is one of the reasons Rose remained an outsider within a group of women where many close friendships flourished.[13]

13. Rose, though not close to any of the women in the movement except Anthony, was clearly respected by the other women, including Lucy Stone. Lucy Stone writes to Antoinette Brown in November 1853, telling her that she had recently spent the night with "Mrs. Rose" and that Rose was "doing us good service by answering newspaper ridicule." See Stone's Nov. 24, 1853, letter in Lasser and Merrill 125.

Less than a month later "all the big guns," including Ernestine Rose and her colleagues from the Tabernacle, were at the October 5–7 national woman's rights convention at Cleveland.[14] Rose was, according to the Cleveland *Plain Dealer*, the "master-spirit of the convention," a speaker known for her "true eloquence" (*BI* Nov. 2, 1853). During the convention, Rose joined Lucretia Mott, Wendell Phillips, Lucy Stone, and Thomas Wentworth Higginson as appointees to a committee to prepare two essays—one on the educational opportunities of women, the other on women's business opportunities. In order to gather the facts they needed, the committee put out a circular asking for a variety of statistics on which schools at all levels admitted women and which types of work women were documented as doing (see the Jan. 15, 1854 Circular, AAS).

Rose attended the convention as the chair of the business committee, her favorite committee, with Abby Kelley Foster, James Mott, Lucy Stone, and William Lloyd Garrison, among others working with her. She spent some of her conference time directing people to the task at hand, often saying "we have a great deal of work to be done" (19) to encourage speakers to leave extraneous subjects such as temperance and to return to the resolutions of the convention.

Despite Rose's warnings, the convention threatened to veer off track on its first morning when H. M. Addison invited the participants to attend the State Temperance Convention that afternoon to listen to Amelia Bloomer give an "admirable" lecture on temperance. Rose, eager to deal with her Business Committee's resolutions, responded by saying "Solomon says—and it is a good saying, not because it came from him, but because it is *true*— 'there is a time and a season for everything.' A time and season has been appointed for a Woman's Rights Convention" (22)—and she moved the resolutions be read. Lucretia Mott, eager to let

14. The "big gun" headline came from the Oct. 12, 1853, *Liberator*. For information on the Cleveland convention, see the *PWRC, Cleveland, 1853*. See the Oct. 12, 1853 *Liberator* for a list of resolutions passed. See also *HWS* 1: 124–52. Page numbers in the text refer to the Cleveland *Proceedings*.

temperance reformers make amends to woman's rights activists, particularly after the recent debacle at the New York City "World" Temperance meeting, chastised Rose: "I think we should receive with a little more courtesy the invitation which has been extended to us" and suggested that the woman's rights convention reassemble later in the afternoon in order to "hear one of our sisters" (20). But backed by Lucy Stone and Stephen Foster, who argued that the woman's rights conference was more important than the temperance one, Rose's position carried.

On the first afternoon of the conference, Rose read the resolutions that her business committee had prepared. The resolutions began by articulating fundamental theoretical constructs: that human rights were "natural" rights; that women were human therefore had human rights; and that because women were human and men no more than human, they had equal rights. Rose spoke often to these resolutions, with her usual force and determination, illustrating that the Cleveland *Plain Dealer* was correct in calling her the "master-spirit" of the convention.

In her first speech to the convention, Rose defends the business committee's resolutions. Employing an argument that Frances Wright had often used in the 1830s, Rose claims all her rights, "without a single distinction," because "humanity acknowledges no sex, mind acknowledges no sex, virtue and vice, life and death, pleasure and pain, acknowledge no sex" (35). Rose alludes to "woman's sphere," that place to which women were relegated without rights. Rose asks: "Is woman alike human with man, or is she not?" (36). If yes, then she deserves the same rights as man; if not like man, then how can man legislate for a being "entirely different from himself?" Neither view, thus, interferes with granting women their rights. Rose agrees, tongue in cheek, with opponents who claim that woman ought to "remain in her sphere," but, she wonders, who can know what a person's sphere is until her own energies and powers are properly developed. And, as Rose pointed out throughout the convention, no college existed where both sexes enjoyed equal advantages, despite the fact that Oberlin, whose president was attending the conference, admitted women.

Rose turns to Owenite theory to buttress her claims, arguing that the subjection of women has caused the subjection of men: "for no one can be truly free, as long as he enslaves another" (39). Rose also broaches the subject of divorce, a subject she had discussed on 1840s platforms, but had avoided on a woman's rights stage for fear of alienating her audience more than necessary.[15] Rose incorporates the same argument that Owenites had often put forward from the early 1820s on when she says "when two beings are so unfortunate as to find, that instead of promoting each other's happiness, they have made that most unfortunate mistake of promoting only each other's misery, that the law of life which should bind the husband and wife, is wanting,—when in fine, it shall be deemed necessary that they shall separate, then, I say, the wife should have a perfect right, to at least one-half the property, and her own children. I ask no more, and will be content with no less" (40). Though Owenite speakers argued throughout the 1820s and 1830s that a marriage should, indeed, promote the happiness of both spouses, and that a marriage that did not promote happiness should end in divorce, Rose, using the cadences of Henry David Thoreau's "Resistance to Civil Government," takes the Owenite argument further, accepting their premises and then arguing that, given divorce, women should be able to retain one half the joint property and custody of her children. Thus, in this speech Rose turns from Owenite proposals to make divorce more easily attainable to more specific demands for women's equal rights. Rose ends her speech by evoking the same imagery as in her August speech at the British West Indian Emancipation meeting when she discussed what it felt like to be enslaved: "from cradle to grave" woman "is another's." Rose concludes: "For here lies

15. Rose expresses her reluctance to bring up the topic of divorce in her second speech to the convention; see *PWRC, Cleveland, 1853* 76. Lucy Stone, Susan B. Anthony, and Elizabeth Cady Stanton had corresponded during the spring of 1853 as to whether to introduce the subject of divorce at the Cleveland convention. Stone, who always considered the politics of the issue, hoped to keep the divorce issue separate from woman's rights issues; Stanton urged including divorce reform into the platform. See Stone to Anthony, Mar. 22, 1853, BFC. Whether Rose knew of this correspondence, we do not know.

the corner stone of all the injustices done woman, the wrong idea from which all other wrongs proceed. She is not acknowledged as mistress of herself. From her cradle to her grave she is another's. We do indeed need and demand the other rights of which I have spoke, but let us first obtain OURSELVES" (41).

This argument illustrates Rose's continued move away from her early 1840s Owenite thought—her belief that socialism would take care of the ills of society. Ten years later Rose maintained that before anything else woman must "obtain herself." No other rights are possible, no other justices can be done, until woman is no longer enslaved by being relegated to a separate sphere, conditioned to influence not act, and left uneducated and content with her enslavement.

In her second speech to the convention, Rose again brought up marriage and divorce, calling it a subject of "vital importance," one that "we must face" despite the fact that dealing with marriage and divorce will engender "more prejudice and in consequence more difficulties than any subject hitherto brought before the public; and hence it is all the more necessary to meet, and discuss it" (76). From the subject of marriage Rose segues into a discussion of prostitution and how women and men can both "sin"—unusual language for Rose—and asks how what is wrong in one sex, can be right in the other. Rose gives an abstract example of "woman" being "drawn into sin often through appeals to her tenderest and best feelings," then being cast out of society while her seducer is not punished in any way. Rose brings the house down when she cries "I ask, if she, the victim, is cast out of the pale of humanity, shall the despoiler go free? (cries of No! No!). *And yet he goes free!*" (77).

The woman's rights movement can help these wronged women, Rose adds, because woman's degradation is caused by ignorance and dependence—evils the woman's movement was trying to eradicate. As Rose says,

> My friends, I speak warmly, because I feel deeply for the degradation of woman. Look into your societies; look into your newspapers; look everywhere, anywhere; look at the helpless beings who crowd our cities! Have these poor creatures been born with

the mark of Cain upon their foreheads? Nature cries no! To what then is it owing, but to the wrongs of which they have been victims! but to the fact, that woman is made to believe that she is created to be only the tool or plaything of man; to be dependent upon him, instead of dependent upon her own rectitude, dependent upon her own faculties. In that doctrine of dependence upon man lies ONE of the great causes at least, of the evils which lead so many young and lovely creatures to a premature and dishonored grave. (78)

This oblique discourse is as close as Rose gets to any direct reference to sexual relationships, and she introduces the subject through the neutral-sounding vehicle of "marriage and divorce," a subject that was a trope for thinking about sexual encounters outside of marriage. In the 1850s, the first public investigations into prostitution were taking place. According to Christine Stansell, more than 5,000 women were "on the town" in 1856, convincing New Yorkers that they were living "amidst an epidemic of female vice" (173). Rose, and other speakers on the woman's rights platform who also hinted about women's "sins," may well have been responding to what Stansell has called the "tensions over gender relations and female sexuality" (171) that colored the way both reformers and the general public responded to women in the 1850s.

In her conclusion to this speech, Rose refers to her own background when, just as Lucretia Mott had in an earlier speech, she urges young women to enter professions that have been closed to them, particularly the law. Rose prods young women "just springing to life, who have a natural capacity for analyzing, reasoning, comparing and judging; whose intellectual faculties are well developed for that profession" to become lawyers because "woman never will be rightly judged, until she is judged by her own sex. Her cause will never be rightly pleaded unless pleaded by herself" (103). Her reasons for this urging come from a story "in a foreign land" where "a girl of tender years" had parents who had "deemed it right to sell her" to an unacceptable man for marriage. Rose relates her story without revealing that she is talking about herself: "This was the case of a girl hardly seventeen, who had to go to law to rescue her property staked on such a contract, which she could not and would not fulfil; and against all the laws of the land, she gained that cause. How came she to gain it? Because she pleaded it, and called down the Justice of Heaven against the Laws." Rose concludes that if her health were up to it, "I should study law" (104).

On the second day of the conference, the two "strongest-minded" women—a phrase that was coined by a local paper when referring to Rose and her colleagues—once again tangled publicly. Rose, talking about the legal system, argued in her typical Owenite fashion that laws construct morality:

> Bad laws always will make bad men. We have had bad laws, hence man has been bad . . . [man] is under the laws of the past . . . framed in ignorance, ignorance of the ultimate end or aim of the human being, man or woman, and ignorance of the relations of the sexes. They were sanctioned by superstition and enforced by power. . . . I blame no one. My creed is, that man is precisely as good as all the laws, institutions and influences, operating upon his peculiar organization, allow him to be. (75)

Rose added: "we [man and woman] are both at fault; and yet we are none in fault. . . . The laws of a country create sentiments. Who make the laws? Does woman? Our law-makers give her ideas of morality" (81).

Unable to remain silent, Abby Kelley Foster insisted that the morality of a people create the laws, not the other way around: "I want to say here that I believe that the laws result from public sentiment. The law is but the writing out of public sentiment" (82).[16] Foster was joined in her criticism of Rose's stance by William

16. See a reference to this disagreement between Rose and Kelley Foster in Elizabeth Clark's 1989 Dissertation, "The Politics of God and the Woman's Vote," 28. Clark adds that Rose grew to intellectual maturity in the freethinking circles of enlightened Europe and was probably the only atheist among the early feminist leaders. Clark's explanation is oversimplified and factually misleading as Rose developed her intellectual maturity in England and in the United States; Frances Wright was an atheist as well. Others reformers like Lucy Stone and Abby Kelley Foster had no use for organized religions, though they were not professed atheists.

Lloyd Garrison, who argued that he, unlike Rose, did believe in "sin" and therefore "in a sinner." Though Garrison praised Rose's speaking ability—"our eloquent friend . . . stood here on this platform and pleaded with such marked ability, as she always does plead . . . [and] told us her creed" (87)—he disagreed with her conclusion that one could not hold any person to be criminal. Rose's notions of the importance of the cultural context—including the laws of the land—for shaping thought set her apart, both from the general public and from her colleagues.

Besides the conflict between Abby Kelley Foster and Ernestine Rose—a tension between two strong, public women who saw the world from different perspectives—another conflict also became apparent at this convention. The issue was whether someone with perfectly good intentions could harm the movement if that person was perceived as too "ultra," or too extreme. Joseph Barker, the former Methodist minister who presided at the Hartford Bible Convention, was one of the woman's rights supporters scheduled to speak at the Cleveland convention. But before he could take the stage, a number of people requested that he step down, or if he spoke, to be very careful about what he said about religion. Barker admitted that one of the most damaging charges made against the woman's rights movement was that it was an infidel movement (133). But Barker went ahead and spoke, to much hissing, asserting that he, too, wanted to support the cause, not injure it. In his speech, Barker argued that if people grant the premises of the priesthood, "their objections [to woman's rights] *are* valid" (136). If, he said, one grants that the Bible is the word of God, that it is true without error, then the woman's rights movement *is* wrong. But in his opinion, the Bible is wrong; he cannot think of a more "revolting" doctrine than that taught by Paul that woman was not "made for herself as man was for himself" (146).

Barker's dilemma illustrates Rose's tenuous relationship to a movement that was, to a great extent, populated with Christians. Other reformers might criticize the "priestcraft," or, in Antoinette Brown's words, the "current Christianity" (163), but most were, nonetheless, believers in the Scriptures and in the main tenets of

Christianity. Rose, as a nonbeliever, shocked her audience merely by the fact of her disbelief. This shock, coupled probably with unstated anti-Semitic prejudices against her Jewish background, led some proponents of woman's rights to argue that a nonbeliever like Rose could not help their cause because the woman's rights movement could only too easily be characterized in the popular press as an "infidel" movement and thus dismissed by the "Christian" nation.

Newspapers across the country responded to the Cleveland convention in just those terms. Some, including the New York *Tribune*, reported on Barker's "blasphemy" and the conference's "attack" on churches and preachers; other reported on the "great confusion" at the conference.[17] The *Commercial Advertiser* opined that Ernestine Rose was "a lady whose pretty name at least is terribly misbestowed upon a strong-minded woman." The editors continued, commenting more on her appearance than on what she said:

> [she] still retains remnants of good looks, set off by very womanly ringlets, and heightened by some coquetry of manner and dress. She wore a black satin dress, open in front, with a lace stomacher, lace undersleeves, and black lace mittens. A broach, a watch and chain, and some sparkling rings, evinced that Ernestine has not arrived at that stage of the strong-minded woman's career when the little vanities of this world are despised. (quoted in the *Liberator* Oct. 21, 1853)

The Cleveland *Plain Dealer* was more sympathetic to Rose and her cause—it called her by her last name and title, rather than by the belittling "Ernestine"—saying that as a Polish lady, she has been known as an earnest advocate of human liberty. Her delivery is both "effective" and "very slightly affected by a foreign accent."

17. See the Oct. 8, 1853, *Tribune* for a brief report on how the conference ended in great confusion following the adjournment, with the president, Frances Gage, fleeing from the hall; but see also the Oct. 10, 1853, *Tribune*, which prints three separate essays on the convention, including one from its own reporter; in these stories we hear of the "perfect harmony" of the convention as well as commentary on Joseph Barker's blasphemy.

The impression she made was "favorable" both to the speaker and to the cause (as quoted in the Nov. 2, 1853, *BI*).

The Cleveland convention and its "strong-minded" women created quite a stir beyond simple reports on the proceedings of the meeting. Pasted in Susan B. Anthony's "Scrapbook" (Vol 1) is a published letter (with no date and no name) from, reportedly, a woman named "Lucretia," who addressed her letter to Ernestine Rose. The letter writer (we cannot know whether it was actually by a woman named Lucretia or by an enterprising newspaper editor) acknowledges Rose's oratorical power as well as fears that power:

> Madam—As you are allowed among the "weak-minded men," to be the bright particular star of the present convocation of "strong-minded women," now gathered together for the purpose of effecting a reform and change in our household, will you allow one of your own sex, a wife and a mother, to propound a question or two for your answer . . . I am informed . . . that sometime since you presided at the Tom Paine supper in the city of New York, and made a speech on the occasion. I am also informed that your views of the marriage relation harmonise [sic] with those of Fanny Wright. It is also said that you disbelieve the Bible as being the Word of God. . . . will our female generals then . . . bring out the golden standard on which is to be inscribed, Paine, Voltaire, Fanny Wright, Infidelity and Amalgamation? Is this the blessed fruit which this glorious "reform" is to produce? Do not, my dear madam consider these questions presumptuous, although coming from a weak-minded woman. I have seen you, madam, with a man's heart beneath the bodice of our sex, rise and address a crowded promiscuous assembly, composed of both sexes and all colors; and amid the double entendres which your words have often elicited from the select portions of your audience, witnessed your unblanching front without a muscle moved, and surely my dear madam, with a courage like this which few of our sex can hope to attain, you cannot be afraid to define your true position in the present efforts to "Reform."[18]

18. One of the reasons I raise the question of authenticity of this letter is the blurb that accompanies it in Anthony's Scrapbook. Above the letter, from the same printed but unnamed source, is a paragraph from a male editor who writes

The anxiety some of the woman's rights activists expressed when they tried to limit what Joseph Barker would say on stage in Cleveland seems strangely appropriate when considering this letter from someone who both praises Rose for her great speaking abilities and strength of character but who is concomitantly apprehensive of Rose's infidelity.

Rose went from the Cleveland national convention to a state convention in Rochester, New York, at the end of November 1853.[19] The Rochester state conference, intended to bring the subject of women's legal and civil disabilities before the legislature of New York, was chaired by Rev. Samuel J. May, who lived in nearby Syracuse. Rose served as the first vice president, presiding over the convention on its second day and giving the closing address. Rose's main speech, a "beautifully touching speech," according to Paulina Wright Davis (*Una* Jan. 1854), was a

---

that he is not responding to a letter Rose sent his newspaper because "a certain lady of our acquaintance, to whom we were married, according to the present wicked dispensation, about a quarter of a century ago, and with whom we have lived very comfortably ever since, insists that she has acquired certain rights, among which is that of an absolute veto power over all correspondence on our part, with the rest of the feminine world. We shall not, therefore, attempt to answer Mrs. Rose, for fear of trenching upon the rights of our 'folks at home.' We have no idea of allowing our gallantry to disturb our 'domestic relations.' These letters from ladies are ticklish things, and are very apt to get confiding and simple minded men, into very unpleasant kettles of fish." So instead of responding to Rose, the editor perhaps fabricated a letter from a "woman" to respond to Rose, thus appeasing his wife.

19. For information about the Rochester conference, see *Reports from the State Convention at Rochester, November 30–December 1, 1853* and *HWS* 1: 577–91. See also the *Una* for January and April 1854, which both discuss the Woman's Rights Convention in Rochester and summarizes Rose's speech. According to Nancy Hewitt (*Women's Activism*), "Rochester ultraists hosted a county woman's rights convention in January 1853 and a statewide meeting the following November. Here Amy Post . . . shared the stage with nationally known feminists Ernestine Rose [who is listed first], Antoinette Brown, Elizabeth Cady Stanton, and Susan B. Anthony" (169). See also the December 8, 1853, *Monroe Democrat* for commentary on the convention—it mentions that Rose spoke in a foreign accent, but added that her comments were "pertinent, forcible, and felicitous."

synthesized version of her Cleveland talk: she discussed the "painful necessity" of having to claim rights because "life is valueless without liberty." In her typical style, Rose added pointed barbs directed at the men in her audience: "at marriage," Rose noted, "the husband says, in effect, 'all thine is mine, all mine is my own' " (*Tribune* Dec. 3, 1853). She added with great optimism that "twenty years from today," she hoped that "it will be a wonder that there was every a necessity for such a convention" (*Una* Jan. 1854).

At this convention Rose met Sallie Holley, a regular lecturer on the antislavery platform. From Holley, we get one of the few intimate glimpses into Rose as a playful person to supplement the public persona represented by conference proceedings and newspaper articles. Holley, like so many of the antislavery speakers, was religious, but her faith did not keep her from appreciating Ernestine Rose. As Holley writes, "Ernestine L. Rose is a charming women and at times playful." She vividly describes their talk about the possibility of an afterlife: "After I had a talk with her about a future life, which she does not believe in, I said, 'But I think I shall meet you in a life beyond and above this.' " Rose responds: "then you will say to me, 'I told you so,' and I shall reply 'How very stupid I was!' "(Chadwick 127). Holley, unoffended, reports that Rose quipped: "Superstition is religion out of fashion, and religion is superstition in fashion." She adds that Rose "has suffered much" and is a "candid, reverent, loving spirit" (127).[20]

Much taken with her new acquaintance, Holley writes in her diary from the Rochester Convention that the strong-minded Rose was "far before any woman speaker I ever heard. She is splendidly clear and logical." Holley paraphrases in her diary what she has heard from Rose:

> I suppose you all grant that woman is a human being. If she has a right to life she has a right to earn a support for that life. If

20. John White Chadwick, the editor of the Holley autobiography, notes that this is an interesting tribute to Rose, "one of the worst-abused women of her time," 127.

a human being, she has a right to have her powers and faculties, as a human being, developed. If developed, she has a right to exercise them. The women who act in this great reform have been stigmatized as "strong-minded women," and for herself she accepted the stigma. If a gentleman flatters a lady you may be sure he does not consider her one of the "strong-minded women."

Holley concludes by exclaiming, "But, oh! I cannot give any idea of the power and beauty of her speech. I can only stammer about it a little." (128)

Holley's response to Rose is genuine. Unlike the probably invented letter-writer, "Lucretia," who had never talked directly to Rose, Sally Holley did engage Rose, and her diary reflects the passion that Rose could engender through her extraordinary oratorical powers, her humor, and her sheer force of character. It was a force that would move other women as well. Susan B. Anthony, who had devoted herself primarily to temperance until the Syracuse convention in September 1852, came under Rose's spell in late 1853 as the two women teamed up to begin a lecture tour.

New York City as it looked when Ernestine Rose arrived in the mid-1830s.
Courtesy of the American Antiquarian Society.

Susan B. Anthony.
Courtesy of the Library of Congress.

Lucretia Mott.
Courtesy of the Library of Congress.

William Lloyd Garrison.
Courtesy of the Library of Congress.

Lucy Stone.
Courtesy of the Library of Congress.

Antoinette Brown.
Courtesy of the Library of Congress.

Horace Seaver.
From Samuel P. Putnam, Four Hundred Years of Free Thought (1894).

Josiah P. Mendum.
From Samuel P. Putnam, Four Hundred Years of Free Thought (1894).

Elizabeth Cady Stanton.
Courtesy of the Library of Congress.

THE EIGHTH

National Woman's-Rights Convention

WILL BE HELD IN

NEW YORK CITY,

AT MOZART HALL, 668 BROADWAY,

On Thursday and Friday, May 13 and 14, 1858,

Commencing at 10 o'clock Thursday A. M.

**Lucy Stone, Ernestine L. Rose, Wendell Phillips,
Wm. Lloyd Garrison, C. Lenox Remond,
Mary F. Davis, Caroline H. Dahl,
Rev. T. W. Higginson, Aaron
M. Powell, Frances D.
Gage, and others,**

will address the several sessions of the Convention.

We regret that so many of the noble men and women, who, in spirit, are fully with us, should have so long withheld from us, kind words of recognition and encouragement.

We earnestly ask all those who believe our claims are just, who hope and look for a higher type of womanhood in the coming generations, to assert, now, their faith in the everlasting principles of justice, that have no respect for age, sex, color, or condition. Is it too much to ask that the BRADYS, the CURTIS', the CHAPINS, the BEECHERS, and the STOWES shall cheer us by their presence at our coming Convention, or by letter make known their position in regard to this movement ? Feeling assured that our cause is just, that our positions are tenable, our platform is FREE for all fair discussion.

Communications for the Convention may be addressed to SUSAN B. ANTHONY, ANTI-SLAVERY OFFICE, 138 NASSAU STREET, NEW YORK.

Notice of the Eighth National Woman's-Rights Convention (1858).
Courtesy of the American Antiquarian Society.

A mid-1850s portrait of Ernestine Rose.
Courtesy of the Library of Congress.

Editorial cartoon satirizing "new" roles for women.
Courtesy of the American Antiquarian Society.

Susan B. Anthony in her study in 1900
with portrait of Rose on upper right wall.
Courtesy of the Library of Congress.

·····×[5]×ל····

Ernestine Rose and Susan B. Anthony

No one knows how I have suffered from not being
understood.

—Ernestine Rose, Baltimore, 1854

Ernestine Rose continued her hectic pace into the new year. In
early January, Rose spoke at the Broadway Tabernacle, as part of
a weekly series of lectures on woman's rights. In the lecture the
week before, Emma Coe had referred to Rose as one of the best
examples to offer those who opposed woman's elevation to their
rightful social and legal position (*Tribune* Jan. 3, 1854). Speaking
again from one of her primary sources of her authority, the Declaration of Independence, Rose talked on the importance to women
of obtaining a good education and of changing the laws that kept
women subordinate. Telling the audience that women who were
left penniless widows were "generously" allowed by the law to
struggle and wear themselves out trying to raise their children
with no help, Rose added that should these women inherit any
property, then the state stepped in, leaving them the income from
only one-third of the property, the family Bible, a bed, a half
dozen tea cups "and so on" (*Tribune* Jan. 10, 1854). Rose ended
her talk by distributing petitions for signatures to be sent to the
state legislature.

After her Tabernacle lecture, Rose traveled to Beverly, Massachusetts, to speak of her own hatred of slavery as the country
turned to debates on the Kansas-Nebraska Act, legislation that
antislavery and Free-Soil reformers feared would introduce slavery
into Nebraska and thus spread slavery to other western states and
territories. In Massachusetts, speaking on the "Causes of our Social

Evils: Slavery, Intemperance, and War," Rose criticized slavery of all kinds and an economic system that accommodated, even encouraged, slavery. Decrying self-interest that promoted selfishness, Rose disparaged the professions of medicine, law, divinity, and trade, calling them all "injurious to the true interests of society" (*BI* Jan. 25, 1854). Physicians, claimed Rose, promoted disease; lawyers created confusion in the laws; clergymen made men slaves of creeds, and merchants taxed the whole world to make themselves rich—all injurious to the true welfare of society. A reporter from the Beverly *Citizen* reported that although her lecture abounded in fallacies, she spoke "our language with considerable elegance and propriety; her manner as an orator is graceful and attractive, and she exhibits great powers of ratiocination" (*BI* Jan. 25, 1854). More than any other Beverly lecturer "this season," Rose, according to the reporter, "set people to thinking."[1]

After giving a speech at the New York Paine Celebration urging underdogs England and France to unite to aid Turkey against the encroachment of Russia (in what would become the Crimean War), Rose traveled to Albany, New York, where she met up again with Susan B. Anthony. Anthony, after leaving the Cleveland

---

1. Rose, then, opens 1854 with what might seem like a paradox to modern readers. How can Rose rail against individualism in the economic system, we may wonder, while promoting with great passion extensive individual rights. For Rose, though, these two ideas, which we in the twentieth century often conflate, were diametrically opposed, and her promotion of one and censure of the other were not inconsistent within her frame of reference. Rose championed social and political rights—basic Enlightenment virtues that formed the philosophical basis of the Declaration of Independence. But she was not swayed by another Enlightenment thinker, Adam Smith. Rose, unlike Smith, believed one's individual gain did not equal a gain for all of society; rather, one's gain often meant that others would suffer more hardships, just as slavery provided an economic boon to owners but hopelessness to slaves. Thus to her, individual social and political rights were quite separate from laissez-faire economics, and what we might call economic "individualism," Rose would call pure "selfishness." In mid-nineteenth-century America an individual's right to make as much money as he could (capitalism) became an ideology that few, save Rose, would question, whereas an individual's right to vote or own property or even own one's self (political liberty) was limited in every state in the union.

woman's rights convention, had spent her time working for temperance in southern New York State. From Albany, Rose and Anthony began their first lecture tour together and initiated a friendship that would last the rest of their lives.

Rose's and Anthony's friendship was quite different from Anthony's well-known friendship with Elizabeth Cady Stanton, who was also present in Albany that February—the first and perhaps only time all three women were together at a woman's rights convention in the 1850s. Anthony, who had met Rose at the Syracuse national meeting in 1852, first met Stanton in 1851. Stanton recalls meeting Anthony: "There she stood, with her good, earnest face and genial smile, dressed in gray delaine, hat and all the same color, relieved with pale blue ribbons, the perfection of neatness and sobriety. I liked her thoroughly" (Stanton, *Eighty Years* 163). The principal detail Stanton noticed first about Anthony was her appearance—Anthony looked very much the middle class, former teacher that she was. With her strong chin, straight posture, and slightly crossed right eye, Anthony reflected her Quaker roots in her bearing and practical clothing. She was, indeed "earnest," "genial," "neat," and "sober"—the attributes that Stanton first noticed about her. Stanton and Anthony from practically the first sight of each other were close friends, recognizing from their appearance that they were like-minded soul mates. Neither Stanton nor Anthony would ever be confused with the gloved, exotic forty-four-year-old Ernestine Rose, with her long, free-flowing, ringleted hair.

Rose's relationship with Stanton cannot be called a friendship. Stanton knew Rose and knew of her work for more than a decade without noticing her. The two women worked together gathering petitions for the Married Woman's Property Bill throughout the 1840s, according to Stanton in her autobiography (*Eighty Years* 150). Yet, Rose never figures in Stanton's life, as is clear from Rose's absence in Stanton's letters. Stanton's anti-immigrant speeches in the mid-1860s suggest that, like so many others in the mid-nineteenth century, she probably harbored unconscious biases against foreigners and, perhaps, Jews that may have rendered Rose's words and deeds invisible to her. Yet, Stanton certainly learned from Rose, who was five years her senior. Many of Stanton's most effective speeches and best ideas of the 1850s were predicted by Rose's talks in the 1840s. Rose and Stanton, the two most brilliant and forceful orators of the movement, were, perhaps, in some ways too much alike in personality and too different in background and manner to ever become close friends.

Ernestine Rose's friendship with Susan B. Anthony was much warmer. In many ways, the women related to each other much as Anthony would relate to Stanton in ensuing decades. Like Stanton, Rose was older, a natural orator, politically savvy, and unafraid to confront men in public spaces. Anthony preferred, at least in the mid-1850s, to work behind the scenes—keeping detailed budgets and receipts, arranging for meeting halls. She did not like public speaking and, by most accounts, was not good at it. She was for Rose, first, and later for Stanton, the amanuensis, the assistant, the arranger.[2]

Even though Rose probably felt closer to Anthony than to any other woman in the movement, the women's friendship was never as intense as Anthony's relationship with Stanton. Historian Carroll Smith-Rosenberg has shown us that extremely close, intimate relationships between women were commonplace in mid-nineteenth-century America, even relationships that seemed to border on the erotic. Women wrote each other passionate letters that sound like love letters to us today; they often walked hand-in-hand; they spent months in each other's company. Though Anthony and Stanton fit this picture well, Rose does not. Rose, as best we can tell from the letters and diaries of her friends and acquaintances, did not write passionate, personal letters. Although she spent months at a time away from home, when she was away she was traveling and lecturing, staying with friends of the freethought movement to save money. And, Rose was also well married to a

2. Griffith in her biography of Stanton writes that "Stanton provided the ideas, rhetoric, and strategy," while Anthony circulated petitions and rented the halls: "Anthony prodded and Stanton produced." Though Anthony certainly had ideas herself and became an efficient strategist, this description could also describe Anthony and Rose's relationship in 1854.

man who, according to Anthony, worshipped her. As Anthony's Diary will reveal, Rose was probably a difficult friend, expecting much from her confidants and brooking no compromises.

Albany

The 1854 Albany convention and appearances before the New York Legislature brought the three women together in one of their rare opportunities to share the same stage during the 1850s. They all played out the roles they were most comfortable with at the time: Rose spoke many times, Stanton spoke once, and Anthony, "though a stranger amongst us," according to the *Albany Transcript*, performed much of the arduous labor including making the contracts for the rooms, advertising in the papers, obtaining the speakers, and publishing the addresses (as quoted in *HWS* 1:606). Stanton, a resident of nearby Seneca Falls, was president; Rose was vice president.[3]

Once again Rose was "the queen of the company," according to the *Albany Transcript* (quoted in *HWS* 1: 606), even though Stanton gave her first speech to the New York Legislature.[4] Stanton's speech, which Stanton herself remembers as "a great event in my life" (*Eighty Years* 187), is an interesting compilation of Rose's issues combined with an argument comparing women to African Americans that Rose never employed. In her address, Stanton appeals to "common sense" over custom to give rights to "the disenfranchised one-half people of this State" (*HWS* 1: 596). Emphasizing the importance of reason, just as Rose did, Stanton turns to woman's position under the law and cites the problems with English common law; she continues by talking about

3. For information on the Albany Convention see *HWS* 1: 591–612; see also the March 1854, *Una;* the Mar. 1 and Mar. 8, 1854, *Boston Investigator;* the February 24, 1854, *Liberator;* and Susan B. Anthony's Scrapbook, Vol. 1.

4. To hear Stanton tell it, both in *Eighty Years and More* and in *HWS* 1: 595–612, her speech was the praised one; Rose's contributions, in Albany, and elsewhere, are almost an afterthought in *HWS*. The local newspapers, though, help to correct this misrepresentation.

woman's position if she is fortunate enough to have inherited
property and if she is unfortunate enough to be a widow whose
husband has died intestate. All these points were details that
Rose had used throughout the 1850s in her speeches at woman's
rights conventions. But Stanton added a different kind of argument to sway the white, propertied men who were listening to her
as well. Stanton opens her speech by saying that women "are
moral, virtuous, and intelligent, and in all respects quite equal to
the proud white man himself and yet by your laws we are classed
with idiots, lunatics, and negroes. . . . yet . . . the negro can be raised
to the dignity of a voter if he possess himself of $250" (*HWS* 1:
595–96). She continues later in her talk along the same lines:
"True, the unmarried woman has a right to the property she
inherits and the money she earns, but she is taxed without representation. And here again you place the negro, so unjustly degraded by you, in a superior position to your own wives and
mothers; for colored males, if possessed of a certain amount of
property. . . can vote, but if they do not have these qualifications
they are not subject to direct taxation" (*HWS* 1: 597). In comparing woman's position to the Negro's, Stanton leads her listeners to see the inappropriateness of giving African-American men
more rights than their own white "wives and mothers." Such a
comparison would result, by the mid-1860s, in a virulent racist
argument that both Stanton and Anthony would employ, to no
avail, in their attempts to prevent the passage of the Fifteenth
Amendment that granted suffrage only to black men.

Although one might assume that Stanton's speech was received favorably, it was Ernestine Rose's speeches that were the
most applauded during the convention by the New York Legislature. Like Stanton, Rose spoke about the legal disabilities of women
and considered some of the objections made against the movement. According to one local paper, she handled her topic "in an
ingenious and plausible manner. Her remarks were listened to
with the most profound attention, and she was encouraged by
frequent and prolonged applause. Occasionaly [sic] a wife might be
seen glancing at her husband, as much to say 'Are all these thing
so?' and now and then a lip would be curled in contempt of her

doctrines. But as a whole, her speech which was of great length and ability, appeared to be favorably received."[5]

Rose's convention speeches were lauded by neutral and friendly newspapers. The February 24, 1854, *Liberator* contained a letter to Garrison from G. B. Stebbins, who has just come from the Albany convention: "The last evening," he wrote, "Mrs. Ernestine L. Rose made the closing address—a most noble and powerful effort." A correspondent to the *Boston Investigator* adds: "I never saw an audience more absorbed in their attention, more hearty in their applause, more subdued at times in their feelings, more carried onward and upward by the exalted sentiments of a speaker" (Mar. 1, 1854). Even the local Albany *Express* observed:

> This woman who attended the convention held in Association Hall, is a remarkable one. She possesses an intellect that lifts her a 'head and shoulders' above the mass of her sex. She is a native of what was once Poland. . . . We heard her speak for upwards of an hour on Tuesday evening. Though we dissented from much— very much—that she said, yet we did admire her eloquence, her pathos, her elocution. She spoke wonderfully well. Her arguments were strong, and well put, and her wit and sarcasm 'told' unmistakably upon the large audience that listened to her. With her foreign accent, and her style of elocution, not less than by what she said, she constantly reminded us of the eloquent and impassioned Kossuth.[6]

5. This passage comes from an Albany newspaper from early March 1854, pasted in Susan B. Anthony's Scrapbook, Volume 1, which contains no page numbers. The clipping has no name and no exact date, but the newspaper is referred to as the Albany *Transcript* in HWS 1: 606.

6. As quoted in the Mar. 29, 1854, Boston *Investigator*. "Kossuth" refers to Lajos Kossuth, the Hungarian patriot whom Rose spoke of often in the 1850s. Kossuth had helped to bring about the revolution in Hungary in 1848; his visits to the United States and Great Britain in the early 1850s were triumphal processions allowing the United States to celebrate "freedom" and "democracy" because Kossuth had, among other things, helped to eliminate serfdom in Hungary. Rose may have been pleased to be compared to Kossuth, but many of the antislavery reformers were unhappy with Kossuth's 1852 visit to America since he avoided the abolitionists' cause on his lecture tour. Cromwell says that Kossuth refused an invitation to Lucretia Mott's home (165).

As the intention of the Albany convention was to influence political action, Rose made several appearances before the New York Legislature following the convention. On March 3, she and Anthony went before the New York State House Committee to argue that the women's right of petition would be of no avail unless their demands be "candidly considered" by the legislators (*HWS* 1: 607), adding that the woman's demands were not momentary but "are the demands of the age; of the second half of the nineteenth century. The world will endure after us, and future generations may look back to this meeting to acknowledge that a great onward step was taken in the cause of human progress" (*HWS* 1: 607–8).

Rose also spoke, along with William H. Channing, before the Senate Committee "of Bachelors" of the New York Legislature.[7] She related some clever incidents of the war in Hungary, when women "amazed mankind by parting with their jewelry, so that the war might go on." She hoped the republicans of America would, at least, grant to women the same rights that are granted to them in Hungary. Refuting the notion that voting would take women away from "the fireside," Rose argued that voting would take no more time than going to a concert or a ball. The only effect Rose's speech produced, according to the unfriendly *Evening Journal*, was a determination by the Senators to remain bachelors in the event of the success of the movement (Anthony Scrapbook Vol. 1).

The local newspapers were not pleased with Rose's and her colleagues' efforts before the legislature. The Albany *Register* of March 7, for example, criticized Rose and, in doing so, clarified just how effective a speaker she was:

> It is a melancholy reflection, that among our American women who have been educated to better things, there should be found

7. The information comes from a March 1854 clipping from a local newspaper, probably the Albany *Register*, placed in Susan B. Anthony's Scrapbook, Vol. 1.

any who are willing to follow the lead of such foreign propagandists as the ringleted, glove-handed exotic, Ernestine L. Rose. We can understand how such men as the Rev. Mr. May, or the sleek-headed Dr. Channing may be deluded by her to becoming her disciples. They are not the first instances of infatuation that may overtake weak-minded men. . . . But that one educated American woman should become her disciple and follow her infidel and insane teachings, is a marvel. . . . This Mrs. Ernestine L. Rose, with a train of followers, like a great kite with a very long tail, has, for a week, been amusing Senatorial and Assembly Committees, with her woman's rights performances, free of charge. . . . The people outside . . . are beginning to ask one another how long this farce is to continue. How long this most egregious and ridiculous humbug is to be permitted to obstruct the progress of business before the Committees and the Houses, and whether Mrs. Ernestine L. Rose and her followers ought not to be satisfied with the notoriety they have already attained. The great body of the people regard Mrs. Rose and her followers as making themselves simply ridiculous. (quoted in *HWS* 1: 608–9)

The editors' churlishness derives, at least in part, from Rose's reputation as a freethinker. As they say, in no other country "would her infidel propagandism and preaching . . . be tolerated. She would be prohibited by the powers of government from her efforts to obliterate from the world the religion of the Cross—to banish the Bible as a text-book of faith and to overturn social institutions that have existed through all political and governmental revolutions from the remotest time" (*HWS* 1: 608).

Rose, incensed with errors of fact in this article about her, wrote to the newspaper correcting the *Register*'s misstatement that she had come to this country "from Poland, whence she was compelled to fly in pursuit of freedom." Rose adds that she indeed did come from Poland, but that she was not "compelled" to leave her birthplace; she left her country quite "deliberately." She chose to make the United States her home, she writes, "because if you carried out the theories you profess, it would indeed be the noblest country on earth" (*HWS* 1: 610).

Washington, D.C.

When the Albany convention and meetings with Senate and House committees concluded in mid-March, Rose and Anthony headed off for a lecture tour to Washington, D. C., and Baltimore, and then a rest with the Motts in Philadelphia. The tour marked Anthony's first trip with the older and far more widely traveled Rose. Perhaps the reason for the trip to Washington came from Rose's suggestion at the end of the Cleveland woman's rights convention that the women's next meeting be held in the nation's capital in order to "exercise a moral influence over Congress" (*Tribune* Oct. 10, 1853). Although the group followed James Mott's advice that the next national meeting be held in Philadelphia, Rose was probably still determined to try to influence Congress.

Washington, D.C., though the nation's capital, was relatively undeveloped in the spring of 1854. Visitors described the Mall as a "cow pasture" and the recently begun Washington monument "a huge stone stump about two hundred feet high."[8] In fact, in 1854 a huge section of the monument, donated by the pope, was stolen. The Capitol was under construction, having its two wings added and its dome enlarged. In many streets, according to a German visitor in 1854, geese, chickens, pigs, and cows seemed to have the right of way (quoted in Reps 112).

Arriving in Washington shortly before the Kansas-Nebraska Act was signed into law on May 30, Rose and Anthony entered a politically charged atmosphere. The Kansas-Nebraska Act, which Rose and others referred to as the Nebraska Question, in effect repealed the 1820 Missouri Compromise, which had prohibited slavery north of latitude 36°30′, by allowing slavery to expand beyond the Compromise's limits. Orchestrated by Stephen A. Douglas, the Act was being hotly debated. Rose and Anthony, along with many antislavery and religious groups,

8. For travel narratives of visitors' description of Washington, D.C., in 1854 see Reps, especially 112–22.

were opposed to the Nebraska question because it allowed the spread of slavery.[9]

As Rose and Anthony traveled to Washington and then on to Baltimore and Philadelphia, Anthony kept a detailed journal of their daily experiences.[10] The pages Anthony wrote while traveling with Rose give us one of our few chances to see Rose up close, from a fellow reformer and friend's perspective. Rose was an intensely private person who did not believe in talking about herself. To her, emphasis on self led to selfishness. She believed in action, not self-revelation. She did not regard her persona as important, for she was only a medium through which reform might be achieved. Her energies went into serving the *public* good: writing letters to the *Boston Investigator*, or speaking at conventions. Thus, the only glimpses we have into Rose's daily activities come when a friend records her impressions.

In the nation's capital and in Alexandria, Virginia, for a week and a half, Rose and Anthony tried in vain to find an appropriate meeting space in which Rose could speak. Consistently denied their requests, the women became more and more frustrated as the week wore on. Slogging through the rain and snow, Anthony asked the Speaker of the House for the use of the Capitol for March 26 for Rose to lecture on the political and legal rights of women. The women were denied the Capitol, supposedly because Rose was not a member of a religious society, but probably because she was a woman, Jewish, and an advocate of woman's rights. Anthony complained that "ours was a country professing religious as well as civil liberty and to not allow any and every faith to be declared in the Capital of the nation, made the profession of religious freedom a perfect mockery" (Diary Mar. 24, 1854). The women continued to appeal to members of Congress to allow

9. The Society of Friends in Pennsylvania, New Jersey, and Delaware, for example, wrote a tract against the introduction of slavery into Nebraska; see "Memorial of the Religious Society of Friends, 1854," Broadside Collection, AAS.

10. Susan B. Anthony's Diary is in the Schlesinger Library at Radcliffe College, I used the microfilm of the Diary, Box 1, Folder 8.

Rose to speak in the Capitol, but to no avail. Frustrated, they traveled to Alexandria to try to persuade a Mr. Millburn to allow them to speak in Liberty Hall in Alexandria, but, according to Anthony, he "assumed great clerical sanctimony and said "NO" (Mar. 25, 1854). A few days later, the women, once again, tried to find a hall where Rose could speak. Rose herself applied to Professor Henry to speak in the Smithsonian Hall, but she was again refused. Anthony wrote that he "very blandly told her that they had to be very careful whom they permitted to speak there— they could not allow any one to speak on any Political question of the day" (Mar. 28, 1854).

Unable to find a large hall in Washington, Rose was relegated to speaking at Carusi's Saloon instead. Her first lecture was to an audience of around 100 on "The Educational and Social Rights of Women." The crowd, small according to Anthony because woman's rights had "never been agitated here," netted only $10 (Mar. 21, 1854). Perhaps the audience in Carusi's Saloon was more used to lectures on "Spiritualism," like those Professor Brittan of New York gave there on March 23 and 25.

Rose spoke at Carusi's again later in the week, on the political and legal rights of women, after giving tickets to her speech to both Representatives and Senators. Few dignitaries attended, causing Anthony to worry about the "thinly attended" lectures. Few people in Washington, fretted Anthony, were interested in any subject of reform; all "seemed afraid of us; if we don't say anything our very presence seems to rouse their suspicions" (Scrapbook, Vol. 1). Told that the numbers who attended were large enough and equal to the number who attended literary or scientific lectures, Anthony nonetheless was not placated because the women's expenses were not even being covered by the admissions fees they were taking in.

At the end of their first week in Washington, still unable to obtain the Capitol or another large hall, Rose spoke at Carusi's a third time to about 500 people on "Women and the Nebraska Bill." Despite the pair's attempts to insert notices about Rose's speeches in the local papers, the crowd of around 500 was not large enough to help them recoup their costs. Anthony lamented the night of Rose's third speech that they were $105 in the hole since leaving Albany, but, ever the optimist, she wrote that she could not "but feel that great good is accomplished notwithstanding this financial loss" (Mar. 28, 1854).

Rose's speech at Carusi's was on the burning issue of the day, the Nebraska Question. Arguing against the bill that she feared would spread slavery, Rose refuted the southern argument that it would be an impossibility, in the present state of society, to bring about the abolition of slavery. But she saved her most pronounced wrath for northerners who, she said, have no excuse for encouraging slavery: "How can northern men promote slavery—what excuse do they have?" Rose queried. Outraged that northerners claimed to live in "free" states and professed principles of freedom for all, Rose questioned how people who lived in the North and who could not even claim the sanction of their laws, could continue to pander to the slave principles of the South.[11]

At least one reporter from the Washington *Globe* was in the audience at Carusi's to hear Rose speak on the Nebraska Bill and that reporter, as did most commentators on Rose's speeches, first noticed her appearance and her Polish accent, though from an unusually sympathetic bent:

> Mrs. Ernestine L. Rose, a lady well known for her eloquence in advocating the cause of woman, delivered a lecture last evening at Carusi's Saloon, upon that somewhat intricate and perplexing subject, the Nebraska question, as deduced from human rights. Mrs. Rose is a lady apparently about forty years of age, sprightly, intelligent looking, and her features strongly marked by a

11. For information on this third speech at Carusi's and Rose's response, see the May 1854 *Una*, which reprinted an essay from what Paulina Wright Davis called the *Congressional Globe* in the *Una* and Rose's response to it. See also the Apr. 19, 1854, *Boston Investigator*, which reprints the same *Globe* article but without Rose's response. The editor of the *Boston Investigator* refers to this daily newspaper as the *Washington Globe* or the *Daily Globe*. See also the pasted copy of the *Liberator* in Anthony's Scrapbook, Vol. 1., where Anthony discussed in an April letter Rose's third lecture on the Nebraska Question, saying that the *Globe* covered her talk but misrepresented her.

thoughtful expression, which at once enlists the attention of her audience. In her manner, during the delivery of her lectures, she is easy, dignified and graceful; and though her sentences are somewhat tinctured by a Polish accent, her correct use of language, and propriety of expression, render every word perfectly intelligible. (*Una* May 1854)

The reporter raved about Rose's speaking abilities. He wrote that the entire lecture was a "credit to the lady" because it was marked "by a display of thought and eloquence rarely to be found in the lectures of this description." This glowing praise for a woman speaking against the Nebraska Bill was unusual for a reporter from the *Globe*, a newspaper that carried primarily the proceedings of Congress and some advertisements, not commentary on lectures. The reporter's admiration, perhaps in spite of himself, lets us see Rose's self-confidence and poise from an unexpected source. Unlike the inhibited Anthony, who fussed about money and knew she was awkward and uncompelling on the speaking platform, Rose comes across as a natural star, someone who had an "easy" manner, along with being "dignified" and "graceful." How difficult it must have been for Rose, who spoke not a word of English until she arrived in London at age nineteen, to learn to speak English so well—to be able to use the language correctly and to have every word "perfectly intelligible."

Perhaps because the reporter was so taken with Rose's appearance and demeanor, he misunderstood her main point, saying that Rose was aware that it was an almost utter impossibility to bring about an abolition of slavery, because it was an institution handed down from generation to generation for a long time. Her sympathies were, said the reporter, with the South.

Rose, not to be deflected by praise of her oratorical style, responded in her typical fashion when reporters got her points wrong. Writing while she was still in Washington, Rose sent a letter of rebuttal to the editor of the *Globe* on March 31:

In the *Globe* of the 29th inst. I perceive, in an article referring to my lecture of Tuesday evening, on the "Nebraska Question as deduced from Human Rights," that the writer mistook, what I repeated as the well known southern argument, for my own. I did not say, "that it was almost an utter impossibility, in the present state of society, to bring about the abolition of slavery." (*Una* May, 1854)

What she did talk about, she added, was asking how northern men could promote slavery without the excuse of laws or institutions, how northerners could pander to the slave principles of the South.

The day after her final speech at Carusi's, Rose and Anthony left Washington for Alexandria where Rose was finally able to speak in Liberty Hall, even without the help of Mr. Millburn. Rose gave two addresses in Liberty Hall on back-to-back nights. Her first talk was on "The Educational and Social Position of Women," and the second on "The Civil and Political Rights of Women."[12] On the first night, Rose talked to a small audience of about 80 people, including 14 women, suggesting that she might have been better off remaining at Carusi's. Rose admitted that her cause was not popular, though she wondered at the prejudice in this country against women's rights in the "progressive nineteenth century." What she found difficult to believe was that women should have to ask for their rights in "this progressive country," a country of comparative liberty and knowledge. Women, Rose proclaimed as she had proclaimed many times before, were not properly educated—not for a profession but to be "a picture in a frame, gilded, perhaps, if rich, to adorn a parlor—if poor to grace the kitchen." She asserted that because women were not educated, society suffered. Men turned to gaming tables and crime because of the want of intellectual companionship, while women were drawn to vice because of their dependent condition and inability to partake in the professions. Urging women to become independent, Rose advocated opening trades and professions to women. Women, Rose added, could measure off six feet or a yard of lace as well as any man, could handle the works of

12. See the Alexandria *Gazette* for Mar. 31 and Apr. 1, 1854, as the source for the quotations within the text.

a watch, could become physicians all just as well, if not better, than men.

This speech illustrates Rose wrestling with a central paradox in her thinking: on one level she believed that the professions were "injurious to the true interests of society"—in fact, she had just lectured on that subject in Beverly, Massachusetts, two months earlier. At the same time, however, Rose wanted to open all the professions and the trades to women, as she advocated in Liberty Hall. Given the realities of the American economic system that equated making money with security, Rose wanted women to be able to support themselves and their children and to be able to choose their work. Given the realities of working life in America in the 1850s, Rose had to accept the paradox that she created: wanting women to be allowed to enter professions that she feared injured "the true interests of society." Rose may well have been aware of William Burns's 1851 book, *Life in New York*, a saccharine account of 40 "charming" occupations open to women, occupations that included dress maker, weaver, straw braider, gold leaf packer, hat trimmer, bazaar tender, button maker, shoe binder, bar maid, fruit vender, wool picker, cook, washerwoman, and chambermaid—all low-paying, anything but "charming" occupations. No job paying enough to support a family was listed in Burns's book.

Living with this paradox also demonstrates clearly Rose's lifelong struggle with her Owenite background, from which she understood the getting and keeping of money as leading only to selfishness and not to the good of the society at large. Rose did believe and continued to believe that search for material gain led to self-centeredness and to an unhealthy obsession that was bad for the individual and bad for the society. Yet her increasing commitment to individual civic and legal rights as a first step in correcting the wrongs of the world forced her to advocate woman's participation in the very professions that she deemed "injurious to the true interests of society." It was for her an unresolvable contradiction.

The second night at Liberty Hall Rose turned to the legal problems for married women. She expressed horror that a man had power over the property and labor of his wife. She defended the reasonableness of allowing women to vote and hold public office because, if women were taxed, they ought to have the right to vote for those who proposed the taxes; otherwise the system was unequal and unjust and in violation of the principle that taxation and representation should be inseparable.

The local reporter who covered her two speeches was, again, taken with Rose, commenting extensively on the way she looked; she was "very good-looking . . . not attired a la Bloomer," but wearing her ever-present white gloves with a neat, plain "sober brown" dress, with no ornaments other than a gold watch chain and a breastpin. Her hair "fell in ringlets about her face." Her age, according to the reporter, was 35 or 40, which was 5 to 10 years younger than her actual 45. Her "graceful" voice had an accent "just foreign enough to be interesting." The sympathetic reporter also noted some of the things Rose did while speaking that made her such an unusually good lecturer: she walked "up and down the stand" when lecturing, stopping at intervals to look "earnestly" at some specific spot in the room, "as though, specially addressing those seated there." The reporter also noted that Rose seemed "indisposed to suffer any deviation," so that when a few men indulged in a quiet laugh, "she rebuked them quite indignantly." Such praise was not enough for Anthony, who wrote that the newspapers all had "spoken well of Mrs. Rose's talents" but none said a word about "the cause" (Diary Mar. 24, 1854).

While in Washington, Rose and Anthony also called on a number of friends and were called on in return. Buoyed by the falsely optimistic news that the Nebraska Bill was referred by the House to a committee, they called several times on Gerrit and Ann Smith, who also opposed the bill. Gerrit Smith, the cousin of Elizabeth Cady Stanton and father of one of the first women to wear and promote the Bloomer costume, had just been elected to Congress in late 1852. The Smiths, who lived in upstate New York, were wealthy supporters of the antislavery movement and of women's rights. In fact, Gerrit Smith himself gave a lecture on April 6,

1854, against the Nebraska Bill only a week after Rose's speech on the same subject.[13] At the Smith's residence, the women dined pleasantly and listened to Ann Smith sing and play piano, even as they discussed more serious matters such as the rights of individuals to their own beliefs. The last time they visited the Smiths, before leaving for Baltimore, Mrs. Smith slipped them a $20 bank note to help make up for the monetary loss of their visit. Gerrit Smith added that he was "very glad that Mrs. Rose had come to Washington."[14]

During their stay Rose and Anthony also called on supporters such as Anna Royal, an eighty-five-year-old writer and former editor, whom Rose called a "living curiosity." Royal gave her visitors two books each that she had written years before. The women also called on Mr. Thompson, a young lawyer from South Carolina, to borrow law books; Thompson expressed surprise that the women would want to look at legal books.[15] The two women also called on a Mrs. Melvin, who told them that slavery was a "humane institution," a notion that Anthony and Rose found "chilling." The women were, in turn, called on themselves by Myrtilla Miner, the founder of the "Colored Girls' School," who was interested in women's rights. Miner's school, begun in 1851, was supported by contributions from such reformers and writers as Wendell Phillips, Arthur Tappan, and Harriet Beecher Stowe. Horace Mann's sister also taught there.[16]

13. See Frothingham 220–23, where he explains that although Smith was opposed to the Nebraska Bill he nevertheless refused to become a party to the Republican plan to prevent voting on the bill. Smith believed that restricting a vote was an infringement on democratic principles.

14. For the three visits to the Smiths recorded in Anthony's Diary, see Mar. 21, Mar. 23, and Mar. 26. Anthony, busy with trying to secure places for Rose to speak, jotted only brief notes about these visits and others during their stay in Washington.

15. See Anthony's Diary for Mar. 27, 1854. Perhaps this was the "young lawyer" whom Rose met on her visit to South Carolina in 1847. See Rose's speech printed in the Aug. 19, 1853, *Liberator*, where she mentions meeting a young lawyer in South Carolina.

16. Today, the school that Miner began is part of the University of the District of Columbia. See Flexner, 99–101.

The women also took time out to listen to lectures and do a bit of sight-seeing despite a late spring snow. On Monday, March 27, they walked two miles while visiting tourist attractions, including the printing office, the patent office, and the original Declaration of Independence. The next day they went to the Capitol to listen to Mr. Millburn, who had refused to help them find a hall for Rose to speak in, speak on "Home Life." He exhibited, according to Anthony, "gross ignorance" by saying that "[i]t is in the home that most men and all women's chief duties lie" (Diary Mar. 26, 1854).

Baltimore

In early April, the women moved on to Baltimore where Rose began a series of four lectures taking place April 3, 5, 7, and 9.[17] In Baltimore, Rose and Anthony stayed at 49 Hanover Street, in a private boarding house, which Anthony called plain but clean. Their servants were slaves, evoking from Anthony her bias that three northern girls could do the work of a dozen slaves in Baltimore, such being the "baneful" effect of slavery upon efficient labor (Diary Mar. 30, 1854).

In their first few days in Baltimore, the two women engaged the lecture halls where Rose would speak, the Temple on North Gay Street and the Maryland Institute. They put notices in the Baltimore newspapers, received callers, and found time for Baltimore sight-seeing, visiting Monument Square (now Mt. Vernon Square) to see Washington's Monument and also going to Greenmount Cemetery. They took tea with Edward Needles, an old acquaintance of Rose's from the "come outer school" (Diary Apr. 4, 1854). Although many moderate reformers remained aligned with Christianity, radicals in the 1840s from the

17. For information on the Baltimore lectures, see Anthony's Diary; also see a letter to the *BI*, printed Apr. 26, 1854, from a Baltimore resident, J. W., who heard Rose speak and reported on one of her lectures. Local Baltimore papers noted Rose's style and advertised her lectures, but none printed copies of her lectures.

"come outer school" viewed churches and governments as corrupt and urged women and men of conscience to "come out"
from the corrupt institutions. Rose, of course, had no Christian
church to "come out" from, but others, like Garrison and the
Fosters, did.

Rose spoke to somewhat limited crowds while Anthony fussed
over the number of tickets that they had sold—only 54 on April
4—while giving away some 60 free tickets. In her first two speeches,
Rose talked specifically on woman's rights: the first was Rose's
familiar speech on woman's lack of education and the second
outlined woman's lack of legal and political rights and lack of job
opportunities. Rose's third speech, on April 7, was on "The Roots
of Evil" that underlie the social system. In it, she talked about the
root of evil: man's greed to acquire that allowed him to enslave
others, to keep others from having a "self." Using the same examples she had used in her Beverly talk earlier in the year, Rose
criticized professional men who were out for individual gain to the
detriment of societal benefit. The only professional Rose did not
lambaste was the schoolmaster, a figure that typically was the subject
of ridicule. It was a "delicate" subject according to one Baltimore
resident who heard Rose speak (*BI* Apr. 26, 1854).

Besides giving her own lectures, Rose joined Anthony at the
Temperance Society of Baltimore, where Anthony addressed the
group. Invited to speak after Anthony finished, Rose did so, urging her listeners to "substitute healthful amusements in the place
of alcoholic stimulus" (Diary Apr. 6, 1854).

The morning before Rose's last talk, the two women attended
the Baltimore Universalist Church to hear a sermon on "Woman's
Sphere," where they heard that women should have rights, but
should not have equal rights with men (Diary Apr. 9, 1854). The
morning sermon influenced Rose's evening talk in the Committee
Room of the Maryland Institute where she spoke of "Charity," or
rather the lack of it as expressed in sectarianism and in the "monstrous cruelties" perpetrated by dogmatic clergymen (*BI* Apr. 26,
1854). Rose also criticized the charitable work done by the women
of the local "Samaritan Society," who distributed garments and
food to the poor of Baltimore, arguing that it would be more

charitable to offer the poor a means of earning their own living rather than just offering them charity without a means of enabling them to become good citizens and useful members of society. With her communitarian-inspired background, Rose judged what appeared to most people as charity to be anything but. One theoretical rationale underlying Owenite communitarianism required giving people the means to support themselves and then letting them do so rather than "giving" the poor-but-able their bread and board. Even Rose's hero, Frances Wright, had attempted to create a utopian community to allow slaves to work long enough to purchase their freedom.

Rose ended her speech by reviewing the morning's sermon and then imploring her listeners to ensure that there could never be a time again when "priestly bloodhounds" would have permission to "hunt down and mercilessly butcher those who may simply differ from them in opinion" (*BI* Apr. 26, 1854).[18] Anthony called her speech a "glorious" one and was immensely pleased that even though the hall seated about 500 people, hundreds were unable to get in because all the seats were taken (Diary Apr. 9, 1854).

Local papers noted Rose's powerful oratorical style. The Baltimore *Republican and Argus* praised "Mrs. Rose's Lecture" as "forcible, nay truly eloquent," though they did not necessarily agree with everything she said. "We had," they wrote, "what we do not hesitate to speak of as the highest gratification, in listening to the lecture delivered at the Temple last evening, by Mrs. Ernestine L. Rose, of New York on the 'Education and Social Position of Woman,' as we are sure the audience generally must have had. Not that they, any more than we, necessarily, coincided fully with the lady in all her positions, but because of her forcible, nay, truly eloquent, style of oratory" (quoted in *BI* Apr. 12, 1854).

---

18. Rose's language in the 1850s as in the 1840s was not meant to signify an anti-Catholic sentiment. To Rose the word "priests" simply meant religious leaders whose words, rather than reason, must be obeyed. Southern Baptist ministers who preached that slavery was a divine institution were some of the best examples of "priests" to Rose.

ल्ल:२००

The nine days that Rose and Anthony spent in Baltimore allowed them time to talk as well. Anthony's Diary reports a number of intense discussions that reveal a great deal about Ernestine Rose's idealism and her inability to compromise or to excuse her friends' and colleagues' flaws. On April 9, Anthony recorded that she and "Mrs. Rose" were talking about the Know-Nothings—the conservative group that promoted Bibles in all classrooms and limitation to immigrants' rights—when Rose suddenly told Anthony that she had heard Lucy Stone and Wendell Phillips express prejudice against granting to foreigners the rights of citizenship. It was a subject that Rose, who was not yet a citizen, felt strongly about.

Anthony, unable to believe anything bad about woman's rights supporters, expressed disbelief that either of them would have "that narrow, mean prejudice in their souls." Rose countered by saying that Anthony was blinded by them, that she could see nothing wrong with "that clique of Abolitionists." Anthony felt compelled to defend Lucy Stone, arguing that there must have been some sort of probable cause of Lucy's "seeming fault." Saddened by the disagreement, Anthony wrote in her diary that "it seemed to me that she [Rose] could not ascribe pure motives to any of our Reformers, and while to her it seemed, that I was blindly bound to see no fault, however glaring." More confrontational than usual, Anthony persisted: "At length in the anguish of my soul, I said Mrs. Rose there is not ONE in the Reform ranks, whom you think true, not one but whom panders to the popular feeling?" Rose answered, "I can't help it, I take them by the words of their own mouths. I trust all until their own words or acts declare them false to truth and right." Rose continued, in great misery: "No one can tell the hours of anguish I have suffered, as one after another I have seen those whom I had trusted, betray falsity of motive as I have been compelled to place one after another on the list of panderers to public favor."

Ten years younger and far less cynical, Anthony responded: "do you know Mrs. Rose, that I can but feel that you place ME too on that list." Rose replied, implying that Anthony was correct: "I will tell you when I see you untrue." Their talk ended with Rose acknowledging that she was often in despair over friends and colleagues who had seemed just and good changing, chameleon-like, before her eyes and repeating, "no one can tell the hours of anguish I have suffered, as one after another . . . betray falsity of motive."

Anthony's response reflected both her conciliatory nature and also her distance from Rose: "It filled my soul with anguish to see one so noble, so true, even though I felt I could not comprehend her, so bowed down, so overcome with deep swelling emotions." Anthony explains with great insight:

> Mrs. Rose is not appreciated, nor cannot be by this age—she is too much in advance of the extreme ultraists even, to be understood by them. Almost every reformer feels that the odium of his own Ultraisms is as much as he is able to bear and therefore shrinks from being identified [when] one [more ultra] says I am ultra enough . . . I don't want to seem to be any more so by identifying myself with one whose every sentiment is so shocking to the public mind.

Anthony's perceptions reveal both Rose's greatest virtue and greatest flaw: her inability to compromise her ideals. As an outsider, Rose registered the bigotry that infused even the woman's rights movement. When she heard what she perceived as prejudice, she spoke out; she did not suffer fools, or even friends, gladly. Rose would have been a difficult friend, so intent was she on her idealistic purposes and duties. Her differences in language (her accent) and her appearance (her long, unbobbed, curly hair) were obvious, but less obvious was Rose's overwhelming need to change the world in the public sphere even if it meant ignoring the "bonds of friendship" that sustained so many women, including the husbandless Anthony and the badly married Stanton. Perhaps Rose's relationship with William, her constant source of emotional and financial support, left her less in need of female friendship and more able to focus on speaking. Even though they rarely traveled together to woman's rights activities, William's work in New York City helped support her cause. Or, perhaps, she rightly registered and refused to excuse intolerance (anti-immigrationism, anti-Semitism) that others, who perceived their biases as "natural," were unable to record. Whatever her motives, Rose was clearly a woman with no mind to compromise, no manner of conciliation. It is not surprising, then, that her reception in both her time and in the twentieth century has been so negative: nothing is more fearsome than a sarcastic, idealistic woman who talks straight and appears to need no one.

Anthony reached out to Rose after Rose revealed her anguish. Copying out a hymn that they had sung earlier, Anthony inscribed it to "her dear friend Ernestine L. Rose," and then after handing it to Rose, both women sat and wept. Rose repeated: "no one knows how I have suffered from not being understood." Being "too much in advance" would keep Rose from being understood throughout her life.

Philadelphia

On April 10, Rose and Anthony continued on to Philadelphia, to the home of the Motts. In Philadelphia they relaxed, calling on friends like the Crowells (Charlotte Crowell was a sister of Josiah Mendum, the publisher of the *Boston Investigator*) and Dr. Wright. Anthony but not Rose visited William Penn's monument because, as Anthony related, "Mrs Rose does not agree with me as regards the worth of Penn, indeed she does not regard the memory of any whom we are accustomed to think of with reverence. She sees good in none save such as the world has traduced—it is well that there are some to bring to light the virtues of the neglected and despised" (Diary Apr. 13, 1854).

While in Philadelphia, the two women spent the evening at Dr. Wright's, where Mrs. Crowell was hypnotized by a spiritualist. Spiritualism, the quasi-religious experience where participants spoke to the dead, was greatly in fashion in the spring of 1854. Many other popular figures involved in reform movements— William Lloyd Garrison, the Grimké sisters, Sojourner Truth, and even *Tribune* editor Horace Greeley—had become converts to Spiritualism in the early 1850s, in the wake of the famous 1848 "Hydesville rappings." There, two preadolescence girls claimed they heard sounds made by a spirit called "splitfoot." Brought to New York City, they gave public exhibitions where they communicated with the dead. Spiritualism may have attracted many reformers because of its antinomian assertion that divine truth was directly accessible to individual human beings. As Ann Braude has described, the spiritualist movement removed the authority of the spirit world from the realm of the clergy, fostering a unique opportunity for women to assume leadership roles.[19] Though many, including Rose's friend Charlotte Crowell, became believers in such communications with the spirits of the dead, Rose was having none of it.

Anthony's account of Rose's response to this fashionable parlor-Spiritualism is amusing and telling. Anthony relates that after Charlotte Crowell was put to sleep, "Mrs. Rose took her by the hands and said 'Charlotte! Look at me!' very sternly—Mrs. C seemed not to be able to open her eyes or control her [movements] but Mrs. Rose will have it that she practiced deception" (Apr. 12, 1854).

Even within her circle, Rose was almost always alone in her opinions about spiritual matters. Concluding their Philadelphia visit, Rose and Anthony dined again at the Motts on April 14, where the table conversation turned once again to Spiritualism. On the "unbelieving side" were Ernestine Rose and Thomas Curtis, who assumed "the spirit inseparable from the body." On the other side were the rest of the party—the Motts, Sarah Grimké, and Anthony herself, who reasoned that "if it is be true that we die like the flower, leaving behind only the fragrance . . . what a delusion has the race ever been in—what a dream is the life of man" (Diary Apr. 14, 1854). As is evident from Rose's reaction to the

19. See *Radical Spirits*, in which Braude examines the nature of the overlap between the nineteenth-century woman's rights movement and Spiritualism. Braude understands Spiritualism to be an antinomian response to the crisis of faith in mid-nineteenth-century America. See also Reynolds 262.

séance, there was not one spiritual bone in her body. She was the complete materialist. Given that she was living in a world where the rationalism of a Tom Paine was growing increasingly out of style, it is little wonder that, even among her friends, Rose was always and forever "too much in advance."

···⊰[6]⊱···

Growing Acclaim and Exhaustion
in the Mid-1850s

I have been told 'your principles are very well to live by,
but will they prepare you how to die'? They little know
what a compliment they pay us by that admission. All
we need is the right principles to live by, and the rest
will take care of itself.

—Ernestine Rose, New York, 1856

Throughout the late summer and early fall of 1854, Ernestine
Rose was sick with what we would call pneumonia or bronchitis
and would remain ill off and on until May 1856 when she and
William went to Europe for a six-month "rest cure." During that
time, for almost two years, Rose traveled and lectured herself into
exhaustion. Her activities during this period demonstrate how
devoted she was to the cause of woman's rights. Constantly in
motion, except when laid up by illness, Rose served as president
of the fifth national woman's rights convention in Philadelphia in
October 1854, then undertook an extensive lecture tour that included stops in New England, 10 upstate New York counties, and
that finally ended in a "western" tour that included speeches in
Ohio, Indiana, and Michigan.

Rose's schedule from the time she and Susan B. Anthony left
Philadelphia until two years later, when she and William left for
Europe, would be enough to exhaust anyone just reading about it,
let alone doing it. The sheer number of talks that she gave—often up
to six or seven a week and sometimes two a day—necessitated that
Rose adopt a series of stump speeches that, with some little variety,
basically reiterated the same major points to geographically different
audiences. To those of us used to new sound bites every day, Rose's

speeches might appear repetitive, but to each audience in the mid-1850s, where few people outside major cities had access to national newspapers, Rose's speeches were novel.

Often alone, Rose traveled by train when she could, but more often she had to resort to walking or taking uncomfortable stage-coaches, wagons, or even sleighs in winter. Writing in late 1854, Rose's friend Joseph Barker tried to explain to Garrison's readers of the *Liberator* just how difficult Rose's journeys were and how dedicated she was to her purpose:

> [Rose] has travelled alone, for months together, along the rivers and lakes, through the towns and cities, the woods and swamps, exposed to the deadly vapors of unhealthy regions, lecturing to Legislative halls and rude log huts, to the highest and lowest, the richest and the poorest, to the most refined and learned, and to the rudest and most neglected of her species. Her eloquence is irresistible. (*Liberator* Nov. 24, 1854)

Rose also traveled as inexpensively as she could, trying to save money from the receipts of her lectures for "the cause." When possible in a strange city or town, Rose stayed with acquaintances in order to save the cost of a room. Susan B. Anthony's careful records in her Scrapbook show us that of all the women on the lecture circuit speaking for woman's rights, Rose spent the least amount of money on her own expenses.

One advantage of Rose's constant activities during this almost two-year period was the increased newspaper coverage she received everywhere she spoke. As one of the "big guns" of the movement who had been the "master-spirit" behind the Cleveland convention in 1853, Rose commanded an audience and subsequent responses from the local and national press. Though few reporters agreed with her, most did notice her, commenting on her looks and clothing. That she had "ringlets" instead of a bun or a bob, that she wore gloves, that she never donned the Bloomer costume, and that she still spoke with a foreign accent drew repeated mention from reporters and editors all across the United States.

Newspaper coverage was a mixed blessing for Rose. Surely, any publicity helped spread the message that Rose and her colleagues were trying to disseminate; but in Rose's case, the attention did not always work to her advantage. Even though the newspapers clearly depicted Rose as the most eloquent of the speakers and portrayed her as standing alone "at the front rank" of the movement, the coverage also revealed a more insidious and subtle message: that Rose was correct when she argued that men did not take women seriously. Focusing often on her looks and her foreignness, the reporters and editors thereby marginalized her even as they valorized her speaking abilities. She was served up to the public, in effect, as another exotic oddity that mid-nineteenth-century audiences so loved to observe. Just as many women in the movement probably excluded Rose from their inner sanctum because of her foreign appearance and manners, so, too, in a more extreme way, the newspapers packaged her as a kind of curiosity, and a foreign one at that.

The main disadvantage to a biographer of this harrowing two years is that, although it is easy to track Rose's many stops across the country, the local newspapers that reported Rose's words did not give their readers entire copies of her speeches, leaving their audiences and posterity with snippets, with aphorisms, rather than with the whole of her logical progression of ideas. And because Rose kept no personal diary of her travels, we have to rely on her letters to Josiah Mendum at the *Boston Investigator* and the letters and scrapbooks of others to look for personal insights during this intensely public time.[1]

---

1. The main source of documents for this time period is volume 1 of Susan B. Anthony's Scrapbook, which is stored in the Rare Books Room of the Library of Congress. Anthony was meticulous about cutting and pasting all articles she found relating to the woman's rights movement. During the mid-1850s, when she was often on tour with Rose or at the same conventions, her newspaper clippings, laid out in chronological order, provide a wealth of contemporary responses to the movement. But despite Anthony's careful collection, she sometimes does not date a clipping; we can only assume, from the careful placement of all the marked clippings, that these unmarked clippings also follow her strict sense of chronological order. Other letters that mention Rose include Martha Wright's letters in the Garrison Family Papers and Lucy Stone and Antoinette Brown's letters in Lasser and Merrill.

Rose, as we have seen, was a private person who rarely talked about her personal life, particularly in such a public period as the mid-1850s. It was clear, for example, by 1855 when Rose was in her mid-forties, that she would not have more children. As might be expected from someone who valued her privacy so much, Rose never talked about her two children who died in infancy. After the deaths of two infants, perhaps Ernestine and William decided they would try no more. Birth control was available to women in the 1830s and 1840s; Robert Dale Owen had, in fact, written one of the first-published tracts on birth control in the United States in the late 1820s. In *Moral Physiology*, Owen discusses in clear language the effectiveness of what we would today call diaphragms, prophylactics, and coitus interruptus, though he criticized the latter because it removed the "control" from the woman, where it should be. Rose could also have been aware of a variety of circulars "to the public" from shop owners selling "cundums" or "preventives" through the mail, both for people to avoid disease and for married couples' birth control.[2] But such personal information about Ernestine Rose must remain mere biographical speculation.

Because her children died in their infancy, Rose had ample uninterrupted time to devote to woman's rights. Like Susan B. Anthony, Rose was able to work nonstop during the decade of the 1850s when other women—particularly Elizabeth Cady Stanton, Lucy Stone, and Antoinette Brown Blackwell—took considerable time out from their activities to bear and nurse children.[3] Rose was free to continue petition drives, to attend the yearly national conferences as an officer and chair of the business committee, and to

2. For example, see the circular from a fancy shop owner in Philadelphia selling "Cundums" at $3 a dozen or $10/5 dozen in the 1855 Broadside Collection at the AAS.

3. Anthony's letters during the 1850s reflect her own unhappiness with her friends' marriages and birthings. As Anthony's biographer Kathleen Barry writes, Anthony was "unsympathetic [with her friends' marriages] because she saw them choosing private satisfactions over the public and collective movement for their sex" (118).

lecture, sometimes for months at a time, across the United States and its territories, spreading the seeds of social and moral reform.

Rose as President of the Philadelphia National Convention, October 1854

After Anthony and Rose returned from their lecture circuit to Washington, D.C., and Baltimore, Anthony tried to get Rose to join her in Saratoga Springs in August 1854, for a hastily called state woman's rights meeting, but to no avail.[4] The pneumonia or bronchitis that would plague Rose for two years kept her from trying to woo a "new class of listeners" who were vacationing at Saratoga during the height of the fashionable season (*HWS* 1: 621).

Rose was so ill that she almost missed the fifth national woman's rights convention in Philadelphia in mid-October, where she was elected president, but she recovered enough to attend and preside.[5] Rose accepted the presidency, though she feared that she might be unable to discharge her duties given her recent attack of "inflammation of the lungs" (*Lily* Nov. 1, 1854).[6] The Philadelphia convention was marked by a wide range of people now involved in the movement: women like Lucy Stone wearing their Bloomer costumes sitting side by side with wealthy Quaker women wearing "mouse-colored gowns and white shawls," or William Lloyd Garrison and James Mott sitting next to "men of the darkest hue" (*HWS* 1: 375). The admission fee of 10 cents during the day and 25 cents at night did not keep people from coming. The *History of Woman Suffrage* reports that the audiences grew

4. See Antoinette Brown Blackwell's Aug. 16, 1854, letter to Lucy Stone reprinted in Lasser and Merrill, 140–41.

5. Rose wrote Josiah Mendum and Horace Seaver at the *Boston Investigator* that she was in "feeble health" at the end of the summer; they remarked in the Oct. 11, 1854, *BI* that she would be unable to attend the upcoming Philadelphia meeting.

6. For information on the convention see *HWS* 1: 375–86; see also the *Una*, Nov. 1854, which includes resolutions. See also the Nov. 1, 1854, *Lily* for a summary of convention activity. I can find no extant *Proceedings*.

larger every session until the last evening hundreds were turned away (1: 386).

As president, Rose called the meeting to order and gave a major address that reflected the concerns of her previous year's speech. She argued for equal political rights with men for two reasons: the principle behind the Declaration of Independence and the principle that taxation and representation are inseparable. First, she proposed, human rights were natural rights. Women, like men, were both included in the phrase "all men are created free and equal." If woman was included in the Declaration of Independence, said Rose, what right did man have depriving her of her rights? Rose added an argument that had impressed her when she had heard it from Harriot Hunt and then Lucy Stone: "we claim our equal political rights with man," said Rose, "from another, equally well-established principle in this country, that 'taxation and representation are inseparable.' Woman, everybody knows is taxed; and if she is taxed, she ought to be represented" (*HWS* 1: 377). Rose concludes by saying that if men can convince us that we are wrong, then we will give up our claims, but if we can convince them that we are right, then we expect them to acknowledge it.[7]

The second day of the convention was dominated by a discussion as to whether to publish a newspaper as the official organ of the woman's rights conventions. Mary Ramsdale, Paulina Wright Davis's sister, had written the convention of her sister's health problems and of the uncertain status of Davis's *Una*, the paper devoted to dissemination of the principles of woman's rights. Thomas Wentworth Higginson, who read Ramsdale's letter to the convention, then argued against her idea of moving the paper to New York City and making it into an official organ, saying that the expense of producing such a paper would be heavy, and given the state of finances of the movement, might become a "mill-stone" (quoted in *Lily* Nov. 1, 1854). Thus, without an official organ, the

7. Rose also spoke at length about the condition of women in Europe and the advantages of education possessed by them compared with American women. See Anthony's Scrapbook, Vol. 1.

participants looked to other, less expensive ways of spreading their principles. Lucy Stone suggested that women could write short stories illustrating the wrongs done unto women under present laws, pointing to *Uncle Tom's Cabin* as an example of how fiction could move people, and she suggested that prizes be offered for the best stories.[8]

The conference ended with a resolution to convey thanks to Rose "for the courtesy, impartiality, and dignity with which she has presided over [the convention's] proceedings" (*HWS* 1: 385). The press reports on the convention attest to the fact that Rose was the speaker among speakers, the most eloquent one, the one standing "at the front rank" of the movement. The Philadelphia *Ledger* of October 18, 1854, wrote that Rose, the president, gave an "eloquent address." The New York *Tribune* reported, "Mrs. Rose, the President, did her duties with great dignity, and her occasional short addresses showed wide experience, and a more highly cultivated mind, perhaps, than any of the other ladies possessed" (as quoted in the *Liberator*, Nov. 3, 1854). The November 15, 1854, *Boston Investigator* related that two years ago not one paper of influence would have thought it worth while to report the woman's rights convention proceedings, but now "lawyers, professors, ministers, merchants, and even medical students were found in numbers among the crowd, all attentively listening to the eloquent and logical statements of a Mrs. Rose." Both Horace Seaver and Josiah Mendum, Rose's longtime friends at the *Investigator*, were thrilled with Rose's national success; they continue:

> Many who came to mock, remained attentive and went away convinced. One of the happiest features of this Convention, was in the fact that our long tried and faithful friend, Mrs. Ernestine L. Rose, presided on this occasion, and by her accustomed ability and dignity gave character and importance to the meeting, while her able advocacy was felt by all present. It is a great source of satisfaction to find one so liberal and so well known

8. Apparently only Matilda Gage submitted a story, "The Household," but no prize was ever given; see *HWS* 1:379.

as Mrs. Rose, standing thus at the front rank of a great movement. It bears testimony to the fact, that a life of practical goodness is able to live down that bigoted spirit of creeds which excludes from the pale of salvation all who are wanting in adherence to theological dogmas.

Rose's friends in the movement also shared their appreciation of Rose's leadership skills. Martha Wright, for example, wrote to her husband during the convention that Rose "makes a beautiful and efficient President" (Martha Wright to David Wright, Oct. 10, 1854, GFP).

The Upstate New York Lecture Circuit

After her successes at the Philadelphia national convention, Rose spent the remainder of 1854 speaking around New York City and then in Providence and Boston. She continued to interject current political affairs such as the Nebraska Bill and the influence of slavery on the North and South into her talks on woman's rights. Then, in January 1855, Rose began a ten-county lecture circuit with Antoinette Brown, who had, after being ordained in the fall of 1853, experienced a crisis of faith and left her pastor's position. Though Brown would soon find her faith restored even stronger, her lecture tour with Rose helped her focus on the importance of woman's rights in her life.[9] Rose and Brown began their tour with speeches at the Steuben County Woman's Rights Convention in Bath, New York. Susan B. Anthony accompanied Rose and Brown on this tour, helping Rose collect over a hundred signatures for a petition to the state legislature and giving one of her infrequent speeches on women's unequal wages. Rose's first speech to the convention was a version of her Philadelphia convention talk: that woman claims the

9. The tour may also have helped her decide later in the year to marry Sam Blackwell. Worried about how one could combine marriage and public work, Brown may well have learned from observation how Rose managed to combine a loving marriage with complete dedication to lecturing for woman's rights.

right to a voice in the laws because the Declaration of Independence provided that all men are created equal. Rose pointed out that it would be doing great injustice to the framers of the Declaration of Independence to presume that by the phrase "all men" they meant only the male sex.

In her second speech, Rose summarized her 1853 Cleveland national convention speech, discussing the degrading effect of poor education and employment opportunities on women, pointing out that 99/100 of the depraved among women were made so because they had no honest means of support. When one voice objected to her speaking on women's education and social position, Rose remarked that she was glad to hear that one "no" for she "knew well how to sympathize with him who stood in so small a minority," having herself been in a "minority of one" very nearly all her lifetime (Scrapbook, Vol. 1). Rose's identification with the man in the audience who did not want her to talk on women's educational and social position is a telling one. First, it recalls that Rose enjoyed onstage arguments, even when her own public disagreements with such people as Lucy Stone, Antoinette Brown, or Abby Kelley Foster erased the illusion of unanimity and accord that many of the women wanted to promote. It also illustrates that Rose continued to perceive herself as alienated and solitary, as she had expressed to Anthony in Baltimore nine months earlier.

From Bath Rose traveled with Anthony to Lockport, New York, for a "Woman's Wrights [sic] Convention," according to the Lockport *Daily Journal* of January 19, 1855. The convention was called to order by Anthony with Rose giving the convention address. Rose talked first about married women's increased rights in New York State, a subject well received by her audience, according to the local paper, and then talked "with equal zeal and eloquence" on the right of female suffrage, a subject that met with less general favor.

Newspaper commentaries on Rose's speeches were mixed, but all reflected the power of Rose's oratory. The Bath *Advocate* wrote that the audience seemed "spell-bound as [Rose] depicted the wretched condition of a large portion of the female sex."[10] In her evening speech the "dense crowd maintained the most perfect silence throughout the discourse not seeming to realize the flight of time," while Rose spent over two hours talking about the legal and political rights of women. Another paper admitted that Rose "displayed a good deal of intelligence" but the writer disliked having "our laws" made fun of by a foreigner. Yet another paper commented that the "strong-minded ladies" of our state, including Rose and Anthony, "appeared to succeed in everything to a charm," as they made money and left behind a good impression of themselves personally. Though much of the community may disagree with them as to their doctrines, Rose, the paper rather grudgingly agreed, was "no ordinary woman."

As usual, commentators noted her striking oratorical powers while lamenting the sentiments she espoused. The *Farmers Advocate* wrote:

> With the evening came an immense crowd. . . . Mrs. Rose proceeded to address the audience, who by the way, were very attentive listeners. Her argument was a powerful one, and she frequently waxed eloquent. How many converts she made to her faith would of course be impossible to tell; but it is a matter beyond dispute that she displayed genius and oratorical powers, which few women have ever exhibited in this country. She is one of the best speakers we have ever heard; and we can only regret that a woman of such brilliant intellect should be wasting her energies in a cause for which there is not a shadow of hope. (quoted in *BI* Feb. 14, 1855)

The *Farmers Advocate* reflected the spreading sentiments about Rose's abilities; she was "beyond dispute" a "genius" and one of the "best speakers we have ever heard." But there is often a "but" following the glowing descriptions of her oratory and her "brilliant intellect." That "but" refers to her message for equal rights for

10. All the newspaper commentaries come from original newspaper clippings in Anthony's Scrapbook, Vol. 1. Although the Bath *Advocate* is named, the other two articles are clipped without their names. None of the paper clippings is dated.

women and men. Encased within an ideology that mandated separate spheres for the sexes because of their immutably different
natures, most people hearing Rose could not recognize her logic
even as they might be impressed with her oratorical powers.

At home briefly for the January 29 Thomas Paine birthday
celebration in New York City, Rose talked about her recent travels:
the object of her mission, she said, was to "rouse the people" to
the evidence of the "immutable truth upon which the Declaration
of Independence is based," namely, that "all men are created equal,
and endowed with inalienable rights to life, liberty, and the pursuit
of happiness and the pursuit of happiness includes women too"
(*BI* Feb. 14, 1855). Admitting that she had interrupted her lecture tour of 10 counties in upstate New York for "the pleasure of
being with you," Rose conceded that "the mind wants rest as well
as the body." Rose ended her speech to the New York Paine
Society by asking its participants to sign her petitions on woman's
rights—one for equal rights to property, offspring, and a trial by
a jury of peers, the other for the elective franchise. She added "if
you don't wish to sign both, then give us your names to the
elective franchise, for if we have that secured to us, we will take
good care to secure to us all the rest."

Following the Paine celebration, Rose traveled immediately
back to upstate New York for a hearing before the Assembly
Committee in Albany and for a woman's rights convention, where
she had been advertised as a speaker. Joined by Antoinette Brown
and Anthony (incorrectly referred to as "Sarah B. Anthony" in a
variety of newspapers), Rose presented a woman's rights petition
to the New York Legislature containing over 13,000 signatures,
some of which had just come from the Paine celebrants.[11]

11. See the Mar. 7, 1855, *Boston Investigator*. For other information on the
hearing before the Assembly, see *HWS* 1:628–29; the Mar. 14, 1855, *BI;* the
March 9, 1855, *Liberator;* and the June 15, 1855, *Lily*—all of which quote the
Albany *Register*, including repeating the *Register*'s misspelling of Anthony's first
name. In 1855 Anthony is still the least known of the three women. During her
upstate lecture circuit, Rose had to return to New York because of ill health,
leaving Anthony to address a few audiences without the help of the more eloquent and gifted Rose.

Anthony, as usual, did little speaking before the Assembly. Antoinette Brown spoke of the injustice of women being taxed without representation and the necessity of women having a jury of their peers, whereas Rose talked about the laws of our land, focusing on the lack of legal rights available to women. Rose described woman, as she had in previous speeches, as a "piece of property, belonging to father, guardian, or husband, transferred from one to the other, her feelings lacerated, from the cradle to the grave." Rose also, in an unusual strategy for her, employed some of the emotional appeals other women had incorporated into their speeches, particularly from temperance talks, such as alluding to the legal right possessed by a husband to take the earnings of his wife and then spend them for liquor, or his right to bind out their children without the consent of his wife. Such examples, Rose may well have believed, would appeal to the representatives who might think of their own wives or daughters in similar circumstances. Ending her speech by countering a commonly held belief, Rose denied that man alone belonged to the "head" and woman to the "heart," claiming that both head and heart were necessary for a human being and that a popular figure of speech ought not be the basis of our laws.[12]

At the Albany woman's rights convention, held in the Green Street Universalist Church on February 13–14, immediately following the women's speeches to the Assembly, Rose was the "great gun of the occasion," according to Anthony's handwriting in her Scrapbook. Rose spoke first on the ineffective education girls received: "the boy was prepared for business, the girl taught music, a smattering of bad French, painting sufficient to spoil a good canvas; or, perchance, to paint her own cheeks, and without the slightest knowledge of life or how to live, her education is pronounced finished and her highest aim thereafter is to get married—if she can." In the evening Rose addressed the convention on woman's present legal position in this state, pronouncing present laws degrading and, according to an unnamed local paper, she

---

12. For the text of Rose's speech to the Assembly, see the Mar. 14, 1855, *Boston Investigator* and the June 15, 1855, *Lily*.

illustrated her talk "with an amusing manner, showing a married woman in law was a nonentity. She exhibited a great deal of research in relation to the law of marriage and property and showed its glaring inconsistencies with much humor and force." Rose received accolades for her convention speech. She was, according to a local (unnamed) newspaper account, "a Polish lady who would do honor to any country. There is nothing masculine about Mrs. Rose,—nothing coarse,—no pulling on of the breeches, but all she says, and the manner in which she says it, is refined and womanly."[13]

From the Albany hearing, Rose traveled to Binghamton, New York, continuing her lecture tour and gathering signatures for the New York Legislature. There she gave a version of her "teaspoon" speech on the lack of legal rights woman has in marriage, including the sarcastic specifics that woman is allowed to keep if her husband dies: "one cow, one bed, six chairs, six cups and saucers, six spoons."[14]

In March, Rose again became ill as she continued her New York lecture circuit and postponed a trip to Boston until May.[15] By May Rose was appearing again on various platforms in New York and New England. The May 18, 1855, *Liberator* reports that Rose attended a "public discussion" on abolitionism on May 9 in New York, joining other antislavery reformers to speak on slaveholders' pecuniary interest in the institution of slavery.

By the end of May, Rose was in Boston to give the lectures postponed because of her spring illness. At the Music Hall, she lectured in the afternoon on "Human Rights and the Result of

13. The quotes from Rose's speech come from an unnamed newspaper clipping pasted into Anthony's Scrapbook, Vol. 1. The commentary on Rose's speech also comes from a local, unnamed newspaper pasted into the Scrapbook.

14. See the Mar. 21, 1855, *Lily* for information about Rose's speech in Binghamton.

15. See the Mar. 28, 1855, *Boston Investigator.* Rose became ill after lecturing in Penn Yan, New York, as reported by the Yates County *Whig.* On her way to Boston she was taken so ill she could not continue. In Boston, Rose had been advertised as lecturing on "Human Rights"—see Mar. 23 and 25, 1855, *Liberator;* but the Mar. 30 *Liberator* notes that Rose was not able to deliver her lectures. "It was a great disappointment," wrote Garrison.

their Violation on the South and on the North as Exemplified by Slavery" and in the evening on "The Education, Social Position, and Legal and Political Rights of Woman." In her first speech, Rose was equally severe on the black laws of the South and the "blue laws" of the North—both the effects of political and mental slavery upon human beings. As always, even though on an abolitionist stage, Rose could not limit herself to opposing only physical slavery and expanded her talks to include the many shapes of slavery possible when bad laws and customs are allowed to shape the thinking of men and women. Specifically, she decried the religion-inspired "blue laws" that prohibited many kinds of behavior on the sabbath. In the evening speech, Rose advocated the equality of the sexes in regard to educational, social, legal, and political rights, and supported each of the claims "in an argument of much ability and ingenuity" (*BI* May 30, 1855). Garrison's *Liberator* also praised Rose's "lucid and able" address on slavery and her "vigor" in her woman's rights speech:

> she spoke for nearly two hours, without notes or reference to any manuscript, with great vigor of appeal, power of reasoning, and masterly ability, keeping the unbroken attention of her audience to the end, and eliciting frequent expression of approbation. Mrs. Rose is one of the most natural, dignified, intelligent and effective speakers, and, for one born and educated in Poland, speaks our language with astonishing precision and accuracy. She ought to have much fuller houses. (June 1, 1855)[16]

Following those speeches, Rose met with "The Friends of Woman's Rights" at Harriot K. Hunt's home, where Rose complained of mistrusting lawyers. Rose reported that she often found it more expedient to take an index and search a statute book herself rather than ask a lawyer a question. At least one woman at Hunt's home argued that uplifting the social condition was more important than repealing laws. Rose, of course, asked her how one could separate social and legal conditions (see *Una* June 1855).

16. See also the May 25 and June 1, *Liberator* for notices of her speeches.

Woman's Rights Conventions:
Saratoga, Cincinnati, and Indianapolis

In August 1855 the New York Woman's Suffrage Committee held another convention in Saratoga Springs in St. Nicholas Hall.[17] As it was "the season" in Saratoga Springs, where fashionable mothers and daughters were vacationing, the location seemed fit to introduce a new kind of audience to woman's rights. The previous August the State Committee had organized a woman's rights convention at the last minute to coincide with two national conventions and, despite the lack of national speakers available to come—including Rose, who begged off because of illness—the conference had been well attended.

Rose, Anthony, and Antoinette Brown, all vice presidents of the convention, stayed together in the Broadway House Hotel (Ellen Garrison to Anna Davis Hollowell, Aug. 20, 1855, GFP). Lucy Stone came in the middle of the meetings, newly married, and the press insisted on calling her Mrs. Blackwell, despite the fact that Stone had publicly renounced adopting or using her husband's name. At the convention, presided over by Martha Wright who lived in nearby Auburn, New York, the typical hecklers were present, but this time they heckled Samuel May, who gave the first set speech of the convention. Rose, joined by Antoinette Brown and Martha Wright, "in a mild but firm matter" told the hecklers that the women would not speak unless the Rev. May were free to finish his speech.[18]

Rose took the stand after May completed his speech, talking for over an hour on woman's disabilities and the consequences on her intellectual, moral, and social condition—one of her set speeches on the differences between the education of boys and girls and the

17. For information on the Saratoga conference see *HWS* 1: 620–28 and the *Lily* and the *Una* for September 1855. Paulina Wright Davis in the *Una* called Rose "the speaker of the evening." Clippings for this conference appear twice in Anthony's Scrapbook, Vol. 1, once, incorrectly, as September 1854, and again, correctly, as 1855.

18. All quotes from the Saratoga Springs convention come from the *Proceedings* reported in the Sept. 15, 1855, *Lily*.

resulting differences in their life opportunities. She ended her speech referring, once again, to the "fallen daughters" that populate "our" cities, women without education to help them escape their helpless position. She cites these women's "shame and sorrow" to illustrate that none of them are being "protected" by a man; in fact, most have been betrayed by men. And without education, they can do nothing but walk the streets.

Rose's speech was well received, at least by the reporter the *Lily* quotes, who both summarized Rose's speech and referred to her foreign accent. Like almost all commentators, the reporter comments on Rose's eloquence:

> She is an excellent talker—clear, logical and eloquent, with just enough of [sic] foreign accent to add increased interest to her delivery. In glowing words, she painted the difference between the education of boys and girls—of the former, adapting them to every vocation and calling—of the latter, confined to a few branches of study, a few light accomplishments, adapting her to no purpose at all. (*Lily* Sept. 15, 1855)

The second evening of the conference provides us with yet another example of how Rose seemed constitutionally unable to hold her tongue when her colleagues on the stage were saying something she disagreed with. Just as Rose had corrected Lucy Stone at the Broadway Tabernacle meeting in the fall of 1853 and had disagreed publicly with Abby Kelley Foster at the Cleveland convention later that year, so too at this meeting she would try to refute Antoinette Brown's point that woman, in effect, deserved her subservient position because it was "equal to her present capacity." Brown explained that this statement was not a concession but a realistic acknowledgement of women's dwarfed capacities in a world that refused to educate them. Rose, who was scheduled to speak next, cast aside her set speech to refute Brown, arguing that it was "fashion, custom and law, that crushed [woman's] natural aspirations, and prevented the manifestation of the powers with which she was endowed."

Brown, according to the *Proceedings*, interrupted Rose to tell her she had misapprehended her meaning, that she only meant it was a general rule, that of course there were exceptions where women had showed themselves vastly superior to their condition. She asked: "Suppose all women possessed the courage, spirit, and clear, analytical mind of Ernestine L. Rose, who believes that the present disabilities of the sex would exist one hour?" Rose acknowledged the intended compliment, but had to have the last word, insisting that there were "thousands of women who were superior to their present position." Rose, demonstrating again her insistence upon logical correctness over all else, in this case behaves in a way that suggests she has little sense of rhetoric as social intercourse.

After the conference, Rose accepted an invitation to visit Martha Wright in Auburn, New York. Wright, who liked and appreciated Rose, was frustrated that her presidential duties had kept her so busy that she had little opportunity to talk with Rose during the convention (Wright to Lucretia Mott, Sept. 8, 1855, GFP). Wright regretted the calumny directed against Rose as an unbeliever. In an earlier letter to her sister, Wright related how a mocking man referred to Rose as "Miss Rose," a woman who did not believe in a God. Wright with asperity replied to him: "I told him I never had heard *Mrs.* Rose express her views on that subject, but that she seemed to be a very lovely woman" (Wright to Lucretia Mott, Mar. 29, 1855, GFP). Wright continues, telling her sister that she had heard that "[Rose] was idolized by her husband (Banthony told me so), beloved by her friends, and that her life was spent in the performance of those duties commonly called Christian. She should be judged by her fruits and not by her belief."[19]

Wright's letter to her sister is revealing. Rose is somewhat of an enigma even to Wright and Mott, who have to learn about William Rose through Susan B. Anthony. That he "idolizes" her is worthy of their comment. Despite not fully knowing or understanding Rose, they certainly value Rose's role in the movement

19. To Wright and Mott, Susan B. Anthony was nicknamed "Banthony," an affectionate term that illuminates how easily and well Anthony was accepted into the "bonds of friendship" that sisters Wright and Mott shared. It also, by omission, shows how Rose, never nicknamed and never called anything but "Mrs. Rose," was not as intimate with any of the women.

and are quick to defend her honor—"Mrs" Rose not "Miss"—to an outsider. But they, too, had to read her "goodness" through a Christian lens. Although Wright says that Rose should be judged by what she does and not by her lack of belief, she also must see Rose's actions as "Christian."

During Rose's brief visit, we see again how Rose is sometimes incapable of allowing storytelling to be merely playful social intercourse, even when visiting with a friend. While talking, Martha Wright told Rose a story about how a woman traveling by train, even with clear directions from a husband, had gotten confused and ended up back where she started. Rose responded with some "amusing instances where *men* as well as women had made mistakes in travelling" (Wright to Lucretia Mott, Aug. 29, 1855, GFP). Rose was always quick to try to discourage any essentialism she heard, even in stories from a friend like Martha Wright.

Rose may also have told Wright on this visit how she had just "baptized" a baby the week before. Immediately after the Saratoga convention and before her return to Wright's home, Rose traveled to Waverly, New York, for a freethinking "Friends of Progress" meeting where Rose met up with Joseph Barker. At this convention, Rose was asked to name a baby, which she did by christening it "Ernestine Frances Lyons," naming the baby for both herself and Frances Wright. Rose commented in a letter to the *Boston Investigator* that the scene was a novel one, "for a woman to name a child in public and that, not in the name of the Father, Son, and Holy Ghost, but in the name of reason, justice, and humanity" (Sept. 26, 1855).

Cincinnati

In mid-September, Rose took a two-month trip west to lecture in a variety of cities and to attend the sixth national convention in Cincinnati and a state convention in Indianapolis. On the way to Cincinnati, Rose lectured in Salem, Ohio, home of Joseph Barker, to the "Progressive Friends" convention. At this convention, Rose opposed those who argued that without a belief in a future heaven people could not be restrained from crime. To Rose, they had it backward: the very belief in a heaven made people neglect their lives and kept them ignorant of their nature and the relation they sustain to fellow men.

From Salem and the "Progressive Friends," whom Rose convinced to change their name to "Friends of Human Progress," Rose traveled to Adrian, Michigan, where she lectured on woman's rights and the formation of character. From there she went to the Michigan Anti-Slavery Anniversary at Battle Creek, speaking on the evils of society. In Ypsilanti, Rose stayed with a friend, Henry DeGarmo, before speaking in Ann Arbor and Detroit. In Michigan, Rose made at least one semiconvert to expanding women's education. The *Daily Watch Tower* wrote that Rose "is a lady of high literary attainments; and possessed of that practical *substance* of education which certainly cannot injure, if it does not benefit the condition of her sex" (quoted in *BI* Oct. 17, 1855).[20]

By mid-October, Rose was in Cincinnati, calling to order the Sixth National Woman's Rights Convention on October 17 and 18.[21] Perhaps because of the location, many of the regular participants such as Susan B. Anthony were not present and the attendance was down.[22] Lucretia Mott and her husband and Frances Gage, recently moved to St. Louis, attended. Also present were Lucy Stone, currently living in Cincinnati with husband Henry Blackwell, and Martha Wright, who was elected president. Rose served this year as first vice president.

To an audience of over 3,000 people, speakers such as Lucy Stone addressed the midwestern crowd in a variety of Bloomer costumes. Wearing a brown Bloomer and no ornaments except a

20. See Rose's Nov. 20 letter published in the Dec. 5, 1855, *Boston Investigator*, where Rose details her recent trip to "the West" and lists the cities she has lectured in. See also the Oct. 17, 1855, *Investigator*, which comments that Rose is "now" on a tour of the West, having lectured in Adrian, Michigan.

21. For information on the convention, see *HWS* 1: 163–67 and the "City News" pasted in Anthony's Scrapbook, Vol. 1. I can locate no *Proceedings*.

22. According to Martha Wright, Anthony was exhausted and needed to rest. Wright tells Anthony that she wishes more were involved in the cause "to relieve those who have heretofore worked so zealously, such as Mrs. Rose, Lucy and yourself" (Nov. 2, 1855, GFP).

gold cross, Stone spoke of what the woman's rights movement was all about: it was, she began, *not* about woman claiming the right to smoke cigars in the streets; rather the movement is about increasing women's salaries, about widening woman's sphere. The newspaper reporters who were there commented more on the Bloomers and on the curiosity of the audience to see women make a speech than on the content of the speeches.[23]

Rose spoke several times at the convention, telling her audience of her efforts to get petitions signed in New York State that would give women the right both to vote and to keep their earnings and their children in the case of divorce.[24] Employing the same images and the same emphasis on woman's lack of education and opportunities that she had been using on her recent lecture tour, which, of course, was new to each audience, Rose urged convention goers to help change the present method of female education. Women were brought up to get married, said Rose, and among the poorer classes the female was taught a little housekeeping, and "oh how little!—to darn stockings, sew on buttons, and if necessity should require, to rock the cradle." Among the upper classes woman's education was equally weak as women were taught "a little music, a little dancing, a little bad French, to paint a little—just enough to practice on her own face." Rose talked about the happy period of courtship—a time bound to end because a man, thinking he was marrying a woman, discovered she was only a child, a feeble being, "with hands too small to use a broom, and with a false delicacy that caused her to faint away at the mention of a leg of a table (Applause and shouting)." With an education, both poor women and rich women would be relieved of the "necessity of selling [themselves] in matrimony or out of it."

While in Cincinnati, Rose attended a class in anthropology several times, as the convention was not, as she wrote to Josiah

23. See *HWS* 1: 163, where Stanton and Anthony comment on the "brief report" in city journals that was all they could find. Such lack of coverage of woman's rights meetings was all too common outside of large cities.

24. For summaries of Rose's speeches, see the Oct. 15, 1855, *Lily* and Anthony's Scrapbook, Vol. 1.

Mendum, "as interesting as our National Conventions in the East" had been (*BI* Dec. 5, 1855). Before she left the city, she and Joseph Barker visited Frances Wright's grave, where Rose felt a strong devotion to the cause of freedom for which Wright had suffered. She had to be thinking of herself, also, when she contemplated Wright's dedication and ostracism from society. She wrote to Josiah Mendum of

> the high-minded woman that rested there, her devotion to the race, her noble efforts to benefit society by the spread of useful knowledge, her love of human freedom and human rights, her opposition to superstition and intolerance, and the bitter persecutions she suffered in consequence, which have not ceased even though she is no more—were very suggestive to my mind and called up deep thoughts, earnest feelings, and a stronger devotion to the cause of freedom and of right for which she had to suffer so much. But more anon. (*BI* Dec. 5, 1855)

Indianapolis

Leaving Cincinnati, Rose traveled by train to Indianapolis, to speak at a state woman's rights convention. There Rose rejoined Frances Gage and Lucretia Mott as well as her infidel friend, Joseph Barker.[25] The local papers were full of criticism, particularly of "weak-minded men" like Joseph Barker, though they were less critical of the women speakers, admitting that the women were talented and knew how to give a good speech, but their cause, they concluded, was a "dead failure." At least one participant of the convention remembers that the two leading papers in Indianapolis did their best to make the movement look ridiculous, with

---

25. Perhaps inspired by Cincinnati and Wright's grave, Rose had recommended to Barker that he read Wright's *A Few Days in Athens*. To Barker's expression of pleasant surprise that the book was an excellent read, Rose responded: "you remark, you had no idea what it was about . . . was it the fact that the book was written by a woman, and recommended by a woman that misled you so as to its character?" (See *BI* Dec. 12, 1855, for Barker's letter to Rose and her acerbic response).

reporters writing about "masculine women" and "feminine men." The reporters spent considerable time describing the dress and appearance of the women, but said little of the arguments of the speakers (*HWS* 1:307). Although neither of the Indianapolis papers reported the speeches, both referred to Rose and her oratorical powers. The Indianapolis *Daily State Sentinel* wrote that, although "we" do not accord with her peculiar doctrines, especially that of infidelity, "we will do her the justice to say that she is in every sense a true orator, her voice being full and melodious and not, in the least, marred by a slight foreign accent. Her gestures were in themselves eloquent, and well suited to the language employed" (Oct. 24, 1855). The Indianapolis *Journal* of October 24 emphasized Rose's foreign accent, her looks, and her age in an extremely negative tone:

> Among the celebrities in attendance are Mrs. Gage, Mrs. Ernestine Rose of New York, and Mrs. Lucretia Mott of Philadelphia, and another lady named Joseph Barker of no where in particular. . . . Mrs. Rose is a Polander by birth, and retains a perceptible foreign accent in her pronunciation. Her face is profusely adorned with ringlets, which don't appear to help her pale complexion in particular. Her eye is very black—a sort of varnished eye, like a bug's back, with little depth or expression in it. She looks like she might be about forty years of age.

Both papers, as usual, comment on Rose's foreign accent—as if her demands are even more obnoxious because she is an outsider. Even when her accent does not "mar" her oratory, it is still worthy of commentary, as is her appearance. A middle-aged, foreign-born orator, who could talk better than the native-born speakers, offended many of the middle-class white men writing for the papers. Responding to all the negative commentary Rose drew across the nation, Horace Seaver and Josiah Mendum of the *Boston Investigator* rather naïvely wonder why Rose has been assaulted by so many newspapers. They write, "we are considerably puzzled to find out . . . what [the] real objection to Mrs. Rose consists of, unless it be that she is of 'foreign extraction.' [Yet] Lafayette was 'foreign.' and the traitor Arnold of native extraction" (*BI* Mar. 12, 1856). Seaver and Mendum either conveniently forgot or purposely overlooked the fact that Rose, as well as being a foreigner, was also an "ultra" woman's rights advocate, who came from a Jewish background, and was known to be an infidel.

Bangor, Maine Controversy

Upon her return from her western trip, Ernestine Rose had little time to relax before she found herself embroiled in yet another controversy. Invited to lecture at an antislavery society meeting in Bangor, Maine, in mid-December 1855, Rose found herself slandered in the Bangor *Mercury*. Opposing her invitation to speak, a local minister, Reverend G. B. Little, a friend of a notorious New York minister who hated freethought and Rose, wrote that Rose was "the President of an Infidel club in New York, whose speeches at the annual Tom Paine festivals have, for half-a-dozen years, surpassed anything with which we are acquainted in ribald blasphemies against the Christian religion." He continues: "For ourselves we do not hesitate to confess that we know of no object more deserving of contempt, loathing, and abhorrence than a female atheist. We hold the vilest strumpet from the stews to be by comparison respectable" (quoted in *BI* Dec. 12, 1855). Rose immediately set the record straight by citing all Little's errors: she was not the president of an infidel club; she had not been a presiding officer for a half dozen years; Christ was not blasphemed at Paine celebrations. She also called upon the Reverend Little to *read* her Paine speeches and to then publish them (*BI* Dec. 12, 1855). The controversy had two good outcomes: first, Rose did travel to Bangor and give her speech and, second, she was championed in print by another minister, the Reverend Amory Battles, who wrote to Reverend Little via the editor of the *Whig and Courier* that Rose should certainly be allowed to speak. He argued that "her right to do this is no more to be questioned than yours is to preach to your congregation or mine to speak on temperance. We live in an age and country where free thought and free speech are acknowledged in theory as they should be in practice.

And you will pardon me if I fail to discover in the facts to which you refer with so much sensitiveness, anything that disqualified one for lecturing in our Course [antislavery] (as quoted in *BI* Dec. 26, 1855).

Rose's speech to the Thomas Paine Society a little over a month later was a lively one as Rose recounted the Bangor incident. She was greeted by "thunders of applause," and then told the group, gathered to dance polkas and quadrilles, eat supper at midnight, and hear speeches and toasts, that "you see, you were implicated with me. Misery, they say, likes company." Rose explained that she received quite a battery of "priestly intolerance" from Reverend Little and his New York counterpart, Reverend Rufus Griswold, who pledged to "use all moral means to thwart Mrs. Rose's influence, so help me God!" (as quoted in *BI* Feb. 13, 1856). Rose went on to praise the Bangor committee that invited her for not violating their word and allowing her to speak, thus earning her and other champions of free speech a "moral victory." Rose described how the same kind of slander befell Thomas Paine, who had enemies that, if they could not destroy him, slandered and vilified him instead, so much so that most people know of Paine "today" only through his enemies' stories about him; thus, we remember him as intemperate. Rose argued that even if that were accurate, which it is not, would the truths he uttered be less true? His death has been painted in the darkest colors.

Rose concluded her talk by asking what does Paine's death or anyone's death have to do with life? Rose added that she had often been told "your principles are very well to live by, but will they prepare you how to die?" She said: "they little know what a compliment they pay us by that admission. All we need are the right principles to live by, and the rest will take care of itself. . . . This senseless talk of teaching man how to die while he is left utterly ignorant how to live—to make the world wiser, better, and happier for his living in it—is as ridiculous as it is pernicious, for it diverts man's attention from life and its duties" (*BI* Feb. 13, 1856). In this talk, then, Rose astutely summarizes the core of her humanistic freethought: one lives by the "right principles"—making the world wiser, better, and happier. One does not live to prepare for death; rather one lives to perform a duty and executing that duty—improving the world in some way—will be enough to prepare for death.

Farewell Letter

Throughout the winter and early spring of 1856, Rose continued to suffer from inflammation of the lungs, even though she did lecture in and around Boston in late February and in Philadelphia in early April. Sometime in the spring, she and William decided to travel to Europe to give her a rest, in the hope that a sea voyage, a change of climate, and a few months without constant lecturing would improve her health and enable her to return invigorated and ready to "perform my part in the great drama of life a few years longer" (*BI* May 7, 1856). On April 30, preparing for her six-month trip to recuperate in Europe, Rose wrote a revealing "farewell letter" to her friends for publication in the *Boston Investigator*. Rose's letter reflects both her status as an important public figure—someone who should and would send a public farewell letter to a newspaper—and her awareness of her primary flaw.

In this letter Rose notes that on May 14 (Robert Owen's birthday), it will be 20 years since she arrived in this country to "serve the cause of progress and humanity." She explains

> I have endeavored, to the best of my powers and ability, to serve the cause of progress and humanity; to advocate what to me seemed the truth; to defend human nature from the libel cast upon it by superstition; to claim human rights irrespective of sex, country, or color—in fine, to devote and direct all my efforts to the elevation of the ignorant, the poor, and the oppressed. In the little I was able to do, I had no ulterior end to serve, no personal interest to gain . . . and if, in expressing my opinions, I have been severe alike on friend and foe, it is because in principle I know no compromise.

Taking a look back at her residence in the United States, Rose says that despite the severe reproach and persecution for daring to oppose the popular superstition called religion, she has always been treated with civility and kindness except at the Hartford Bible Convention, at an antislavery convention in Boston (blue laws and black laws), and at the 1853 woman's rights convention in the Broadway Tabernacle where "a few silly boys" kept interrupting the women trying to speak.

Rose's letter is a self-revelatory one. First, it is written in the past tense, as if her public life were over, not merely being temporarily interrupted. Perhaps her choice of tense had much to do with the dangers of traveling by ship across the Atlantic. We can also see from the letter that she understood how "severe" she appeared to her friends and acquaintances. She admits her lack of compromise but links it, rightly so, with her principles. She reiterates that she has never sought personal gain, as she might have felt others were. In fact, she will tell Jenny d'Hericourt two months after writing this letter that Lucy Stone and Antoinette Brown were always paid wherever they lectured, but she traveled and gave talks "at the expense of her health and her purse" (d'Hericourt, "Madame Rose" 139).

Rose writes that she will be gone for six months, leaving on May 6 and planning to return in November. Even a six-month absence worried her colleagues in the woman's rights movement, however. Martha Wright feared that without Rose the national convention would be "a failure" (Wright to Anthony, June 14, 1856 GFP). In England, Rose hopes to see Robert Owen and to consult other liberals about a forthcoming World's Bible (or anti-Bible) Convention to be held in New York City. She ends her farewell letter with great self-awareness by asking her friends to excuse her shortcomings, the most notable being equally her most noble trait: her inability to compromise.

⋯⊱⟦ 7 ⟧⊰⋯

A Trip and More Conventions in the Late 1850s

All woman asks of man is space to grow in, that and nothing more.

—Ernestine Rose, New York, 1859

Exhausted by more than a decade of activism for women's and human rights, Ernestine Rose left for Europe with William on May 7, 1856. Hoping that a change of climate might improve her health, Rose must also have believed that traveling to England and Europe would afford her her first extended vacation in almost two decades. Having lectured in 23 states, often giving multiple talks in a single day, Rose needed a rest. But she was not to find rest and relaxation. As she wrote in her first letter back to Horace Seaver and Josiah Mendum in Boston: "Sightseeing is the hardest labor that can be performed."[1]

Rose was, at the time she left New York, a celebrity. Most of the country knew what she looked like: brown hair that was greying naturally, with her ever-present curls in the front but with the rest now pulled back. She dressed simply, always wearing either a grey, brown, or black dress, a bit of lace, and a gold brooch at her neck. She was a small, slight woman, but her intelligent face, a half-smile, soft eyes with a great light in them, and a lyrical voice

---

1. See the Aug. 30, 1856, *Boston Investigator* for the quote. All of Rose's letters on the trip come from the *Investigator*. But because of the delays in mail service, some of the letters were published after Rose had returned to the United States. The parenthetical dates after all quotes refer to the publication date of the letters, not the date they were written.

suggested the power behind her outward appearance. Her first lengthy biographical sketch by L. E. Barnard had recently appeared in the *Excelsior*, and it was quickly reprinted in both the *Liberator* (May 16, 1856) and the *Boston Investigator* (July 9, 1856). Returning to London and Paris—cities she had lived in during her early twenties—as an international leader in the burgeoning woman's rights movement, she and William were feted there and in most cities they visited by leading infidels and woman's rights activists. Her arrival in various cities was announced in newspapers in London, Paris, and across Germany. Despite her wish for relaxation, Rose, the ever-active activist, must have been at least privately pleased at her enthusiastic reception.[2]

Though the Roses were certainly not wealthy, Ernestine was careful with money, often staying with friends and acquaintances during her travels in the United States. This six-month trip to Europe, which may sound extravagant to us today, was not so for the Roses, as they stayed with friends and freethinking colleagues whenever they could and at inexpensive lodgings where their network of friends ran out. The Roses, who owned no property, kept no servants, and lived in rented rooms, found living expenses to be less dear in Europe than in New York City.

Rose's status as a well-known public figure is reflected in the letters she wrote while on her six-month vacation/tour. She wrote 11 long letters "home" to Horace Seaver and Josiah Mendum at the *Boston Investigator*, and, as are most of her extant letters, they were written for the public, not for the private perusal of Seaver and Mendum. The insights she shares, the glimpses she gives into herself are those of a public persona who understands the responsibilities of her status, who has agreed to an implied contract that makes her actions accountable to all. Even her "vacation," then,

---

2. For example, Anthony Collins wrote in the June 1, 1856, *London Reasoner* that Ernestine Rose "will arrive shortly in this country. . . . Mrs. Rose is one of the most courageous, honest, intelligent, and womanly of the woman's rights agitators—the friend of Garrison and Barker, an American successor in theological controversy to Mrs. Emma Martin. It is only our duty to welcome Mr. and Mrs. Rose to England and English Secularists by a public meeting in London, as we did to the late Mr. Carlile (quoted in the June 18, 1856, *Boston Investigator*).

becomes a tour with events to be reported with Rose's typical wit and insight.

The Trip

Their voyage to England was a long one—five weeks of cold, bucking waves that left Rose perpetually seasick. Unable to work or read, Rose stayed in her cabin, like the others on board. She writes in her first letter home on June 29 that everyone was, "amusing themselves with each other's discomfort" (July 30, 1856). Rose describes her discomfort in a way that anyone who has ever been seasick will recognize: "For those unfortunates who are sick, sea sick, there is nothing to enjoy, except at intervals, when they have a little rest; then they enjoy a very faint gleam of hope, which seems to be so very far off, that they can hardly perceive it, of just living long enough to be able to put a foot once more on terra firma" (July 30, 1856). The few days of respite came when the sea calmed, stalling the boat, and the ship's passengers then spent their time on the deck wishing for wind to send them on their journey.

Her fellow cabin passengers consisted of one young woman and a Darby family of three, who were traveling with a "little menagerie" consisting of a dog, a cat, two parrots, and eight other birds. Rose writes that the little time the family could spare from eating and drinking was spent with their animals. In her usual acerbic manner, Rose characterized the family's devotion to their animals (and their religion): "They were very unselfish in their nature, for they gave us the *full* benefit of the perfume and music of the menagerie, accompanied by a long and loud prayer twice a day" (July 30, 1856). In addition to being religious, the family was also "loyal . . . expatiating with admiration and delight on the virtue and piety" of such rulers as Louis Napoleon, the emperor of Russia, and Queen Victoria. When Ernestine and William suggested that all three monarchs could be more virtuous, they nearly got themselves thrown overboard (July 30, 1856).

Her constant seasickness did not stop Rose from meditating upon the ocean, seeing in it a metaphor for her life's work. She wrote that the ocean at rest was illusory, like poor countries where nature had been polished over to hide the inequalities beneath the surface. She preferred "the sea to be in motion." Although the waves look threatening when the breezes begin, and although they may "be against us" for the moment, at least they are favorable to someone else and will soon be so again "for us." Rose favored anything but "a dead calm," be it physical, mental, or moral. A "dead calm" was "conservative, anti-progressive. In it there is no health, no hope, no life" (July 30, 1856).

Rose was three weeks in England before she had a moment to write, busy as she was sightseeing, visiting old friends, and being entertained. The first friend she mentions visiting is Robert Owen, then 86 and living 27 miles from London at Seven Oakes in rented rooms with gardens and parks available to walk in. In the nine years since Rose had seen Owen, he had become a believer in Spiritualism. Exasperated with him, Rose writes that "needless to say, his endeavors to convince me *into* it, and mine to convince him *out* of it met with equal success" (Aug. 6, 1856). As a tourist, Rose visited many of the most popular attractions, including Madame Tussaud's Exhibition of 378 wax figures, Hampton Court Palace, the British Museum, St. Paul's, the Tower of London, Westminster Abbey, Windsor Castle, and the Crystal Palace at Sydenham, which she found to be a light, airy, "magnificent" structure.

Visiting Parliament House, Rose contrasted its architectural beauty with its antediluvian policies concerning women. Women could visit the structure, but could not attend the debates unless they obtained a permit, applied for in writing. Then, if their petition was approved, women could observe only in a special small gallery enclosed with metal wire, "like that of a prison window," which allowed women to view the debates with only one eye at a time. Unable or unwilling to wait the two weeks it took to obtain a permit, Rose relates that, as she had a desire to hear a debate in the House of Commons, she just "went in . . . without any permit" (Aug. 6, 1856). Rose thought that of all of English policy, it seemed to her the strangest that women should be virtually excluded from the House of Commons, but she added "let silly men do all they can to keep woman out, she can always outwit them," as Rose had herself done.

Besides her detailed descriptions of London's attractions, Rose also commented on the people and culture of England; it was a world full of "heavy and dull" people. She wrote that "the buildings are massive; the animals strong; the people heavy and dull, and as long as they have enough beer to drink, they are quite content to be taxed heavily to support a most extravagant aristocracy, who despise them for it" (Aug. 20, 1856). She saw a world where hardly "a ray of sunshine can penetrate the fog and smoke that constantly overhang the city." Rose adds that England boasts that the sun never sets on her dominions: "we might with equal justice say that the sun never rises clear on London. In fact, if he ever rises at all, he has to get up very early" (Aug. 6, 1856). Attracted to the glories of London and yet despairing of the pollution and poverty she found, Rose wrote that London was "teeming with glory and degradation, splendor and wretchedness, the highest cultivation and refinement, and the almost barbarian ignorance and rudeness, the immense wealth with all its pride, and the lowest depth of poverty with all its abjectness, and of the tyranny, oppression, apathy, indifference, and subservience and submission which the terrible misrule of such extremes must naturally engender. It would require more than the graphic pen of a 'Trollope' to do it justice" (Aug. 6, 1856).

This city of extremes depressed Rose because of its exaggerated class system. The railroads, she noted, had three classes, the first being very comfortable but very expensive, the third being affordable but extremely uncomfortable, and the second costing nearly as much as the first and as being as uncomfortable as the third. The English people, unlike Americans, Rose found, did not indulge in as many sweets or pastries but did drink alcohol with three of their five meals a day. The upper classes drank wine, the middle, beer, and the lower, gin, and it was these drinking habits that separated the classes of society. Nevertheless, each class looked down "with contempt" on those below and with "slavish subserviency" on those above (Aug. 20, 1856).

While in London, Rose attended "fashionable" literary parties where she heard that reform movements were "dead" in England. Petitions to improve married women's rights had been presented to the House of Lords, but had not been acted upon, much as in the United States. A member of Parliament confided to Rose that "we can do nothing with the present Parliament; we must wait until it is broken up" (Aug. 20, 1856). But Rose was pleased to see that at least music could now be played in the parks on Sundays, despite religious opposition.

Rose left London on July 9 for Paris, where she stayed another four weeks. Her time there, as in London, was occupied with sightseeing and private parties. Remembering her life in Paris during the glorious days of revolution in July 1830, Rose revisited important sites such as the Louvre, the Palace of the Tuilleries, the Palace d'Elysée, Luxemburg Gardens, and the Hotel de Ville, where she had seen General Lafayette present Louis Phillipe to the people from one of its central windows in 1830.

As well as detailing the sights that Paris is known for, Rose also commented on its current condition, as one of a "vast barracks": soldiers patrolled every street. From 1852 through 1860, France's Second Empire was a highly despotic government with rigid censorship and an authoritarian control of all printed materials. Rose's letters about (but not from) Paris give us her insightful impression of that repressive time. Paris was, in September 1856, a "city full of soldiers" (Nov. 26, 1856). But the city was full also of spies, "against which you cannot guard except by a dead silence on all subjects connected with freedom" (Nov. 26, 1856). These spies were "everywhere"—in private and public, indoors and out.

Rose's friends and acquaintances did talk of political freedom but only behind closed doors. While in Paris, Rose became part of a literary and reformatory circle that included Charles Lemourier, a St. Simonian; Felix Etienne, the president of a philosophical society; and Jenny d'Hericourt, a physician and author who was interested in woman's rights and freethought, as were all the reformers who befriended Rose. On one of the nights Rose visited the circle, the group read a poem from Victor Hugo's "Judgment," which found its way into Paris by manuscript and which was read cautiously in private homes and small assemblies. But before reading and discussing the poem, Rose noted that the group had to "lock their doors and windows before they dare unlock their hearts" (Nov. 26, 1856). In fact, Rose was urged not to write letters from France, as "everything is known, not only what takes place, but what is going to take place!" (Nov. 26, 1856). Since a letter she was expecting from Owenite George Jacob Holyoake from London and a number of editions of the *Boston Investigator* had not reached her and may have been interrupted by the authorities, Rose took her friends' advice and posted her letters about Paris from Berlin.

Despite the lack of political freedom in Paris, Rose remained enamored of the French people. She wrote that she had always liked the French and liked them more now. She commented that most French people work hard and live "still harder; but they have the arts, the sciences, the beautiful, the elevating. No country so abounds in these elements, and no people on earth enjoy them as much as the French" (Dec. 3, 1856). Particularly impressed by the easygoing French response to alcohol, Rose contemplated bringing American temperance lawmakers and blue law supporters to Paris to learn a lesson of sobriety and good behavior. In the four weeks she was in France, she never saw one single drunken man or any rudeness or impropriety. She speculated about why the Americans and the British could not have the same uncomplicated attitude toward alcohol and concluded that it is England and America's Puritan influence: "[Puritanism] has prohibited enjoyments; it has made public amusement and recreation low, because it has made it a crime . . . and as human nature will not entirely be stifled, it seeks excitement in other ways" (Dec. 3, 1856).

At some time during her visit in Paris, Rose sat down with Jenny d'Hericourt and told her about her life.[3] Not only did she tell her the familiar story about her precocious childhood and her father's religiosity and her rebellion from it, but she also must

3. D'Hericourt wrote her biography of Rose sometime after meeting her in Paris in September 1856; it was published in *La Revue Philosophique et Religieuse* in Paris in 1856. D'Hericourt also wrote a briefer sketch of Rose in June 1869, shortly after the women met again in May at the anniversary of the Equal Rights Association. In that sketch, published by both the *Revolution* and the *Boston Investigator*, d'Hericourt writes that after she met Rose in 1856 and introduced her to Parisian reformers, she wrote her biography, which "was translated into Italian."

have told her about the births and deaths of her two children, children who had lived long enough to be nursed, but who, as far as we know, were never spoken of to anyone else at any time in any extant letters, diaries, or speeches. Perhaps Rose found herself comfortable with d'Hericourt in ways that she was not with American women; d'Hericourt was only one year older than Rose and, like Rose, was a European-born and educated freethinker. Perhaps being on holiday in Paris encouraged Rose to make these unusual revelations about her private life.

From Paris, Ernestine and William traveled to Lyon, France, and then on to Geneva and Chamberry, Switzerland, where they ascended a high mountain near Mont Blanc. From there they went to Strasbourg, France, and Baden, Germany ("a terrible gambling place"). They then toured Germany, going from Heidelberg to Frankfort, taking a Rhine trip to Coblenz. From there they traveled to Berlin, Dresden, Prague, and then Vienna. They crossed the Alps to Italy, visiting Milan, Turin, Genoa, Leghorn, Florence, Rome, and as far south as Naples.[4] Rose found the most interesting cities to be Venice, Rome, and Naples, though she was depressed by the number of priests, soldiers, and beggars that predominated in Rome and on the roads to and from Rome. In a letter she wrote October 20, Rose speculated that the priests were necessary for the other two groups—to direct the beggars to think of an afterlife and to give absolution to the brigands (Dec. 10, 1856). From Naples, they took a steamer to Marseilles.

After a few days back in Paris, the Roses returned to London and then went to Liverpool, where they spent some time with John Finch. A lifelong Owenite reformer, Finch was, according to Rose, a "true socialist" opposed to all creeds and superstitions as well as an advocate of "knowledge, freedom, and right, without distinction to sex, country or color."[5] Finch, who, like Rose, had

---

4. What is missing from this long list of cities and countries that Rose relates visiting is a trip home to Poland. Did she visit her homeland or her relatives, I wonder? If she did, she left no known record of it.

5. The information comes from a letter by Rose, dated Mar. 27, 1857, and printed in the Apr. 17, 1857, *Liberator*.

become a follower of Robert Owen in the early 1830s, had been an officer in Owen's Association of All Classes of All Nations in Liverpool; he was perhaps best known for his extensive tour of intentional communities in the United States during the mid-1840s. A dedicated Owenite until he died in early 1857, he hosted the Roses during their brief stay in Liverpool.

The Roses sailed home on November 1 on the Europa, a steamer whose speed cut their five-week transatlantic crossing down to thirteen days. The exhausting and stimulating six-month tour was not the restful vacation Rose needed. Rose writes aptly in her final letter home on October 20 that "the plain fact is" that "we have been in too many places, seen and heard too many things, examined too many dead and living ruins, witnessed too many wrongs, admired too many wonders, grieved over too many follies, beheld too much wealth and too great poverty and wretchedness, and frowned at too many priests, their altars and gods, to have had time left for anything else" (Dec. 10, 1856). Unhappy to be disappointing the many people in London, Liverpool, and Glasgow who had wished her to speak before she left for the United States, Rose, nonetheless, returned home without lecturing in England or Scotland because the winter was "close at hand" and sea travel could not be delayed any longer.

Seventh Annual Woman's Rights Convention, New York, 1856

Ernestine Rose returned to New York City on November 13, 1856, just in time for the seventh annual woman's rights convention in New York City. Less than two weeks after her return from her grand European tour, Rose was again an active participant in the movement, much to the pleasure of her friends, who had feared her trip would force her to miss the convention.[6] Lucy Stone was the president, with Lucretia Mott first vice president;

---

6. For example, see Martha Wright's July 9 and Aug. 30, 1856, letters to Susan B. Anthony in the GFP. Wright feared for the convention if Rose were not present; she considered Rose to be one of the movement's "true workers."

Rose was, as usual, the leader of the "Business Committee." At this year's conference, the business committee brought resolutions to the participants that stressed the primacy of suffrage and also offered a hint of a threat. Being neither "a slave or . . . an equal, taxed but not represented, authorized to earn property but not free to control it," the women resolved this was a transitional period they could not "long endure" (7).[7]

On the first day of the convention, November 25, participants talked about the benefits of such gatherings and responded to the audience's questions about the movement. At this convention at the Broadway Tabernacle, as at others, many in the audience attended only to watch the spectacle of women speaking about woman's rights; others came to heckle or disagree with the speakers. Yet, sometimes people who came just to observe or to disagree became converts to the cause. The conventions, then, were vital for disseminating the women's words. "Compare public opinion," said Rose on the first morning of the convention, "seven years ago with public opinion now" (13). The difference in support was striking to all. And, Rose added, such a gain in public opinion was just and right because the woman's rights movement was also a human rights movement; there was, said Rose, not one claim set forth by women that did not benefit men as well.

Lucy Stone, the president, gave a congratulatory speech, lauding all the changes in laws that have come about because of the women's activism in the past decade—"now almost every Northern State has more or less modified its laws" (4) and the young

7. For information on the convention, see *PWRC, New York, 1856.* All page numbers in the text come from the *Proceedings.* See also *HWS* 1: 631–35; the Dec. 5, 1856, *Liberator;* the Dec. 1, 1856, *Sibyl;* the Dec. 15, 1856, *Lily;* and the Nov. 26 and 27, 1856 New York *Tribune* and *Times,* which both commented on the large attendance and gave lengthy summaries of the proceedings. The women also resolved that the Republican party (the party that opposed the spread of slavery), was pledged to do justice hereafter in those states where it held control, while the Democratic party, "must be utterly false to its name and professed principles" because it did not advocate suffrage for "both halves of the human race" (7). Rose, a lifelong Democrat, but horrified that the Democrat party was in the mid-1850s the party that supported the Kansas-Nebraska Act, probably had something to do with that particular resolution.

states like Ohio, Illinois, Indiana, and Wisconsin have "materially" modified their laws (5). Stone went on to talk about what still needed to be done, including clarifying what the women meant by "woman's rights," which was not the right to "go down to Stewart's and run up a big bill, and my husband would have to pay it" nor was it taking men's rights away from them (16). Thomas Wentworth Higginson added that despite surprise that men should speak at a woman's rights gathering, he believed that "there was no place where a man could redeem his manhood better than on the Woman's Rights Platform" (9). Wendell Phillips argued that the woman's rights movement was one of only three movements (the other two being antislavery and socialism, which he did not accept) that questioned what is right and wrong in society. He added that "silent power"—women's traditional power "behind the throne"—is power that is not responsible: "I do not want half the race concealed behind the curtain and controlling without being responsible" (23).

Next responding to a letter read aloud that suggested that more men than women were in favor of woman's rights, Rose argued that although the statement appeared, at first glance to be true, if the movement were put "in its proper light," women would be in favor of it. Rose argues:

> Ask [a woman] if she is not entitled to self-government, to the full development of her mental powers, to the free choice of her industrial avocations, to proper remuneration for her labor, to equal control of her offspring with that of her husband, to the possession and control of her own property, and to a voice in making the laws that impose taxes upon property that she may hold—ask her a few simple straightforward questions like these, and see if an immediate, hearty and warm assent is not elicited. (13)[8]

8. The argument sounds familiar today as well. In the 1850s, women claimed they were not "woman's rights women," even though, when presented with the platform, they might agree with all of it. Similarly today although the premises of feminism—equal pay for equal work, a woman's right to the autonomy of her own body, equal access to education and jobs—are commonly accepted by most Americans, few call themselves feminists. Perhaps this discrepancy is a telling revelation about the way the issue of woman's rights is shaped and presented by the media and voices of authority in a culture.

Rose continued during the first day to counter opposing voices. A writer—a Mr. Johnson—argued that mothers did have legal control over their children. Rose disagreed, saying that in none of the states has she equal control with the father: "In this state," Rose corrects him, "up to the age of eighteen months, the child was under the control of the mother, but beyond that age the father could bestow [the child] on another by will; could apprentice it without the mother's consent or knowledge, and could place it beyond the mother's reach" (13–14). She added that she had been all over the country and in countless places she saw men trying to tear children away from their mothers, not because a father cared about a child, but to "tantalize" its mother (*Liberator* Dec. 5, 1856). Another speaker argued that it was not true that a woman had no right to control her earnings. Rose again corrected this misconception, responding that "all that [woman] may acquire by herself after marriage, she has no power to control. Her person, her talents, her labor, all belong to her husband" (14).

On the second day of the convention Rose spoke about how, although she was in Europe during the recent presidential election, the "fire of freedom" spread across the ocean. She commented that American political parties had "ceased to exist. There is no longer Whig and no longer Democrat—there is freedom or Slavery" (28). The presidential election of 1856 did, indeed, see the final dissolution of the Whig party as well as the emergence of a new party made of up ex-Whigs, Free-Soil Democrats, and antislavery groups. The new party, the Republican party, opposed the extension of slavery and would win the national election in 1860. Although James Buchanan, the Democrat who won the 1856 election, supported the Kansas-Nebraska Act and followed a "noninterference" policy with slavery, his days and the days of the supporters of Kansas-Nebraska were numbered.

During this second day, Rose spent much of the time on stage, first talking about woman's rights in England and France and then giving a major speech. She argued that in England the woman's rights movement was not "dead," as someone had suggested, but that the movement was in a difficult stage because the class system thwarted reform movements: every petition in Parliament had to first be supported by the upper class. Rose also spoke in support of the cause of women in Paris, the worthy successors of Pauline Roland and Jeanne Deroin, the two women whose revolutionary exploits had been one of the subjects of the second national woman's rights convention in Worcester in 1851. Rose said that if difficulties surrounding English women were great, the difficulties surrounding French women were even greater. She knew from her own recent personal experience that French women could write their thoughts, but their writings could not be published in France. Madame Roland, Rose continued, had been imprisoned and lost her arm because of her desire to "utter the truth." Jeanne Deroin was exiled and now lived in London where she supported herself and her three children (35).

When Rose finished, a young man challenged her, asking whether woman's rights claims were based on "Nature" or "Revelation" (36). Higginson responded, saying that the basis of this movement was not in a creed. Included in the movement were Calvinists (Wendell Phillips), professed atheists (Rose being unnamed, but implied), and Congregationalist ministers (Antoinette Brown) (36–37). The young man, not to be assuaged, continued to argue with the speakers on the platform, claiming that woman was not fitted for the pulpit, the rostrum, or the law course as her voice was not strong enough: "God gave [woman] a mild, sweet voice, fitted for the parlor and the chamber, for the places for which he had designed her" (39).

Despite the young man's arguments, there was some evidence that at least some of the practical goals of the woman's movement were being heard. In the afternoon of the first day a Dr. Wellington spoke, who first stated baldly that it was an undeniable fact that woman was not "free to act and to live as she desired. She had neither the social, political, nor religious privileges and rights that men had. It was useless to argue to evident a proposition as that" (47), but he turned into a mild advocate for woman's economic rights when he considered his daughter's impending employment. As a father anxious about his daughter's future, he could not see why a male school teacher should receive up to five times more pay for his duties than his daughter—such discrepancies were "unjust" (47). When letters were read, Horace Greeley wrote to the convention that employment for women was far too restricted (55).

Rose's speech on the final evening was, according to her friends, one of the best of her career. It was a speech that in connecting women's education, their available professions, their legal rights, and their political rights, Rose offered her strongest attack on marriage without love: when women married out of economic necessity, such a union was little better than prostitution. Although none of the subject matter was new to her or to her colleagues on stage, Rose wove specific details into her colorful oratorical style that were crowd-pleasing, even to an audience not universally enamored of woman's rights.

Claiming her authority from the Declaration of Independence, Rose begins her talk by discussing woman's first claim—the claim to education. Most women believe, have been taught to believe, that a woman's aim in life is to please men and that "all that is needed to complete her destiny, is to enter into fashionable life, place her name on the matrimonial list, and then, like a picture that has received the last finishing touch from the artist's hands, to which nothing more can be added, she is placed in a frame, perchance a gilded one, to grace the drawing-room, or a rude one for the use of the kitchen; but thenceforth there she is" (69). Just at the time a man's life becomes wider, a woman's, says Rose, is believed to be finished.

Furthermore—Rose moves to her second claim—men can study the professions, the arts, the sciences, or engage in a business. Should a man not be fit for one profession, he can choose another. Women are "assigned" the kitchen, the needle, and the school-room. "The fact is, man has a choice, woman has not" (71). If the kitchen, the needle, or the schoolroom cannot "supply the de-mands of her physical, mental, or moral nature, what other re-source has she to fly to except the last sad alternative: to sell herself in matrimony, or out of it?—and it would take the wisest heads, and the best hearts, to decide which is the worst. Both are evil, and productive of incalculable vice and misery in society"

(71). Rose urges women in her audience to do their "duty" in the name of poor, downtrodden, and outcast sisters—who were once as pure as "you." When a minister asks for money for missionary purposes, Rose tells her audience to tell him there are better missions to be performed at home; when he asks for colleges to educate ministers, tell him women must be educated; when he speaks of a hereafter, tell him to enable women "to live a life of intelligence, independence, virtue, and happiness here, as the best preparatory step for any other life" (73).

Rose then lays out her third claim: legal rights for woman, a subject she has dealt with before many times, but which, she believes, remains crucial to each new audience. Rose admits that some states have given limited property rights to married women, particularly allowing a woman to bring property to a marriage, but she adds that few women have much property to worry about. The vast majority of women, she says, begin married life with nothing more than the "united capital of head, hand, and heart" (74). During the lifetime of her husband, she cannot claim as her own one dollar resulting from her own efforts—it still belongs to the husband. As evidence of wrongs under current law, Rose evokes some of the horrifying examples all the women activists peppered their lectures with: even an idle, dissipated and vice-ridden husband has complete power over his wife and can retrieve her earnings from an employer to use for buying whiskey instead of feeding their starving children. And, even worse, the laws rob women not only of their identity, their property, and their earnings, they also rob mothers of their children. Fathers have complete control over their children and could bequeath, bestow, or sell a child without consent of the mother. Rose concludes that women must have political rights to be able to alter the unjust laws.

Admitting that there is a great prejudice against women's claim to political rights, Rose contends that such rights are morally grounded. She dismisses the heroism of soldiers in the battlefield, saying that standing before a cannon with death in front and disgrace behind and encouraged by a leader and stimulated by a trumpet and sustained by the empty sound of "glory" requires no great heroism. True heroes, she suggests, are the women and men in the woman's rights movement who have faced the fire of unjust prejudice and attacked the "adamantine walls of long-usurped power, to brace not only the enemy abroad, but often the severest of all enemies, your own friends at home" (77). Reflecting upon her own and Frances Wright's experiences in the 1830s, Rose adds: "you cannot realize what it was twenty-five and twenty years ago to call public attention to these wrongs, and prepare the way for such conventions, and such audiences; and yet, woman had the moral courage to do it, and do it as fearlessly as now; for though she had nothing else to support her, she had the consciousness of possessing the might of right to sustain her" (77).

Rose concludes her speech by turning the popular concept of the "true woman"—a woman who was idealized as pious, pure, submissive, and domestic—to her own use. She asks her audience if educational, social, and political rights will corrupt woman's nature? She asks if similar rights have "debased" men. Only with equal rights, Rose concludes, will a woman be "capable of being an intellectual companion . . . a useful member of society, and to sum up the whole, a true woman" (79).

At the end of the conference, Lucy Stone seconded Rose's notions of the importance of education, referring to Greeley's letter where he wrote to support economic opportunities for women, although he added that woman's intellect was not equal to man's. Stone imagines: "suppose [Greeley] had been told by his mother, as she placed her hand upon his little head, with all the tenderness that gushes from a mother's heart, 'My son, here is your brother; he shall grow up in the world of society, and no school or college shall be closed against him . . . but for you none of these places will be open." Do you think, asks Stone, that Greeley would be where he is today? (85). Stone adds that she is reminded of what Frederick Douglass has said about Negroes: "you shut us out of the schools and colleges, you put your foot on us, and then say, Why don't you know something?"(86).

Activities in 1857 Through June, 1858

When the Roses returned from their European trip, they moved to 72 White Street, where they lived until the end of the 1850s. Immediately following the 1856 national woman's rights meeting, Rose urged freethinkers reading the *Boston Investigator* to unify themselves through a national convention. Worried that people who did not mix with different classes, particularly lower classes, had no idea of the "tenacity with which the mass of people here and in England blindly cling to the very name of that book [the Bible]" (*BI* Jan. 28, 1857), Rose argued for a large meeting, saying that in 1850, when the first woman's rights convention was called, few people knew of woman's rights or supported them. Now, she said, repeating what she had said at the November woman's rights convention, woman's sphere of action was enlarging and some oppressive laws "have already been altered, and more will be, until full justice will be done to her" (*BI* Mar. 25, 1857). All this, Rose wrote, resulted from conventions.

Rose also spoke at the annual Paine birthday celebration in January 1857. Her talk, though ostensibly on Paine, sounds as if it could be about her as well. Rose told her audience that a prophet is not honored in his own country: "he who can be fully appreciated in his own age and generation, proves conclusively that he cannot be far in advance of the society he lives in" (*BI* Feb. 18, 1857). The language sounds remarkably like Anthony's when she described Rose during their talk in Baltimore. At that time Anthony wrote in her diary that "Mrs. Rose is not appreciated, nor cannot be by this age. She is too much in advance of the extreme ultraists even to be understood by them" (Diary Apr. 9, 1854). Rose's speech continues to describe both herself as well as Paine: "Society seems to resent as an insult any one to be too far in advance of them" (*BI* Feb. 18, 1857). It is no wonder that Paine was misrepresented and persecuted in his lifetime because, not only was he "in advance of his own age," but few people possessed the "common sense" to be able to appreciate him. Rose laments that most people prefer ease, popularity, and profit to a life of martyrdom. "We cannot," she says, "expect to have many possessed of the moral heroism to place themselves in accordance with their highest convictions, in the advance guard of society; hence the world can record so few bright meteors in our social and moral horizon who have shed an unfading lustre on the race, and like a beacon-light illumined the dark and intricate pathways to a higher and nobler state of human progression" (*BI* Feb. 18, 1857). In this talk Rose comes closest to linking herself with Paine, one of her few heroes (along with Robert Owen and Frances Wright). There were striking similarities between Paine and Rose: both were driven by the same freethinking idealism, both of their intellects were informed by the rationalism of the Enlightenment, both were uncompromising, both were "outsiders." Surely Rose, who disdained ease, popularity, and profit, was herself one of those few uncompromised bright meteors of nineteenth-century America.

The fall of 1857 was less busy than usual for Rose because the annual woman's rights convention did not meet this year, the first time since the first Worcester conference in 1850. Susan B. Anthony complained that too many women were marrying and having babies instead of dedicating themselves to "the cause." In some ways, the lack of a convention may have benefited Rose as she was ill again, but she was not so ill as to miss communicating her rage at a recently passed English Divorce Bill.

The bill contained several passages that Rose believed treated women unjustly under the law. Specifically, in a letter to the *Boston Investigator*, she cites how a husband seeking a divorce needed only adultery as grounds, but a wife seeking a divorce needed to prove that her husband's adultery had been incestuous, "that is, adultery with any woman whom, if his wife were dead, he could not lawfully marry" (Oct. 21, 1857). In addition, anyone seeking a "judicial separation"—almost always a wife—could never marry again. For Rose, obsessed with fairness, this "reform" legislation demonstrated only the "vitiated taste, the unblushing shamelessness exhibited by these civil and ecclesiastical law-givers" (Oct. 21, 1857). Rose tells the *Investigator*'s readers that three years ago at the Cleveland woman's rights meeting she argued that both the civil and moral codes were created by men and for men and that "depravity" in a woman would often be pardoned in a man. She cites the English Divorce Bill as evidence that the law-givers in

England are still "shielding and fencing around the depravity and corruption of their own sex, to the detriment and destruction of ours" (Oct. 21, 1857).

By January 1858 Rose had recovered enough to help plan and take part in the festivities for the Paine celebration.[9] The celebration that year was sparked by Gilbert Vale's theory that the Declaration of Independence was drafted, not by Thomas Jefferson, but by Thomas Paine. Vale claimed that he had an original of the Declaration and, when he compared the handwriting of it with Jefferson's and Paine's, it resembled Paine's more than Jefferson's. Rose added her comments on the "sublimely ridiculous" stories in the Bible that people believed simply because they were found in a book called "the Bible" (*BI* Feb. 17, 1858).

Following the Paine celebration, Rose lectured on a variety of subjects and planned a benefit in Boston. During the winter of 1858, Rose spoke on such subjects as "Philosophy and Merit of Religious Belief," "Consistency and Influence of Religion," "Distinctive Characteristics Between Religion and Morality," and "The Virtues and Vices of man, or the Fundamental Course of Social Evil." Planning a benefit for Horace Seaver in Boston, Rose urged readers of the *Boston Investigator* to contribute to Seaver's "testimonial," as Seaver (and Mendum) had both struggled for years to put out the *Boston Investigator* while earning no more than a common journeyman (*BI* May 26, 1858).

In early May 1858 Rose was part of the eighth annual woman's rights convention in Mozart Hall in New York City.[10] Rose joined

9. In early December Rose wrote the *Boston Investigator* that "friends who will help in making arrangements" will meet in "our house 72 White St, on Sunday, December 20th at 3 p.m. I hope that in spite of the 'hard times,' the friends and admirers of Thomas Paine all over the Union, will imitate the good example of the Liberals of our city and celebrate the birth-day of that grossly libelled and shamefully abused, good and noble man" (*BI* Dec. 16, 1857).

10. For information about the convention, see the May 12, 1858, *Boston Investigator*; *HWS* 1: 668–72, but note that *HWS* states, incorrectly, that this was the "ninth" convention; it was, in fact, the eighth, as no convention was held in 1857; see also the June 1, 1858, *Sibyl* for a general summary of the convention and the May 14, 1858, New York *Herald* and the May 14, 1858, New York *Tribune* for general commentary; no extant *Proceedings* appear to exist. See also the 1858 Broadside announcing the convention at the AAS.

many of the woman's rights regulars including Lucretia Mott, Wendell Phillips, William Lloyd Garrison, Susan B. Anthony, Lucy Stone, Frederick Douglass, Antoinette Brown Blackwell, and a number of new faces on the platform including George William Curtis and Parker Pillsbury.

According to Rose, in a letter she had written the *Investigator* a few months earlier, one of the best reasons to have a convention was to create the conditions of a "mental and moral laboratory, where the various metals and elements are thrown together into the crucible of reason, which is such as to cast the base and noxious ones out, and leave the others purer" (Mar. 25, 1857). In fact, at most conventions Rose conducted herself such that her actions complemented her thinking. Not only did she give persuasive, logical talks, but she also refuted anyone else on stage who, she perceived, was creating an imperfect ore, one that would not test true to the trials of reason. At this convention, in one of the few extant dialogues that are available to us, Rose once again corrects a speaker on stage. The ensuing dialogue and the description of laughter that infuses the exchange shows us that Rose's "corrections" were sometimes humorous. It is evident from this exchange that Rose, even in "correcting" someone, could do so with good will and that did have a sense of rhetoric as social intercourse.

Rose also, it is clear from these brief glimpses, possessed a playful sense of humor. When a speaker on stage used one of Rose's favorite subjects—the articles allowed to a widow when her husband died intestate—Rose broke in with laughter, correcting her, telling her that the law did not allow even ONE tea-pot:

> Mrs. Rose protested ONE tea-pot; the law didn't mention tea-pot at all. (*Great laughter.*)
>
> MRS. HALLOCK: Oh yes! but not a coffee-pot. (*Renewed laughter.*)
>
> MRS. GAGE: In Ohio they give twelve spoons. (*Convulsive laughter.*)
>
> MRS. HALLOCK: We'll get up a delegation to Ohio, then.
>
> MRS. FARNHAM: I would say that I will give up all these things if the state will only give us in return one of our children. (*Applause and laughter.*)

MRS. HALLOCK: Isn't it a pity that our laws—are they ours?
MRS. ROSE: No.
MRS. HALLOCK: When, then, your laws. It is a pity that those statutes should not be revised so as to give a widow a carpet and other smaller articles of luxury. (*Great laughter*) (*HWS* 1: 672)[11]

According to the New York *Herald*, Rose gave a rousing opening speech that alluded to her childhood. She told the audience that she had been a "rebel" since she was five years old, wanting to ask questions about the meaning of what she read. She could not understand, she explained, why a little girl should not ask questions as could a little boy. Paying tribute to one of the world's great female rebels, Frances Wright, who had been mentioned earlier in the day by another speaker, Rose pointed out that it was courageous even to mention Wright's name as she had been subject to great slander, abuse, and persecution during her life. Rose also alluded to her own decades of work in the movement, mentioning the occasion in 1837 when, at the Broadway Tabernacle, she dared to question the Reverend Breckenridge for being oblivious to the issue under discussion. Rose reminds her audience that since 1837 she has never ceased raising her voice for woman's rights as she has followed in Wright's unpopular footsteps (*Herald* May 15, 1858).

Rose also gave a major speech that concluded the conference. She spoke on one of her standard topics: how women deserved their rights because human rights included women's rights. Happiness, asserted Rose, had everything to do with social rights, which depended upon civil rights, which were based on political rights. Suffering all the burdens of government, women should

11. Despite her good humor, Rose did not trust Eliza Farnham, who, she believed, did not identify sufficiently with the movement. Martha Wright confided in Lucretia Mott shortly after the convention that "I found Mrs. Rose distrustful of her [Mrs. Farnham]; she formed the same opinion of her that I did in Philadelphia as one who wished to avail herself of whatever had been done, [but] not caring to identify herself fully with the movement." See Wright to Mott, May 17, 1858, GFP. Farnham's belief in the theory that "woman is superior to man" (see the *Liberator* June 4, 1858) would not have appealed to Rose nor, probably, did her elaborate and quite fancy dresses.

have all its privileges. Rose acknowledged to detractors that the world had produced no female Newtons or Shakespeares, but she foreshadowed Virginia Woolf's famous essay on "Shakespeare's Sister" by one-half a century when she said that there was no telling how many female geniuses were buried in their graves, having been unable to get educations or live productive lives. Men had crushed genius in woman, but if men would free woman, she would show them greater beings than Shakespeare and Newton.[12]

Free Convention at Rutland, June 1858

In late June, Rose attended a reformist "Free Convention" in a large tent in Rutland, Vermont, that drew several thousand people.[13] The convention was a somewhat unusual one for Rose to attend, although its promoters did claim it to be a celebration of free speech where participants would come together with no "symbol or doctrine" (7). Perhaps Rose believed that this large gathering would help spread the freethinking message in the same ways that the woman's rights conventions had spread their ideas. With most of its resolutions—including resolutions on individual authority (as opposed to biblical authority) and on women's rights in and out of marriage—Rose could agree; however Rose, Horace Seaver, and Parker Pillsbury were greatly outnumbered by believers in Spiritualism, who took charge of the meeting. Speakers promoting and proclaiming Spiritualism were allowed unlimited time for their talks, whereas the infidels were strictly limited to 10 minutes.

12. See the May 14, 1858, *Tribune* and *Herald* for summaries of Rose's speech. The skeptical Boston *Courier* reviewed Rose's speech: "Mrs Rose declared as her unalterable opinion that women had a right to win the same fame as Shakespeare and Newton—and so they have, we suppose, if they choose, but it is doubtful whether they can attain it by holding Conventions from now till doomsday" (as quoted in the June 4, 1858, *Liberator*).

13. For information on the "Free Convention" see *The Proceedings of the Free Convention held at Rutland, Vt, June 25, 26, 27, 1858*; all page numbers in text refer to these *Proceedings*. See also the *Boston Investigator* for July 7, 14, and 21, 1858; also see Braude, 69–73.

Rose spoke early in the convention, urging women as well as men to vote on motions placed in front of them. In her first 10-minute speech she rebutted a previous speaker's arguments for Spiritualism: even if her longtime friend Robert Owen, who had recently converted to Spiritualism, told her that he had seen a mouse draw a three-decker through the streets of New York, she still would not believe it: "I would say 'I cannot believe it.' 'But am I not Robert Owen?' 'Why certainly; and I believe that you believe you have seen it; but that can be no authority for me [Hear! hear!]' " (30). For Rose, the eternal materialist, authority came from what she could learn through her senses, what appeared reasonable to her. Even though the Spiritualists were not calling upon a scriptural authority, they were still assuming the existence of a spirit world; for Rose the spirit world had no reality. Whether at a séance with Anthony in Philadelphia or with Robert Owen in England or at the Rutland Convention surrounded by Spiritualists, Rose refused to waste her time on "mere speculation" when so many real-life wrongs needed to be corrected. Why argue about life after death when there were serious problems—slavery, lack of woman's rights, increasing crime—to worry about in this life? "Time is not ours" to simply "spend . . . in mere speculation" (31). Rose urged her Spiritualist listeners, in effect, to pray on their own time and use convention time to work on serious issues. She illustrated her point with an example from her past. "Fifteen years ago," she told the audience,

a society of women was formed in New York, called the "Prison Reform Society." I attended one of the meetings, and a lady read a chapter from the Bible and then knelt down and offered a long prayer. True to my own convictions of duty to humanity, I protested against it as an outrage. I said "If anyone wants to pray or read the Bible, I have no objection, but let her read and pray at home; but the moment we cross the threshold of this chamber, called together to do something for the relief of the poor convict, from that moment the time is not ours, even to pray, but to work." I will say the same to this Convention. (31)

Rose believed the subject matter of Spiritualism was "too slippery; it is like a live eel, which, if you think you have it by the head, the tail slips out of your grasp; and if you catch it by the tail, the head creeps out" (*BI* Oct. 13, 1858). It is little wonder that Rose felt out of place at this "free" convention.[14]

On the second day of the convention, Rose talked about marriage, speaking to a resolution proposed by Stephen Foster to add the words "perfect equality" to the following statement: "Resolved, That the only true and natural marriage is an exclusive conjugal love based on *perfect equality* between one man and one woman" (*BI* July 28, 1858). Even though she said she had steered clear of the subject of marriage in the past because she wanted to focus on unequal laws first, Rose agreed to support Foster's addition because she believed that without equality in a marriage the notion of conjugal love was an impossibility (61). In this same talk Rose spoke for the first time on any stage about her husband, William. Saying that she hardly ever alluded to herself, Rose told the audience:

> I am a married woman: have been married over twenty years; have a husband, and, as far as individual rights are concerned, I have as many as I ought to have. But I do not thank the laws for it. And why? Because it happens that my husband is "a law unto himself," and being a law unto himself, there is no need of any other law; and, therefore, we might say, Abolish all laws, because there is one who is a law unto himself. But what are laws made for? Not for my husband, nor for myself either; but for those who recognize no law but their own passions and lusts, and their own rights, at the expense and sacrifice of the rights of everyone else. (61)

14. Rose wrote in the Oct. 13, 1858, *BI* that she had not written on Spiritualism because "I dislike to have to do with ghosts." Anne Braude, writing on Spiritualism and women's rights in nineteenth-century America, notes that Rose was isolated at the Rutland convention: "only the indomitable atheist, Ernestine Rose, argued that Spiritualism was incompatible with the convention's reform objectives" (71).

Within her marriage, then, Rose implies an egalitarianism—she has "as many" individual rights as she "ought," that is, as many as her husband has. Rose has these rights because of their relationship, not because of any state law granting women equal protection under the law with men. Rose suggests that William, a "law unto himself," is the opposite of the kind of men whose "passions and lusts" promote their own interests. Her husband, then, by implication does consider others, especially her, and scorns the societal laws that give men unequal power over women.

From this acknowledgment of her own egalitarian marriage, the New York *Times* somehow deduced that Ernestine Rose was an advocate of "free love" and publicized the entire convention as one advocating free love. Outraged as usual when she was so misunderstood, Rose sent off a letter to the *Times* (and a copy to the *Boston Investigator*) patiently explaining what she did say and denying, emphatically, that she was a believer in free love. She took the opportunity to add, summarizing from her 1856 National Woman's Rights Convention talk: "when the laws proclaim woman civilly and politically equal with man, and she is educated to enable her to promote her own independence, then she will not be obliged to marry for a home and a protector, for she well knows that she can never be protected unless she protects herself, and matrimony (not a matter of money) will take place from pure affection" (*BI* July 28, 1858).

Despite being surrounded by believers, Rose rejoined the Spiritualists in Utica, New York, the following month. The large attendance (estimated at 5,000) and the group's dedication to individual authority, as expressed through woman's rights and antislavery sentiments, was probably enough to convince Rose to speak even on a predominantly Spiritualist platform.

Activities from Fall 1858
Through Winter 1860

In early October 1858 Rose joined her fellow freethinkers at an Infidel Convention in Philadelphia. There, encircled by her familiar freethinking friends such as Horace Seaver, the Mendums, and Joseph Barker, Rose must have felt more at home than at the Spiritualists' conventions. Immediately after greeting the participants, convention president Horace Seaver invited Rose to address the assemblage, which she did, talking about how the purpose of the meeting was to remove error and advance truth. On the second day Rose spoke on how the theological idea of God is man's own conception and thus as men grow in wisdom, so will their ideas of God change.

Rose's close and continued association with the infidels was probably one important reason why Rose did not often seek the companionship of other women activists outside the woman's rights conventions. While in Philadelphia at the infidel convention, for example, Rose did not visit Lucretia Mott. Martha Wright wrote to Mott on October 26, 1858, sad that "you did not see Mrs. Rose when she was in Philadelphia." Wright added that "there are so few who dare to be friendly toward her. She [Rose] said to me . . . 'it is so seldom that I see a face that expresses so much sympathy as yours.' "[15] Rose found the sympathy she needed with her freethinking friends and, of course, with William, who often helped her organize the freethinking events and attended those with her. The distance that Rose kept between herself and other women—women who did not dare express as much sympathy to her as did Martha Wright—exacerbated her isolation and made her less involved in the day-to-day work of the woman's movement.

The following month Robert Owen died in England and Rose opened her home at 72 White Street to help make arrangements for a public testimony of respect to his memory. The testimonial was held on December 27 at Stuyvesant Institute at 659 Broadway. There Rose gave the major eulogy, as she had known Owen

15. See the Garrison Family Papers. Another example of missed opportunities for Rose to visit with woman's rights activists occurred during the woman's rights convention in New York City in May 1858. While in New York for the convention, Martha Wright thought about visiting Rose, but when she saw she lived at 72 White Street, it was "so far" that she did not go for fear that Rose might be out. She was "greatly disappointed not to see Mrs. Rose" (Wright to Mott, May 17, 1858, GFP).

for over 25 years. She recounted the main accomplishments of his life and added that, even though he had not achieved all he set out to do, "he who aims at the sun does not accomplish his object when he hits only the nearest star" (*BI* Jan. 12, 1859)—an allusion that could refer to herself as well. Though Owen had not succeeded in changing this state of society, he left the principles by which to do it and, like a giant tree with invisible roots, his principles "have spread all over the subsoil of a garden." Owen's crowning glory, according to Rose, was his truthfulness and consistency: "History, as well as every day's experience, proves that unexpected prosperity is a far greater tempter and corrupter than adversity. . . . Where shall we look for one who, born in humble circumstances, has passed through the fiery ordeal of unexpected, unheard of prosperity, without being contaminated?"(*BI* Jan. 12, 1859). Rose asserted that Owen, despite the temptations and allurements of wealth and honor, the adulation of the worlds' greatest and best, had remained true to himself and to the cause of humanity. In this speech to an audience that included her close freethinking friends as well as many others, Rose does not mention Owen's foray into Spiritualism—the one specific way Rose believed him to have erred.

A month later Rose was back at the yearly Thomas Paine celebration in New York City, speaking on "the rights of man." After ridiculing the absurdities of the blue laws that punished a man for working in his garden on the sabbath, Rose attacked the clergy, many of whom refused to share a public stage with an infidel—fearing the exposition of pantheism, materialism, and other sophistries. Clergy should fear materialism, said Rose, as it accepted the universe as it was while spiritualist lecturers spoke for "the man in the moon." One spoke for life, the other for death: "morality, the Infidel's text-book, teaches man how to live; superstition, the priest's weapon, teaches him how to die. Let us, then, my friends, be content, by reason, justice, and truth, to secure a happy life, and they are welcome to the rest" (*BI* Feb. 16, 1859).

After a spring of illness, Rose attended the ninth annual woman's rights convention, again held in Mozart Hall in New

York City on May 12, 1859.[16] The meeting included the usual "strong-minded women" who were no longer wearing the Bloomer costume on the platform, according to the *Herald*, though several in the audience were wearing it. After Anthony called the meeting to order, the participants discussed approaching each of the state legislatures on the subject of granting women equal rights. A committee appointed for that purpose included Rose, along with Wendell Phillips, Elizabeth Cady Stanton, Antoinette Brown Blackwell, Thomas W. Higginson, and Anthony.

Caroline Dall, who offered a historical perspective to the woman's rights movement by talking about Mary Wollstonecraft's ideas, gave the first speech, followed by Lucretia Mott expressing gratification at all the interest the movement has created. Antoinette Brown Blackwell followed, speaking of the unfairness of asserting the mental inferiority of women (one of Horace Greeley's favorite premises), as there was no proof for such an assertion. It was not woman's mind that was inferior; it was her legal and social condition that made her seem inferior.

The fourth speaker, Ernestine Rose, agreed with Antoinette Brown Blackwell and then gave a version of her speech on the importance of woman's education, beginning with making fun of old attitudes that denied woman an opportunity for education: "arithmetic was deemed entirely superfluous, for what, indeed, had woman to count? Her children she could count on her fingers!! (Laughter)" (7). Rose notes that "now" public opinion has it that women need to be educated; but Rose argues here, as she has argued before, for a particular kind and quality of education—an education comparable to the one a man receives. The destiny of too many women is to "be[come] a toy in the drawing room, or a drudge in the kitchen, as the case may be; henceforth legally annihilated"(8). When women are educated physically, morally,

16. For information about the ninth convention see the *PWRC, 1859*; all page numbers in text refer to these *Proceedings*. See also *HWS* 1: 672–76 and the June 1, 1859, *Sibyl* with reports on "Women's Rights Anniversary" and a summary of Rose's talk on page 562; see also newspaper clipping from New York *Herald* in Anthony's Scrapbook, vol. 1.

and intellectually they will not have to protect themselves with revolvers. Asking what a well-educated woman needs from a man, Rose answers in one of her typically pithy and quotable phrases: "all woman asks of man is space to grow in—that and nothing more" (*Sibyl* June 1, 1859). Rose inserted some of her trademark wit into her speech by responding to a disturbance in the gallery. Pointing to the disturbance, Rose said "Yonder you have an evidence of the education woman has received. Had she been educated fit for the domestic sphere, those rude boys would know how to behave themselves (laughter and applause)" (8).

The *Sibyl* called Rose's speech "a strong, manly speech, with many delicate womanly touches of wit" (June 1, 1859). The *Boston Investigator* also commented on the events of this convention and specifically on Rose's history in the movement. Horace Seaver wrote that woman's rights are nothing new for their readers: the movement dates back further than the current women know of; Mary Wollstonecraft—70 years ago—was the first woman to speak "boldly and singly, and claimed the equality of the sexes." Next and the first in America was Frances Wright, who possessed uncommon nerve and heroism. Finally, Seaver points out that Rose had been laboring for more than 20 years for this reform and "may justly be regarded as one of its pioneers in this country. She was busily employed in advancing its doctrine when many who now support them were among her opposers. . . . Mrs. Rose is a lady of fine abilities—a fine lecturer, and remarkably clear and logical as a reasoner and debater, with no deficiency of quiet humor and sarcasm when it is needed for the rebuke of bigotry and intolerance" (July 13, 1859).

In the late summer of 1859 Rose fell down stairs, severely spraining her wrist and bruising her forehead, leaving her unable to attend the summer Saratoga women's meeting. Lucy Stone wrote that "we waded through the four sessions as best we could without her" (Lasser and Merrill 156–57). Rose was also unable to attend the early October National Infidel Convention, again held in Philadelphia, though her wrist, which had kept her from writing, was improved enough that she penned a letter to the convention. She called on convention participants to counteract the superstition of Christianity in all its forms because religion is "a hindrance to the elevation and progress of the race" (*BI* Nov. 23, 1859).

That same autumn in New York she and William attended several Sunday talks at Hope Chapel. Listening to the Rev. George F. Noyes expound on his opposition to the blue laws and on "enlarged freedom" on Sunday as well as any other day (*BI* Oct. 12, 1859 and Dec. 28, 1859), Rose was at first delighted that she had found a group of religious men who would entertain discussion of "reason." One young Unitarian minister from Rochester said to Rose: "You are the only person I have ever met who believes less than I do; I had no idea that any person entertained these views" (*BI* Dec. 28, 1859). Rose spent several Sundays correcting some of the men's impressions of "license and intemperance" in Paris. She told the group in no uncertain terms that there was no license or intemperance in Paris. On hearing Rev. Noyes's regrets on the Harper's Ferry insurrection, Rose responded that the cause that produced the insurrection (slavery) was more to be regretted than John Brown's actions. After several Sundays Rose became disillusioned that Noyes did not have the "moral courage" to continue free and open discussion when the group ended with a resolution to start "a Sunday School to develop the belief in God in our children" (*BI* Dec. 28, 1859).

In the fall of 1859, John Brown went on trial for his raid at Harper's Ferry. His early December execution marked the climax of a decade of growing antislavery sentiment. When the Republican party adopted a plank on their platform calling for black male suffrage, the response both in the South and in the North was often negative. For example, in February 1860 the Albany *Atlas/ Argus* editors argued "this is a government for white men—intended, of course, to afford protection in person and property to other races, but not to endow them with political control—the Republican party now proposes to abandon and overturn, and to establish in its place the theory of a government controlled and conducted by an intermixture of races, which shall place the Negro, the Indian, the Fejee Islander . . . alongside of the whites at the ballot box" (Feb. 18, 1860). In the winter of 1860, the country appeared more divided than ever and soon the woman's rights movement would be as well.

···⋙〖 8 〗⋘···

The Nation and the Woman's Rights Activists at War

In a republic based upon freedom, woman, as well as
the negro, should be recognized as an equal with the
whole human race.

—Ernestine Rose, New York, 1863

The winter of 1860 when Ernestine Rose turned 50, the country
seemed more divided than ever. Unknown to Rose or to any of
her colleagues at that time, the woman's rights activists would be
irrevocably divided themselves by the end of the decade. Just as
the antislavery movement split into factions in 1840, so would the
woman's rights movement splinter into two distinctive organizations with different missions by 1869. Already divided over the
presence of freethinkers like Joseph Barker and Rose on their stages,
the women and men who made up the core of the woman's rights
movement would soon take opposite sides on the Republican Party's
attempt to give black men, but not women black or white, the right
to vote. Their split would widen throughout the 1860s, plunging
the reformers into a crack just as devastating to the woman's rights
movement as was the Civil War to the United States.

Ernestine Rose began the decade of the 1860s with the cus-
tomary Paine birthday celebration. Rose continued to participate
in these infidel events even though the term "infidel" itself was
unpalatable to the American public. Wendell Phillips went to great
trouble in the spring of 1860 to defend his friend William Lloyd
Garrison from the "calumnious denunciation" that Garrison was
an infidel. Phillips wrote that Garrison's character was too well
recognized to need defense against the "odious" ridicule of such

a term.[1] The anniversary party in January 1860 was the usual festive occasion with oyster soup, duck, and pastries. Women celebrants outnumbered men. Rose was particularly pleased that many young people were present, though the New York *Herald* noted that some women, "hovering on the borders of the realm of fourscore," were dancing as energetically as the young people (quoted in *BI* Feb. 15, 1860). Rose gave a typical speech, asserting, as always, the importance of the rights of humanity "without distinction of sex, country, or color."

Tenth Annual Woman's Rights Convention, New York, May 1860

Although in later decades other women, particularly Susan B. Anthony, Elizabeth Cady Stanton, and Lucy Stone, would become the reformers most often associated with the movement, Ernestine Rose was, in 1860, the winter of her 50th birthday, one of the best known of the woman's rights activists. A letter writer to the New York *Tribune* in February 1860 commented that Rose "is too widely known to need comment" (quoted in *HWS* 1: 677).

The events of the Tenth National Woman's Right Convention foreshadowed the ideological differences that would fragment the movement. The convention was held in the just-completed Cooper Union, which had been constructed to unify the arts and the sciences, the rich and the poor, the immigrant and the native-born. Its grand hall was a spacious and aesthetically pleasing space for woman's rights speakers. The convention reunited Rose with Anthony and Stanton for the first time on a woman's rights platform since the state convention in Albany in 1854, just before Anthony and Rose left for their lecture tour of Washington and Baltimore. Anthony and Rose had appeared on dozens of stages together since February 1854; in fact, in the mid-1850s when Anthony despaired that most of her colleagues were too busy getting married and having babies to travel, she and Rose were the

1. See the Broadside, dated Apr. 20, 1860, "Wendell Phillips in Defence of William Lloyd Garrison," at the AAS.

dependable circuit riders, so to speak, who spread the word of woman's rights across the nation.

Stanton had experienced a different life story in the 1850s. Following her Albany speech in 1854, she became what she herself called a prisoner of "domestic bondage," occasioned by giving birth to four children during the decade of the 1850s and, perhaps, by not finding essential support from either her father or her husband.[2] Stanton's unexpected final two pregnancies in her 40s kept her away from woman's rights activities longer than she had hoped or planned and led to her feeling increasing disappointment and insurrection. She wrote to Anthony in mid-1858: "How rebellious it makes me feel when I see Henry going about where and how he pleases . . . as I contrast his freedom with my bondage, and feel that because of the false position of women, I have been compelled to hold all my noblest aspirations in abeyance in order to be a wife, a mother, a nurse, a cook, a household drudge" (quoted in Griffith 95). The six years leading up to the national convention in 1860 had taxed Stanton's patience. From her position, women's work often meant being a "household drudge"; it was husbands, not wives, who were free to do as they pleased. Marriage, at least as Stanton had lived it during the 1850s, was not an institution designed for women's happiness.

The convention began inauspiciously enough with Martha Wright elected president, Susan B. Anthony on the finance committee, and Rose, along with Stanton, Antoinette Brown Blackwell, William Lloyd Garrison, and Wendell Phillips on the business committee.[3] The conference began with a self-reflexive question: "what is the use of the conventions?" Rose answered with an extemporaneous

2. For a description of Stanton's unhappiness during her six years of relative exile, see Griffith 86–107.

3. For information on this convention see *PWRC, 1860*; the page numbers in the text refer to these *Proceedings*. See also *HWS* 1: 688–737 and the May 15, 1860, *Sibyl* and the *Herald* and *Tribune* for May 10–15, 1860.

speech on "agitation," little knowing at the time that this particular convention would, indeed, agitate many people. The purpose of any convention, said Rose, was to stir up the waters—to agitate and thus make pure: "It is a well known fact, that stagnant atmosphere and stagnant waters can only be purified by agitation" (7). The queen of agitation, according to Rose, was Frances Wright, the first woman "in this country who spoke on the equality of the sexes" (8). Her reward was sure: "the same reward that is always bestowed upon those who are in the vanguard of any great movement. She was subjected to public odium, slander, and persecution" (8). Rose then chronicled her own work beginning in 1837, when she went from house to house gathering a few signatures to allow married women to hold property in their own names. How different from "now," as women had won some property rights in New York in 1848 and had more educational institutions open to them and work available to them. Even popular ministers were speaking out for woman's increased rights. These changes, Rose pointed out, were the results of the cultural work of the conventions.

The dissention began after Elizabeth Cady Stanton gave a speech on the importance of divorce law reform. Arguing that it was the inalienable right of an individual to be happy, Stanton claimed that women (and men) should have the right to divorce. Just as Robert Owen had argued in the 1820s, and Rose had argued at the 1853 woman's rights convention in Cleveland, Stanton declared that marriage was a social contract that could, and should, be broken when it failed to produce or promote human happiness. Stanton concluded that one kind of marriage had never been tried—"a contract between equal parties to live an equal life, with equal restraints and privileges on either side" (72). Such sentiments were old hat to people like Rose who had come to the woman's rights movement from Owenite reform, but the topics of marriage and divorce were not often raised on woman's rights platforms.[4] Rose usually avoided raising the issue of

4. In her biography of Susan B. Anthony, Ida Husted Harper has claimed, incorrectly, that Stanton was the first to ever speak on the subject of marriage and divorce reform (1: 193). Stanton's speech was mild by Owenite standards.

marriage and divorce for tactical reasons: she wanted to focus on inequitable laws before turning to divorce. She also knew from personal experience at the Rutland Free Convention two years earlier what newspapers would write if women talked about marriage or divorce: they would call women who spoke on such matters "freelovers." Men like Robert Owen and Robert Dale Owen might be able to get away with advocating premarriage agreements and less restrictive divorce laws, but women could not. But given Stanton's speech, particularly her rather embittered claim that no one had ever experienced a marriage with equal restraints and equal privileges, Rose felt compelled to defend her ideology *and* her own marriage.

Stanton brought up this divisive topic for a number of possible reasons. Certainly she might have been disposed toward divorce reform for the same personal reason that Robert Owen was inclined to it: being in an unhappy marriage. In Stanton's case, at least according to her accounts in letters written during the 1850s, her domestic life left her frustrated and stifled.[5] But Stanton probably talked about divorce when she did because the New York State Legislature was contemplating making divorce easier to obtain and the topic was in the air. Beginning in March 1860, New Yorkers had been reading the sometimes passionate debate between *Tribune* editor Horace Greeley, who argued against reforming the New York divorce laws, and Robert Dale Owen, who defended his help in reforming Indiana divorce laws some years earlier. Greeley, who argued that although he did support increasing women's rights, offering more grounds for obtaining a divorce would only "invite the sensual and selfish to profane the sanctions of Marriage whenever appetite and temptation may prompt"; Owen contended that increasing the grounds for divorce to include divorce for habitual drunkenness was conducive to public morality (Greeley 605).

For two months the men disputed each other's premises in a series of editorials and letters that New Yorkers followed avidly.

---

5. Stanton also had had an affair with a married man—her brother-in-law—before she had married Henry Stanton, according to Lutz. Perhaps her youthful desire that he could be free also influenced her advocacy of divorce reform.

Greeley, who based his authority in the Scriptures, posited that "the Saviour's" doctrine of marriage was "the chief reason for the moral, intellectual, and even material, supremacy of Europe over Asia" (Greeley 604), and he added, in emotion-filled rhetoric: "I insist that one who truly comprehends the nature and purposes of Marriage will not seek to marry another while the father of her children is still living. I do not think she could look those children in the eye with all a mother's conscious purity and dignity while realizing that their father and her husband, both living, were different men" (Greeley 605). Owen countered by agreeing that it was indeed, a misfortune that a mother should look her children in the eye and think that their father and her husband were different men, but "far greater is the misfortune when she looks upon them with the bitter consciousness that they are daily, hourly, learning to know in their father a sot, a brute, a ruffian, the desecrator of the domestic sanctuary" (Greeley 609).

After hearing Stanton's speech, Antoinette Brown Blackwell responded with great horror, basing her rebuttal on the sacredness of marriage vows from a biblical perspective. Rose quickly defended Stanton's speech; it was, after all, Rose's own argument, one she had believed in for more than two decades and had delivered forcefully in Cleveland in the early 1850s. Responding to Blackwell with her usual asperity, Rose quipped that Reverend Blackwell "treats women as some ethereal being" when she suggests that marriage "is a union of equals." Rose adds, "it is very well to be ethereal to some extent, but I tell you, my friends, it is quite requisite to be a little material, also. At all events, we are so, and being so, it proves a law of our nature" (81). Women, *not* being equal with men, must be able to remove themselves from a marriage "when the husband hold the iron heel of legal oppression on the subjugated neck of the wife until every spark of womanhood is crushed out" (82).

Once Stanton had brought up the subject, Rose did not shirk her duty to tell the truth as she perceived it. First, she notes that merely talking about divorce would cause critics to label her a "Free Lover," which she was not. Rose explains that she asked for reformed divorce laws to "prevent" free love, because "too often" adulterous love was carried on because the parties were badly married. Free love, she notes, acknowledges no marriage and thus requires no divorce. She, a believer in "true marriages," asks for a law to "free men and women from false ones" (84). Given that marriage is but a human institution, she wonders why such an institution has to be binding for life. Rose points out that if one removed the impossibility of dissolving marriages there might well be fewer separations: "We are a good deal the creatures of habit, but we will not be forced. We live (I speak from experience) in uncomfortable houses for years rather than move, though we have the privilege to do so every year; but force any one to live for life in one house, and he would run away from it, though it were a palace" (84).

Rose, then, in responding to Antoinette Brown Blackwell also responds to Horace Greeley's question that she had read in the *Tribune*: "How could the mother look the child in the face, if she married a second time?" Rose gives a slightly different answer than Robert Dale Owen did:

> with infinitely better grace and better conscience than to live as some do now, and show their children the degrading example, how utterly father and mother despise and hate each other, and still live together as husband and wife. She could say to her child 'As, unfortunately, your father proved himself unworthy, your mother could not be so unworthy as to continue to live with him. As he failed to be a true father to you, I have endeavored to supply his place with one, who, though not entitled to the name, will, I hope, prove himself one in the performance of a father's duties.' (84)

Rose concludes her impromptu rebuttal of Blackwell's arguments and support of her own and Stanton's by saying that with good educations, women could promote their own independence and not be obliged to marry for a home and subsistence. "Give the wife an equal right with the husband in the property acquired after marriage, and it will be a bond of union between them . . . a gold band is more efficacious than an iron law. . . . A union of interest helps to preserve a union of hearts" (84). Rose, thus, used the occasion to promote her political agenda of equal rights for women. In doing so, she also tried to close the political pandora's box that Stanton had opened.[6]

Phillips, speaking immediately after Rose, moved to table the discussion because the topic of marriage and divorce was "inappropriate" for the woman's rights conventions. The appropriate topics for such convention, for Phillips and for others such as Lucy Stone—who, according to Andrea Kerr, probably did not attend the convention because she knew that Stanton was going to bring up the divisive topic of divorce—were the laws that discriminated against women. Even Rose had consciously decided not to speak about divorce on a woman's rights platform since the Cleveland convention because she wanted to focus on correcting inequitable laws first, but once the subject was brought up, she alone felt compelled to defend Stanton's speech.

Although Rose did not succeed in preventing divorce from becoming a divisive issue, her oratorical ability at this convention, as at others, received considerable praise. One person in the audience wrote that he had heard Ernestine Rose for the first time and, unlike the weary, biblically based speech before hers, Rose's address was given with "a good delivery, a forcible voice, the most

6. Stanton had thought about divorce reform before; from the early 1850s she and other women on temperance stages talked about adding "habitual drunkenness" to grounds for divorce in New York State. In 1856 she sent a letter to the national convention attacking current marriage practices. In her letter, Stanton foreshadows her 1860 talk by writing that marriage, "as we now have it," is "opposed to all God's laws" (*PWRC, 1856* 89). Although marriage was intended by God for the greater freedom and happiness of both parties, it was not, Stanton added, as currently constructed, an equal partnership; women lost "everything" (89). Having no identity, a married women either shines in her husband's reflection or hides in his shadow. She is nameless—she is "Mrs. John or James, Peter or Paul, just as she changes masters; like the southern slave, she takes the name of her owner" (89). Though many people might consider taking a husband's name a "small matter," Stanton writes that it is "the symbol of the most cursed monopoly by man of all the rights, the life, liberty, and happiness of one half of the human family—all womankind" (89).

uncommon good sense, a delightful terseness of style, and a rare talent for humor . . . in about two minutes she managed to infect her two-thousand-fold audience with a spirit of interest—an audience which mere dry morals and reason had succeeded in reducing to the comatose state" (*BI* May 30, 1860).

Commenting on the convention, Horace Greeley had nothing good to say. Writing in the March 14, 1860, *Tribune* that from now on the annual conventions should be called "Wives Discontented," Greeley argued that Mrs. Stanton's notions of divorce reform, would "destroy the family" because the possibility of divorce "contemplates no married life at all, and no parental relation." Greeley's position, not Rose's or Stanton's or Robert Dale Owen's, was to become the one the New York Legislature agreed with when it eventually voted against divorce reform.

The 1860 convention highlighted more than anything else the different political strategies and beliefs of the participants in the woman's rights movement in dramatic ways. Some of the activist women, writing to each other following the convention, acknowledged that raising the "divorce" issue had injured the movement. Martha Wright wrote to Anthony that "it seems to me our present position is precisely that of the hated Garrisonians," who had "insisted on tormenting people" about issues before the people were ready to hear about them, thus frightening timid people "from our glorious platform" (July 17, 1860, GFP).

Although many believed that Rose herself was detrimental to the woman's movement and had frightened people from the platform because of her atheism, Rose had been careful to avoid talking about religion on the woman's rights stages, saving her freethought comments primarily for Infidel and Owenite conventions and for the pages of the *Boston Investigator*. She had avoided controversial topics like divorce for the same reasons. Stanton's advocacy of divorce reform caused a rift among believers in the woman's rights cause. It pitted Rose and Stanton and Anthony against most of the rest of the women and men in the movement. Just as Frances Wright had doomed her reform attempts in the mid-1820s when she lost the support of her mainstream male supporters by advocating miscegenation and suggesting that sexual pleasure should be possible for women as well as men, so too did the women fighting for increased woman's rights lose momentum when their ranks began to splinter on the issue of divorce.

Final Meetings Before the Civil War

The late summer of 1860 through the winter of 1861 found Rose immersed in freethinking causes and the final woman's rights meetings in New York State before they were interrupted by the Civil War. She wrote long letters to the *Boston Investigator* carefully taking apart arguments in favor of Spiritualism and Christianity. When vacationing in August on Long Island Flats, where she had gone for "a change," Rose was approached by several men asking her to speak to children and then to a larger adult group. A local minister, horrified that "*such* a woman" would be speaking to his parishioners, stirred up considerable interest in Rose and increased her audience. Rose relates that she had been innocently unaware of the shock church people had received "from the very thought of my speaking" (*BI* Aug. 29, 1860). Once at the hall, she was agreeably surprised to find a large audience of women and some men. She was "proud" of the courage shown by the women to come to her talk, saying "when woman is once roused, she has always more moral courage than man." Although she had planned to speak only on education, Rose added comments on how religion was "manufactured." One man, a deacon in the church, was so distressed at Rose's talk he urged his wife and sister to leave, but Rose writes that "the disobedient daughters of Eve refused!" The talk caused "quite a little stir" and gave the people of Long Island something else to think and talk about "besides prayer meetings and potatoes" (*BI* Aug. 29, 1860).

In early October Rose was the first vice president and served on the business committee at the Infidel Convention at 446 Broadway. The convention was close to the Roses' new rooms at 95 Prince Street, where they had moved in late 1859 and remained until the mid-1860s. The New York *Herald* accused Rose of "another of her characteristic speeches, teeming with blasphemy and profanity" (quoted in the Nov. 7, 1860 *BI*). Rose quickly responded to the *Herald* and sent a copy of her letter to the *Boston Investigator*, saying that she did, indeed, test the consistency of the biblical account of the creation and if that was blasphemy, so be it. She added that the only profanity she was guilty of was quoting a few passages of Scriptures so if she was profane, the Scriptures and "not I ought to be responsible" (*BI* Nov. 7, 1860).

In early February 1861 Rose spoke at the final New York State woman's rights convention before the Civil War induced the women to cancel their conventions for the duration of the war. This Albany convention coincided with the liberalized divorce bill then pending before the Judiciary Committee of the New York State Legislature. Since the previous May, when Stanton created such a furor by advocating liberalized divorce laws, the Stanton/Anthony/ Rose triad had managed to gain the support of Lucretia Mott, who, though she had cautioned Stanton and Rose to "be as moderate as possible" on the subject of divorce (Bacon, *Valiant Friend* 177), nonetheless argued that "before woman can have any justice by the laws of England, there must be a total reconstruction of the whole system. . . . So Elizabeth Stanton will see that I have authority for going to the root of the evil" (quoted in *HWS* 1: 746).

In Albany, in addition to testifying before the House, Rose took part in back-to-back conventions—an antislavery convention, February 4–5, and a woman's rights convention that followed it. The antislavery convention was marked by threats of violence that began when the mayor of Albany, George Thatcher, received an anonymous letter telling him to prevent the upcoming antislavery meeting because of possible "disorderly demonstrations" (Albany *Evening Journal* Feb. 2, 1861). The mayor refused, explaining that when he took office he promised to uphold the Constitution, which prohibited Congress from passing any law abridging the freedom of speech.[7]

7. For information about the conventions, see the Albany *Evening Journal* for Feb. 2, 6, and 9, 1861; see also Rose's Feb. 21, 1861, letter to the *Investigator* and reprinted in the Mar. 22, 1861, *Liberator*.

From the beginning the convention was in confusion. Speakers were hissed and not allowed to speak. Stanton was treated with hostility when she talked about the Garrisonians as "pure and worthy people, engaged in a holy crusade against a monstrous and gigantic inequity" (*Liberator* Feb. 15, 1861). When Rose spoke the second day of the convention in a way that attendees perceived as strongly condemning the South, she practically brought down the house, but not with applause. Despite the northern location, many people in the audience were strong supporters of states' rights and of national unity at any cost. To a predominantly Democratic crowd Rose declared herself a Democrat, but a Democrat who had helped Lincoln be elected because she considered antislavery principles to be the true basis of democracy. Calling the crowd favorite, former President James Buchanan, a "miserable coward" for the compromises he had made, she prophesied that Mr. Seward would never be elected president if he were in favor of compromising with the South.[8] Interrupted by someone who claimed that because he had contributed when the hat was passed around he had the perfect right to demonstrate disapproval, Rose shot back that the convention "had every right to hold its meetings without interference." Rose explained that a boarder in a hotel "might as well take it upon himself to disturb the whole house, because he paid his $2.50 a day for board, as for one of the audience to undertake to interfere in a meeting of this kind" (*Liberator* Feb. 15, 1861).

That night, after the speeches were over, Rose wrote in a letter that leaving the building in the evening, "all Bedlam was let loose," and were it not for the . . . mayor and 60 policemen who escorted us home, the "mob demon would have done his work" (*BI* Feb. 21, 1861). The editors of the Albany *Evening Journal* agreed with Rose on the potential for violence, pointing out that "the mob amused themselves by hissing and hooting the colored men and

---

8. William Seward of New York had been the front-runner at the Republican convention in 1860 but conservatives feared he was too liberal concerning slavery and liberals feared his moral principles; thus, Lincoln, a compromise candidate, was nominated instead.

women as they passed out. And but for the continued presence and interposition of the Police, violence might have manifested itself" (Feb. 6, 1861).

Although the Mayor and many of the convention goers may have agreed with Rose on the importance of free speech, their response to the antislavery meeting and the woman's rights meeting that followed it is illustrative. As the editors of the Albany *Journal* wrote on February 5, "we had hoped for a different re-sult—that they [the antislavery and woman's rights speakers] would be permitted to come and go unheralded and unnoticed; for such a reception is the only thing they fear." Indeed, the Albany *Journal*, though it did report the events surrounding the antislavery meeting, never printed a word about the following woman's rights meeting. The negative attitudes of the local press and local attend-ees were only exacerbated by the fact that it was women speaking on the hated topics, women like Rose, who criticized their hero Buchanan. The editors of the Albany *Journal* wrote, tellingly, that "there was not, among all those who either hissed or stamped, one [who] would strike a woman—except when irritated—even though she were an abolition lecturer" (Feb. 5, 1861). The news-paper editors concluded that they hoped the abolitionist and woman's rights speakers "might be let alone—to pour out their vials of ultraism and vituperation to empty benches" (Feb. 6, 1861). It was a hope that was shared by many in the mainstream culture, in the North as well as in the South.

After the insults of the Albany meeting, Rose had a brief respite when she and Lucretia Mott visited Martha Wright at Wright's home in nearby Auburn, New York. Wright enjoyed the visit, happily getting up at 5:30 A.M. the morning Rose and Mott were leaving to fix them breakfast before their long train trip back to New York. (Wright to Ellen Garrison, Feb. 10, 1861, GFP).

A decade of morale-building and information-disseminating con-ventions ended with the attack on Fort Sumter on April 12, 1861. The all-consuming presence of the Civil War prevented the women from holding another national woman's rights convention for five years. For numerous reasons many of the primary reformers turned "politic," arguing that they could have no conventions during "the crisis." Martha Wright, for example, felt it "unwise at this time, when the Nation's whole heart and soul are engrossed with this momentous crisis," to hold a convention because "it is useless to speak if nobody will listen—and everybody now is absorbed in watching the course of our politicians, [and] calculating the effect of every action on the future of the nation . . . how then is it possible to think of a Convention?" (Wright to Anthony, Mar. 31, 1862, GFP). Though Rose and Anthony believed such cessation was ill conceived, they were in the minority. Anthony wrote to Lydia Mott that Garrison, Wendell Phillips, Lucretia Mott, Martha Wright, and even Elizabeth Cady Stanton argued to "wait until the war excitement abates. . . . I am sick at heart, but I can not carry the world against the wish and the will of our best friends" (quoted in *HWS* 1: 748–49).

During this lull in activity, the New York Legislature quietly repealed several of the reform laws that had improved rights for women. Specifically, they repealed the law that allowed a mother a right to equal guardianship of her children with the father, replacing that liberal and significant change with veto power, which could keep a father from binding out or willing away a child without the mother's consent. Such behind-the-scenes activities substantiated the need for women to have voting rights. It also illustrated just how effective the woman's rights conventions had been at rousing public opinion and compelling legislators to enact laws that treated married women more fairly. Without the "agitation" of the conventions, the legislators felt they could do whatever they wished with impunity. One can only speculate how much more quickly American women would have received the franchise had the Civil War not slowed the momentum achieved by the yearly conventions.

Rose's Continued Activity

Despite the lack of national and regional woman's rights meetings for five years, Ernestine Rose, opposed to waiting out the Civil War, did not cease her activities. She turned to freethinking causes, possibly because there was less pressure on freethinkers to be "patriotic" than on the women of the woman's rights movement to appear self-sacrificing and devoted to their country. Rose continued lecturing throughout the winter and spring of 1861, speaking in New Jersey, in New York City, in Boston, and in various Massachusetts towns.

As always, the Roses helped organize the annual Paine Celebration in New York City in January 1861. The people who attended saw a portrait of Paine suspended in front of the hall and on either side of it were the portraits of Voltaire, Abner Kneeland, Robert Owen, and Frances Wright. After dancing, the party adjourned to the banquet hall where William Rose supervised the light supper. Ernestine gave her usual speech, though the subject was not Paine, per se, but the events that were stirring the nation. Rose argued that freedom and slavery could not live in harmony, that slavery must eventually destroy freedom. Rose urged the North to compromise no longer—no more Fugitive Slave Acts or Missouri Compromises. The danger, as she saw it, was not that the South might secede from the North but that the North might secede from the "self evident truth of man's right to life, liberty, and the pursuit of happiness. Let that danger only be averted, and all will be well" (*BI* Feb. 20, 1861).

While on a lecture tour of Boston and surrounding towns, Rose gave a major lecture entitled "A Defense of Atheism," in Mercantile Hall in Boston on April 10, 1861, two days before the attack on Fort Sumter. Today, the speech, reprinted several times as a broadside, is Rose's most frequently found extant speech in libraries across the United States.[9] It is particularly well written, full of the freethought issues important to Rose throughout the 1850s and early 1860s.

Rose begins her talk simply, saying she is undertaking to inquire into the existence of a God, an inquiry she knows is fraught with difficulty. Using a style of argument similar to Thomas Paine's

---

9. The essay was first published in the May 8, 1861, *Boston Investigator*. It was then published separately by J. P. Mendum in 1889. Page numbers in the text refer to the separately published essay.

in *The Age of Reason*, she finds no record of a God's existence in the world of matter, only in the mind of man. That mind, she continues, has made God in his own image—"according to man's knowledge, his experience, his taste, his refinement, his sense of right, of justice, of freedom, and humanity,—so he made his God" (6). Rose then turns to the so-called word of God, the Bible, and asks whether it can withstand the test of reason and truth. God, we are told, is omnipotent, omniscient, omnipresent. This ever-present, all-seeing, all-powerful God created men and women "in his image" and a paradise garden for them to live in; yet, after the serpent successfully tempted Eve and she, in turn, tempted her husband, they were expelled from paradise. Rose asks:

> Did not God know when he created the Serpent, that it would tempt the woman, and that SHE was made out of such frail materials (the rib of Adam) as not to be able to resist the temptation? If he did not know, then his knowledge was at fault; if he did, but could not prevent that calamity, then his power was at fault; if he knew and could, but would not, then his goodness was at fault. Choose which you please, and it remains alike fatal to the rest. (10)

Thus, the Bible tells us, says Rose, that God made man perfect, but found him imperfect; he—and Rose specifically used a lower-case "he" when referring to God—pronounced all things good, and found them bad. Even after he tried to clean up his act and destroyed the entire world save Noah, his family, and a few household pets, the world was still "not one jot better after the flood than before. His chosen children were just as bad as ever, and he had to send his prophets, again and again, to threaten, to frighten, to coax, to cajole, and to flatter them into good behaviour" (11).

In fact, Rose continues, the world is still full of ignorance, vice, poverty, sin, and crime. Why does God permit these horrors? Does omniscience not know all? Is omnipotence not all-powerful? Would infinite wisdom allow children to suffer? To a believer's response that God saves children "hereafter," Rose responds by saying "what a mockery": "If a rich parent were to let his children live in ignorance, poverty, and wretchedness, all their lives, and hold out to them the promise of a fortune some time hereafter, he would justly be considered a criminal, or a madman" (12). The testimony of the Bible has, thus, "failed." The account of the creation is disproved by science; God can be neither all-seeing nor all-powerful, given the evidence. Similarly, the "evidence" that believers use to prove God's existence is simply the result of humans mistaking effects for causes. For specifics, Rose cites the Methodist minister who proved the wisdom of God "in always placing the rivers near large cities" (17).

Rose then refutes some common notions about religion. To the idea that religion is "natural" Rose responds that if it were natural, we would not have to teach it: "We don't have to teach the general elements of human nature—the five senses, seeing hearing, smelling, tasting, and feeling" (19). To the idea that, without religion, man would become a monster, living in a cha-otic, confused world, Rose says, nonsense. In a world without religion, the seasons would still follow each other, the stars would still shine just as brightly and man's nature would remain just the same: "his affections would be just as warm, the love of self-preservation just as strong, the desire for happiness and the fear of pain as great" (20). "Morality," Rose adds, does not depend upon belief in any religion, as she refers to the "present crisis" brought on by slavery that was sanctioned by religion.

Rose ends her talk in an upbeat, humanistic way. "Though I cannot believe in your God," she says, she does "believe in man. . . . I have faith, unbounded, unshaken faith in the principles of right, of justice, and humanity" (24). She says: "whatever good you would do out of fear of punishment, or hope of reward hereafter, the atheist would do simply because it is good" (24). Doing good, for the sake of doing it, concludes Rose, constitutes pleasure and promotes happiness.

The speech that would be one of her most famous received little attention in the spring of 1861, probably both because of its subject matter and its timing. The *Boston Investigator*, ever the faithful reporter of Rose's activities and ever her supporter, wrote that the talk "afforded much satisfaction" and showed her reason-ing to be "very able, logical, and ingenious," arguing that Rose "could not have been successfully refuted by any theologian in the land" (*BI* Apr. 17, 1861). When he printed the lecture in early April, Horace Seaver wrote that this lecture "is about the best she has ever given, and they have all been good. From first to last, it is marked by a train of argument which is at once thorough and conclusive, and the impression left by the reading is, that she is a woman of uncommon moral courage and a remarkably logical and penetrating mind" (*BI* May 8, 1861). Similarly, Rose received a positive review in Garrison's *Liberator* from a Christian attendee of her lecture. G.W.S. of Milford, Massachusetts, wrote to Garrison that "last Sabbath evening, I listend [sic] to a lecture from the gifted and intellectual mind of Mrs. Rose." The lecture hall was crowded with an audience that gave Rose a "respectful and patient hearing." The letter writer hypothesized that at least part of the cause of Rose's notoriety came from a slanderous essay that had appeared in the *Milford Journal* charging Rose with being an advocate of "free love," an accusation based on false interpretations of the Rutland Convention. G.W.S. finds it painful to acknowledge that Rose is an atheist but understands that her objection to Christianity is founded upon what he or she calls "pseudo Christianity, which talks so much about glorifying God in the *abstract*, and leaving his children to suffer and die." The letter writer believes that Christianity, "shorn of its false and heartless appendage," was in Rose's heart, because true Christianity meant worshiping and serving God by blessing our suffering brother—which is what G.W.S. saw Rose doing in her lecture (*Liberator* Apr. 10, 1861).

In 1862, discouraged by the continuation of a war that was supposed to end quickly and decisively, Rose nevertheless continued her freethinking activities. At the Paine Celebration in January 1862, Rose used the occasion to talk about the desolating effect of a civil war, a war that was instigated by people who wanted to "trample the immortal declaration of human equality under foot" (*BI* Feb. 5, 1862). She likened Paine's projections of "when the Empire of America shall fall" with current, pessimistic feelings brought on by the war that newspapers had all predicted would be over in a matter of months. Rose notes that what Paine had deplored was not the possibility that Fifth Avenue palaces or State Street mansions might be destroyed, but that man's right to life, liberty, and the pursuit of happiness might fall. Rose urged her fellow infidels to remember that the first of rights is the right of man to himself.

In May 1862 Rose went to Boston and spoke both at the Infidel Convention, which had been postponed from the fall of 1861 until the end of May 1862, and to the New England Anti-Slavery Society. Her speeches were dramatically different, reflecting how well she knew her audiences. At the Infidel Convention, Rose urged her audience to remember that the primary cause of slavery was religion. In accordance, she introduced a resolution that read: "Resolved, That it is the bounden duty of every lover of freedom and justice to discard the irresponsible power which has enslaved the human mind,—and to aid in emancipating the slaves wherever found, and of whatever color" (*BI* June 4, 1862). To the Anti-Slavery Society, however, she talked about how Lincoln had not yet gone far enough—all slaves needed to be emancipated. She averred that Lincoln and Congress needed to be pushed: "if the President cannot move without pushing, push him on. I stand here to push you on." Even Wendell Phillips, who feared that Rose's atheism detracted from the antislavery and woman's rights planks, followed her speech by saying that he was much pleased with what she had to say; he could assent to almost every word of it (*Liberator* June 6, 1862).

Woman's National Loyal League, 1863–64

By the spring of 1863 the women's rights advocates had organized themselves into a "Woman's National Loyal League," ostensibly to gather a petition to urge the emancipation of the slaves, but perhaps also to unify themselves once again. Led by Elizabeth Cady Stanton, who had moved with her family to New York City, and Susan B. Anthony, who kept an office for the League in room 20 of the Cooper Union, the National Loyal League had its first national convention in May 1863. The New York newspapers loved this woman's group because the women "wisely" limited themselves to promoting national loyalty and encouraging freedom for all slaves. The New York *Tribune* wrote "Let all loyal women . . . join their ranks, and devote what spare time they may have to this noble work." The New York *Times* deemed the women "prudent" and doing a great amount of good (as quoted in *HWS* 2: 894).

The women's choice of a name—the "National Loyal League"—was a clever one, as it played right into the way men wanted to think about women. A great number of "loyal" leagues made up of women had sprung up during the early 1860s, often to send packages of blankets, quilts, socks, pillows, and slippers to the Sanitary Commission. The woman's rights activists latched onto a useful and nonthreatening term when they chose "loyal league." The name signified that they were first, and most important, "loyal" to the unity of the nation, and second, loyally part of a group of women who acted as auxiliaries to perform necessary work. But just what the purpose of the group was became a source of conflict at this first national convention among participants with differing agendas. The very term "loyal league" drew to the meeting women who were interested, not in women's rights, but in promoting loyalty to the nation.

The May 14 convention began in the Church of the Puritans at Union Square and later that night moved to the Cooper Union.[10] Many of the women who had attended the 1860 national woman's rights convention were there, in addition to some new faces. Lucy Stone was president and Stanton was a vice president; both Anthony and Rose were on the business committee, along with Antoinette Brown Blackwell and Amy Post. The women approved Lincoln's proclamation, which gave freedom to the slaves in the seceded states, but they urged the president to emancipate all slaves. They also resolved that "all citizens of African descent and all women are placed at the mercy of a legislation in which they are not

10. For information on the meeting see the *Proceedings of the Meeting of the Loyal Woman of the Republic in New York, May 14, 1863*; page numbers in the text refer to these *Proceedings*. See also *HWS* 2: 53–78; the June 1863 *Sibyl* and the May 14, 1863, *Herald*, *Times*, and *Tribune*.

represented. There can never be a true peace in this Republic until the civil and political equality of every subject of the government shall be practically established" (15). This resolution, the only one linking women's rights to African American men's rights, was the only one not to pass unanimously.

This simple resolution, innocent-sounding to twentieth-century ears, created considerable dissention at the meeting. Its debate and passage illuminate how this meeting, rather than joining the women together, instead highlighted their differences and fore-shadowed the split that was to come in 1869. After letters were read, after Stanton had spoken on how "the Northern neck must never bow again to the yoke of slavery" (7), after Angelina Grimké Weld had revealed that southerners really believed that slavery was a "divine institution" (13), after the Hutchinson family had sung "the Contraband Song," the women argued over whether to endorse the resolution that asked for equality of every subject of the government. One speaker, Mrs. Hoyt from Wisconsin, argued that "anything which could in the least prejudice the interest in this cause [establishing a national "loyal" league] which is so dear to us all" should be eliminated. Another speaker, Sarah Halleck of New York, agreed and said that supporters of the resolution should "give way" because "the negroes have suffered more than the women, and the women, perhaps, can afford to give them the preference" (21).

Ernestine Rose quickly challenged Halleck's logic by stating clearly and succinctly: "I, for one, object to throw women out of the race for freedom." Encouraged by applause, Rose continued:

> And do you know why? Because she needs freedom for the freedom of man. (Applause) Our ancestors made a great mistake in not recognizing woman in the rights of man. It has been justly stated that the negro at present suffers more than woman, but it can do him no injury to place woman in the same cat-egory with him. I, for one, object to having that term stricken out, for it can have no possible bearing against anything that we want to promote; we desire to promote human rights and hu-man freedom. . . . In that resolution it simply states a fact, that in a republic based upon freedom, woman, as well as the negro,

should be recognized as an equal with the whole human race. (21–22)

Rose's point—that it could do black men no harm to "place woman in the same category with him"—was one that she argued from before the war until long after the war was over. From Rose's idealistic (and, as always, uncompromising) perspective, the logic of her position was quite clear: universal suffrage was simply the moral and logical imperative.

At the 1863 Loyal League meeting, the core of women who had joined each other at the yearly conventions in the 1850s sided with Rose. But many of the newcomers to the meeting—"loyal leaguers" as opposed to "ultra" woman's rights advocates—sided with Mrs. Halleck, being more concerned about establishing a national Loyal League than in pressing for woman's rights. As Mrs. Hoyt from Wisconsin said in her first public speech, in the West there was a "very strong objection to Woman's Rights." Fearing that the convention was in the hands of the "woman's rights ladies," Hoyt added that she was sorry to see it because "I know women from our State . . . who will take no part if these ideas prevail" (26). To Hoyt, the Woman's Loyal League needed to do three things: encourage people to retrench their household expenses, strengthen the loyal sentiments of people at home while instilling a deeper love of the flag, and finally, write soldiers in the field to help them keep their spirits up. Such a version of a Loyal League—loyalty to flag, letter writing to boost morale—was not what Rose and the other women had been working for. It is little wonder that the convention proceedings reflect a deep ideological split in the participants. It is also little wonder that Rose, though she lived within walking distance of Anthony's Loyal League office in Cooper Union, took part in few Loyal League activities. To Hoyt's point, Rose responded: "It is exceedingly amusing to hear persons talk about throwing out Woman's Rights, when, if it had not been for Woman's Rights, that lady would not have had the courage to stand here and say what she did" (27). Rose implores the women not to "wrangle" simply because "we associate the name of woman with human justice and human rights." Even though she admits to liking opposition on any subject because it elicits truth better than any single speech, Rose prods the women to accept the debated resolution, arguing that it would be "exceedingly inconsistent," to throw out the resolution because "some women out in the West are opposed to the Woman's Rights movement—though at the same time they take advantage of it" (28).

In the evening session, held at the Cooper Union, Rose's major speech to the group explained what "loyalty" meant. Unlike women such as Mrs. Hoyt, who wanted women to support the northern "cause" as symbolized by the flag, and Mrs. Halleck, who wanted to give black men suffrage before women, Rose criticizes Lincoln for prolonging the war by retaining McClellan, an inept commander, and for not freeing the slaves of the border states. Despite the fact the Lincoln had issued a proclamation emancipating all the slaves of the rebel South, Rose accurately tells her audience that none of the slaves in the border states were freed and the slaves in the South were not yet free. She likens the southern slaves' not being free despite the proclamation to a story she had once heard:

> A gentleman once found himself of a sudden, without, so far as he knew, any cause, taken into prison. He sent for his lawyer, and told him, "They have taken me to prison." "What have you done?" said the lawyer. "I have done nothing," he replied. "Then, my friend, they can not put you in prison if you have done nothing." "But I am in prison." "Well that may be; but I tell you, my dear friend, they can not put you in prison." "Well," said he, "I want you to come and take me out, for I tell you, in spite of all your lawyer logic, I am in prison, and I shall be until you take me out." (43)

As Rose is saying, the slaves are still in slavery, Emancipation Proclamation or not, and she urges the women in the audience to goad northerners, no matter how much they wanted the war ended, not to compromise. One single seed of slavery, argues Rose, stifles freedom.

Not sympathetic to abstract outpourings of "loyalty," Rose asks her audience what they are "loyal" to? She explains that she is not loyal to the administration in a blind way; she is only loyal to justice and humanity. She also cautions the women not to give their loyalty "unconditionally" to the administration: "We women need not be [loyal] for the law has never yet recognized us" (44). Rose concludes by saying that "we must work. And our work must mainly be to watch, and criticize, and urge the Administration to do its whole duty to freedom and humanity" (48). History would prove that Rose's caution was prescient; unquestioning loyalty to their country did not help women achieve their rights. At the turn of the century, Susan B. Anthony would look back at the Woman's Loyal League meetings and recollect that the women had hoped that when slavery was out of the way, men would be able to see the great wrong done to women and would remedy it. But nothing of the kind happened.[11]

The women came together again the following year for an "anniversary" meeting of the Loyal Women of the Republic held again at the Church of the Puritans in New York City, on May 12, 1864. Elizabeth Cady Stanton was the president; Rose gave a "soul-searching" speech.[12] In the intervening year, the number of women in the "Loyal League" had grown to over five thousand. They had gathered over two hundred thousand signatures on their petition to abolish slavery, but the number was not close to the

11. See Susan B. Anthony's handwritten notes in the Library of Congress's copy #1 of *Reports of Woman's Rights Conventions* where she wrote, "the annual conventions were abandoned in 1861–62, 62, 64, 65 on account of the war—a very poor reason. But we had the Women's Loyal League in New York—and called up a petition to Congress of 265,000 names—for the *black* men . . . thinking—when slavery was out of the way—men would be able to see the great wrong to women of the nation—they would see the degradation of disfranchisement." Anthony dated her note Jan. 11, 1907.

12. Information on Rose's speech comes from Harper 1: 237–38. For information about the "anniversary" meeting see *HWS* 2: 87. See also the brief article on the meeting in the May 13, 1864, *Tribune*. There is no extant copy of Rose's speech and only one brief clipping about the meeting in Anthony's Scrapbook, Vol. 1.

one million they had hoped for. They discovered that many people had refused to sign because they believed slavery to be a "divine institution" or because they denied the right of Congress to interfere with states' rights.

The work for this convention was, according to its call published in the May 6, 1864, *Liberator*, to educate thirty million people about the idea of a true republic. Because the war had "thrown on woman new responsibilities, and awakened in her new powers and aspirations," women needed to develop a "deeper and higher range of thought and action than has of late been realized" (*Liberator* May 6, 1864). The women's resolutions were much more moderate this year; they asked only for the right to vote for black men (*HWS* 2: 85). Instead of giving much coverage to the Loyal League, newspapers in New York covered the following week's "anti-silk" dress movement more extensively. This was a meeting at Cooper Union where women were asked to sign a pledge to make sacrifices for the war effort. Speakers like Susan B. Anthony urged women to give up luxuries, like silk, for the duration of the war (*Herald* May 17, 1864).

The Seaver/Rose Conflict, 1864

During this year of inactivity for woman's rights issues, Rose had a quite public debate in the winter and spring of 1864 with Horace Seaver, the editor of the *Boston Investigator*. The disagreement began when Rose responded in print to what the *Investigator* had recently published about Jewish people: that "even the modern Jews are bigoted, narrow, exclusive, and totally unfit for progressive people like the Americans among whom we hope they may not spread" (*BI* Feb. 10, 1864). Outraged that such bigotry would appear in the freethinking *Investigator*, published and edited by her close friends, Rose accused the *Boston Investigator* of "too much of the Puritan spirit that whipped and hung the Quaker women." Rose asked if "you would drive [the Jews] out of Boston—out of 'progressive America' as they were driven out of Spain?" (*BI* Feb. 10, 1864).

Rose crafted a long essay on "The Jews" to enlighten Seaver and his readers on Jewish beliefs and practices. She insists that a

Jewish person is governed by the same laws of human nature as anyone else. In Europe, in spite of barbarous treatment and deadly persecution, Jewish people have lived and spread and outlived much of the prejudice against them, and Europe has been "none the worse on their account." Jewish people are sober, industrious, good citizens and do not hunt after proselytes. As bad as believing in one God is, at least the Jewish people believe in only one God, without promises, threats, and potential rewards for the future. Christians, Rose points out, believe in three Gods (Father, Son, and Holy Ghost) along with damnation, "the crucified Savior, the blood of the Lamb, the Devil, and the rest of the faternity [sic]" (*BI* Feb. 10, 1864).

The series of letters—nine from Rose and nine responses from Seaver—grew increasingly acrimonious. First they argue as to the "barbarity" of Jewish circumcision. Rose contends that the best that could be said on the subject is that it is "ridiculous" and no more barbarous than piercing girls' ears. Rose reveals that she was "a victim" of ear piercing, that "irrational practice," and she knew great pain and suffering to follow for months (*BI* Feb. 17, 1864). Seaver responds that circumcision is more of a barbarity than pierced ears, especially since Christians do not make pierced ears a religious obligation as the Jewish do with circumcision. Their arguments increase in intensity, with Seaver defending Universalists as believers of a liberal religion and damning ancient Jews as "completely vile, worthless, miserable, contemptible and abominable" (*BI* Feb. 24, 1864). To Rose, the Universalists still believed in the Bible and the Bible's God, so how could they be a better people than the ancient Jews? The ancient Jews, at least, constructed a god long ago ("before the discovery of steam—the invention of the printing press . . . before the *Boston Investigator* existed") and thus were more to be excused for the "rude and barbarous God they made" than the Universalists in the nineteenth century, with all their current privileges, "who still accept Him" (*BI* Feb. 24, 1864). Angry that Seaver continued to damn the ancient Jews, Rose urges him to talk about "modern Jews" unless he knows nothing about them; Seaver responds that Jews not only believed in Moses, Joshua, and David, but that they also believed in a Devil in chief and also in minor devils (*BI* Mar. 9, 1864).

As the tone of both Rose's and Seaver's letters becomes more caustic, Rose loses her usual sense of humor and accuses Seaver of being "uncandid, silly . . . making false insinuations and [raising] false issues" (*BI* Apr. 13, 1864). She calls him "mean and cowardly" because, after being unjust to the Jews, "you now must be unjust to those who defend them" (*BI* Mar. 9, 1864). To Seaver, Rose becomes "tenacious" and a "scold" who keeps repeating herself. Rather peevishly Seaver says "when we follow her example and intimate in the same jocular manner that perhaps she may be thinking of turning Jew, she gives us such a scolding as we have no recollection of ever receiving from any man, and we know we never did from any woman" (*BI* Mar. 9, 1864).

Convinced that Seaver does not know what he is talking about, Rose tells him so in the following week's installment: "whatever you may know of the ancient [Jew], you evidently know nothing of the modern Jews, and don't accuse me of going to the moon or to some other wonderful thing simply because I don't like your prejudice against the Jews, nor against any other people; and above all, keep your temper in an argument" (*BI* Mar. 16, 1864). Not to be outdone, Seaver responds that it is "amusing" to be told to "keep our temper" when the one giving the advice shows "by her abusive personalities [sic] that she can scold bravely, if she cannot use convincing arguments." Arguing that he bases his beliefs of modern Jews in "facts"—from reading Jewish books and personal acquaintances with Jews—Seaver refuses to "allow Mrs. Rose or any one else to scold us out of a certain, positive, unmistakable truth . . . [that Jews are] ignorant, bigoted, and antiprogressive." Seaver adds he has no prejudice against Jews as human beings, but as a sect of religionists he hopes "never to see them increasing in the United States" (*BI* Mar. 16, 1864). Yet, this very comment reveals Seaver's intense (and unconscious) anti-Semitism. Though he says he has no prejudices against Jews "as human beings," he then talks about their alleged characteristics, such as ignorance and bigotry, instead of their religious beliefs.

In their final interchange, Seaver agrees that he will stop writing on the subject "provided the Jewish champion is willing to retire upon her laurels—such as they are," but he adds that "if

Mrs. Rose sees anything in that religion which requires her to defend it, she is more attached to Judaism than we had supposed" (*BI* Apr. 6 and Apr. 13, 1864). Rose, in turn, agrees to let the subject rest because she has not the least desire to "scold you out of certain, positive, unmistakable truth," but she does have a strong desire "to reason you into it." She concludes, "satisfied in having done my duty in defence of justice" (*BI* Apr. 13, 1864).

It was a strange interchange, public for all the world to see. Rose, obviously connected to her Jewish heritage in ways she could not joke about, lost her sense of humor and for good reason. Seaver, trying to tell a person born in the Jewish faith what Jews were like, turned patronizing, labeling Rose "a scold" several times, thus dismissing her arguments as those of a mere fussy old woman. Under pressure, Horace Seaver the woman's rights advocate and freethinker revealed deep-seated prejudices against Jewish people and also against women. That he would patronize Rose and reduce her arguments to what he termed "scolding" is indicative of his prejudices; that he would question whether Rose was thinking of "turning Jew" suggests how deep his anti-Semitism ran. To Rose, it must have seemed that she could never get away from being reminded that she was Jewish—even with her closest friends who understood and supported and agreed with her atheism.[13] At just the time Rose needed her freethinking friends the most, one of them revealed a striking contradiction in everything he stood for—a poisonous inconsistency that highlights just how pervasive anti-Semitism was in nineteenth-century America.

The following January, for the first time, the *Boston Investigator* organized the annual Infidel Convention on Thomas Paine's birthday, so the Convention and the birthday celebration were one and the same. Rose, perhaps still distant from Seaver, did not attend,

13. See Kaplan who, writing about nineteenth-century Germany, says Jewish women in Germany could never simply locate their identity as female; they were, instead, constantly reminded of their Jewishness (ix).

citing her increasing age—"though ladies never get old"—and the inclement weather. She mused "had Paine only been born in a warmer season of the year, I could promise myself the pleasure of dancing with you (for I am as fond of dancing as ever)" (*BI* Feb. 15, 1865). She did send a letter that declared never was there a time when an Infidel Convention and a Paine Celebration were "more appropriate or more needed than at the present struggle between freedom and despotism, which 'try men souls' " (*BI* Feb. 15, 1865).

The Woman's Rights Split Widens

When the Civil War ended in 1865, the conflict in the woman's rights movement escalated. In a split foreshadowed by the debate over Stanton's advocacy of divorce reform and the battle in the Woman's Loyal League about enfranchisement of black men as well as women, Rose, together with Stanton and Anthony, stood together on what was increasingly perceived as the "radical" side of the movement. The end of the Civil War signaled a triumph of nationalism, and the passage in 1865 of the Thirteenth Amendment to the Constitution that abolished slavery portended the triumph of freedom. The question for the woman's rights activists was, whose freedom? From the end of the Civil War until the Fifteenth Amendment to the Constitution was passed in 1870, giving the right to vote only to black men, the woman's rights meetings became the sites of increasingly opposing camps.

At first, most of the women who had been active in the 1850s national conventions sided with Rose, Anthony, and Stanton. In January 1866, hearing that the pending amendment to the Constitution proposed only enfranchising black men, a group of women led by the first five signers—Rose, Stanton, Anthony, Blackwell, and Stone—sent a petition for "universal suffrage" to Thaddeus Stevens. Stevens, long an opponent of slavery, was the leader of the House of Representatives and chair of the Committee on Reconstruction (See *HWS* 2: 97 for petition and signers). In addition to gathering names for the universal suffrage petition, the women also organized the first woman's rights convention since

the war began. The eleventh annual national woman's rights convention took place at the Church of the Puritan, in New York City
on May 10, 1866.[14] The call for the convention promised speeches
by Ernestine Rose (first on the list), Frances Gage, Wendell Phillips,
Elizabeth Cady Stanton, and Lucretia Mott. The main business of
the convention was to discuss and adopt an "Appeal to Congress"
that demanded "equal rights to all" (32–33), which was, indeed,
done. It was an idea that, according to Stanton, "has never yet
been tried."[15]

The conference was dominated by male speakers, a heretofore
unusual occurrence in the woman's rights conventions. Although
there were certainly men on the platform in the 1850s, the 1866
convention seemed strangely populated by long-winded Christian
men. After President Elizabeth Cady Stanton spoke, Theodore
Tilton demanded the ballot for women for "men's" sake because
"we shall never have a government thoroughly permeated with
Christianity, thoroughly humane, thoroughly noble, thoroughly
trustworthy, until both men and women shall unite in forming the
public sentiment" (15). Tilton's talk was followed by an even
longer speech by the Reverend Henry Ward Beecher, who agreed
with Tilton and added that women would bring to public affairs
"peculiar qualities, aspirations, and affections which society needs"
(25). Moving away from the notion of woman suffrage as an
important "right" for women, a right that was predicated upon
their humanness, Beecher emphasized woman's separate, moral
offering to the world. Woman's very difference would help improve politics and the world. The next address was by Wendell
Phillips, who, again, reminded the audience that suffrage was not
woman's right but woman's duty. Arguing, as he had in previous
conventions, that woman's power should be "dragged to the light
of day" (43), he urged lessening woman's power, not giving women
any more influence: "let us trace home the evil to its very source.

14. For information on the convention, see *PWRC, New York, 1866*; see also
HWS 2: 152–82. In-text pages come from the *Proceedings.*

15. See the broadside, "The Eleventh Annual National Woman's Rights
Convention," dated Mar. 31, 1866 at the AAS.

Let woman know that nobody stops her but herself. She ties her own limbs. She corrupts her own sisters. She demoralizes civilization, and then folds her arms, and calls it religion (applause), or steps back and christens it taste" (43).

It is not surprising that when it came her turn to speak after Phillips, Rose had left the platform, telling Frances Gage that the subject was "exhausted." Rose's lack of a speech, despite being billed first on the list of speakers, is telling.[16] Perhaps she had had enough of pompous, religious men telling women that they were such separate, distinct beings: both so moral and pure that voting is their "duty" to clean up the world, or so "evil" and "corrupt" that they "demoralize civilization" by their very existence. Or perhaps she saw in the men's speeches an underhanded campaign to keep her off the woman's rights platform because of her professed atheism.[17]

At the end of the convention, the participants voted unanimously to dissolve the Eleventh Annual Woman's Rights Convention and to create the American Equal Rights Association. The change in name reflected much behind-the-scenes lobbying and was clearly an attempt to respond to the rumor that it would only be "male citizens" who would be included in the Fourteenth Amendment. As Anthony explained, the women and men involved in the woman's rights conventions throughout the 1850s had looked only to state action to recognize those rights. But because of the war and the proposed Fourteenth and Fifteenth Amend-

---

16. Lucretia Mott's letter to her sister telling her that Rose "made a good speech" is perplexing as neither the *Proceedings* nor any newspapers reproduce or cite any speech by Rose (May 8, 1866, GFP). Mott also wrote in the same letter that Rose at this convention gave her a photograph of her and her husband and had asked her for Mott's photograph as well, which Mott promised to send her.

17. Anthony revealed late in life that several of the men who spoke on the woman's rights platform did not want Rose speaking because of her "radicalism" as an atheist: "Forty years ago one of our noblest men said to me, 'You would better never hold another convention than allow Ernestine L. Rose on your platform;' because that eloquent woman, who ever stood for justice and freedom, did not believe in the plenary inspiration of the Bible. Did we banish Mrs. Rose? No, indeed!" (Harper 2: 853).

ments to the Constitution, the group needed to be more broadly based and to urge the adoption of a Constitutional amendment—a national equal rights amendment—rather than look solely to state action. The object of the new association was to "secure equal rights to all American citizens, especially the right of suffrage, irrespective of race, color, or sex" (*PWRC, New York, 1867* 52).

The following year the American Equal Rights Association held a well-attended National Convention in the Church of the Puritans on May 9 and 10, 1867.[18] In the intervening year, there had appeared to have been some progress in woman's rights. In Kansas, amendments circulated that would enfranchise both women and blacks. Lucy Stone and her husband Henry Blackwell were, in fact, in Kansas during the equal rights convention. But a vote in the United States Senate on a pending suffrage bill resulted in only nine senators voting in favor of extending suffrage to women as well as to black men.

Participants in the convention focused on obtaining the right of suffrage for women. Susan B. Anthony opened the convention with a secretary's report bemoaning the lack of financial resources the women had available to them, saying "money [is] the vital power of all movements" (6). Rose builds upon Anthony's point in her major speech: "give us one million of dollars and we will have the elective franchise at the very next session of our Legislature" (43). Rose talks about the necessity for either money or influence: "If we had had the money, we could have bought the Legislature and the elective franchise long before now. But as we have not, we must create a public opinion, and for that we must have voices" (43); if women had had enough money, they would not have had to hold "these meetings."

Rose continues by saying that "recently" she had seen the need for suffrage even more. Having noticed that Senators and members of the House were touring the South talking to the

18. For information on this convention see its *Proceedings of the First Anniversary of the American Equal Rights Association . . . 1867*, as well as *HWS* 2: 182–228. All in-text quotations come from these *Proceedings*.

recently freed black men, Rose asks why no one bothered with these men before. Her answer is that these men were about to get the vote and are therefore worth talking to, worth courting, worth spending time and money on. Rose concludes her speech by demanding that women have the franchise along with black men. Her argument, as in the past, goes back to the rights of man and the Declaration of Independence:

> [Americans] have proclaimed to the world universal suffrage; but it is universal suffrage with a vengeance attached to it— universal suffrage excluding the negro and the woman, who are by far the largest number in this country. It is not the majority that rules here, but the minority. White men are in the minority in this nation. White women, black men, and black women compose the large majority of the nation. Yet in spite of this fact, in spite of common sense, in spite of justice . . . Congress can prate so long about justice and human rights, and the rights of the negro, [but] they have not the moral courage to say anything for the rights of woman. (44)

Anthony supported Rose's position, arguing that even though abolitionists believed the time had come for black men to get their rights, "others, with whom I agree, think we have been sowing the seed of individual rights, the foundation idea of a republic for the last century, and that this is the harvest time for all citizens who pay taxes, obey the laws and are loyal to the government" (60). Sojourner Truth, as well, eloquently supported Rose's position:

> There is a great stir about colored men getting their rights, but not a word about the colored women; and if colored men get their rights, and not colored women theirs, you see the colored men will be masters over the women, and it will be just as bad as it was before. So I am for keeping the thing going while things are stirring, because if we wait till it is still, it will take a great while to get it going again. (20)

Elizabeth Cady Stanton's rationale for including women with black men's suffrage, stated clearly and forcefully during this convention, differed from Rose's and is more problematic for modern readers. As she had argued from the early 1850s on, Stanton demanded the ballot for all because the wisest order of enfranchisement was to take the educated classes first. She asserted: "if all men are to vote, black and white, lettered and unlettered, washed and unwashed, the safety of the nation as well as the interests of woman demand that we outweigh this incoming tide of ignorance, poverty, and vice, with the virtue, wealth, and education of the women of the country." Stanton urged educated women not to stand aside while "two million ignorant men are ushered into the halls of legislation" (55).

Abby Kelley Foster, who said she was in New York for medical reasons rather than speech making, took the stage to argue that given the slave status of black men, people with any sense of justice would not postpone the black men's "security against present woes and future enslavement" by waiting for women to also obtain political rights (55). Otherwise, opposing voices were primarily absent from this convention, so the women drafted a resolution aimed at convincing the absent men that women's suffrage was just as important as black men's suffrage: "While we are grateful to Wendell Phillips, Theodore Tilton, and Horace Greeley, for the respectful mention of woman's rights to the ballot in the journals through which they speak, we ask them now, when we are constructing both our State and National governments, to demand that the right of suffrage be secured to all citizens—to women as well as black men, for, until this is done, the government stands on the unsafe basis of class legislation" (52).

Following the 1867 American Equal Rights Convention, Stanton and Anthony journeyed to Kansas to help the woman's suffrage amendment pass. There they met George Train, a wealthy self-promoting Democrat who championed the woman's rights cause as a way of dividing the Republican ranks. As the Republicans had decided to support only black male suffrage, both Stanton and Anthony thought Train and the Democrats offered them their best opportunity of winning Kansas. The amendments lost in Kansas several months later, but Train helped Stanton and Anthony finance a woman's rights paper, *The Revolution*, which began publication on January 8, 1868. Stanton and Anthony's association with Train separated them even further from their former friends. The men of the abolitionist movement, with few exceptions, backed the Republican party, which vouchsafed for black male suffrage as it was "the negro's hour." Meanwhile, Stanton and Anthony, perhaps influenced by Train, a notorious racist, wrote more and more racist rationales for woman's suffrage.[19] Ernestine Rose, though, managed to remain true to her ideal—universal suffrage—without casting aspersions on black men.

The following year, everyone was back together again for more disagreement at the annual anniversary meeting of the American Equal Rights Association, held in the Cooper Union, in New York City, May 14, 1868.[20] Rose, who served on the executive committee and also on a "resolutions" committee with Stanton and Stephen Foster, was billed, along with Lucy Stone, Susan B. Anthony, and Frederick Douglass, as one of the "distinguished friends of equal rights for women" who were to be on the platform (see the May 15, 1868, New York *Tribune*). The Hutchinson Family was there, as at many of the conventions, singing utopian songs such as "A Hundred Years Hence," songs that seem ironic to us in retrospect.

19. Train tried to play on people's worst fears and prejudices. Warning people against enfranchisement for blacks, he prophesied "carry negro suffrage and we shall see some white woman in a case of negro rape being tried by 12 negro jurymen" (quoted in Kerr 128). Anthony went off on a statewide lecture tour with Train; when Anthony spoke of woman's rights, Train offered racist invective.

20. For information on this convention, see *HWS* 2: 309–12 and the New York *Tribune* and New York *Herald* for May 15, 1868. There were no "Reports" or *Proceedings* published for the years 1868 and 1869, according to Susan B. Anthony, who wrote the information on the bottom of page 80 of the 1867 *Proceedings* in Copy #1 of *The Reports of the Woman's Rights Conventions* in the Susan B. Anthony Collection in the Rare Books Room of the Library of Congress.

Frederick Douglass tried to bring the warring groups together by arguing that it was not one good cause in opposition to another but a matter of timing. He explained to the people gathered that he championed the right of women to vote and the right of the negro to vote, but the negro's emancipation was a matter of "urgent necessity." Women, he argued, were not hated by the Ku Klux Klan like black men were. Black men were hunted and killed while "the government of this country loves women. They are the sisters, mothers, wives and daughters of our rulers; but the negro is loathed" (*HWS* 2: 311). Black men needed the vote for their safety.

The Reverend Olympia Brown, disgusted with the Republican party for refusing to support the enfranchisement of women, argued that there was no difference in principle between the Democrats opposing the enfranchisement of two million negro men and the Republican party opposing the suffrage of seventeen million white women. Douglass disagreed, declaring that the Democratic party opposed suffrage to both groups while the Republicans favored enfranchising the negro and was "largely" in favor of enfranchising women (*HWS* 2: 311). "Where is the Democrat who favors women's suffrage?" asked Douglass. "Train," a voice from the crowd shouted, and Douglass responded bitterly, "Yes, he hates the negro, and that is what stimulates him to substitute the cry of emancipation for women" (311).

Rose seemed strangely oblivious to the issues at hand at this convention, speaking on practical matters such as education and employment for women, topics she had discussed many times before. Perhaps her talk on women attracted to the frivolities of dress was her way of trying to diffuse the tensions of the meeting.[21]

By 1869 the quarrels in the American Equal Rights Association appeared insurmountable. Both Stanton and Anthony were using openly racist language to urge Americans to give women the right to vote, and they took a two-month tour of the West to

---

21. See a summary of Rose's speech in both the *Tribune* and *Herald* on May 15, 1868.

argue against ratification of the Fifteenth Amendment.[22] At a suffrage convention held in Washington, D.C., in January 1869, Stanton's call for woman's suffrage was mixed with appeals to her audience's fear of immigrants and negroes:

> If American women find it hard to bear the oppressions of their own Saxon fathers, the best orders of manhood, what may they now be called to endure when all the lower orders of foreigners now crowding our shores legislate for them and their daughters. Think of Patrick and Sambo and Hans and Yung Tung, who do not know the difference between a monarchy and a republic, who can not read the Declaration of Independence or Webster's spelling-book, making laws for Lucretia Mott [and] Ernestine L. Rose. (*HWS* 2: 353)

Rose, who did not attend and hear Stanton talking about "Patrick and Sambo and Hans and Yung Tung," did write a letter to the convention. In it Rose answered a number of arguments against suffrage for women. She wrote that the "childish argument" that all women do not ask for suffrage is silly: "there never has been a time when all men of any country—white or black—have ever asked for a reform. Reforms have to be claimed and obtained by the few, who are in advance, for the benefit of the many who lag behind. And when once obtained and almost forced upon them, the mass of people accept and enjoy their benefits as a matter of course" (*Revolution* Jan. 28, 1869). Rose concluded by urging Congress to wipe out the purely biological distinction from the Constitution. It was, Rose argued, a terrible mistake to introduce the word "male" into the Constitution (as had happened in June 1866, when Congress passed the Fourteenth Amendment) as the term "male" and "female" simply designate the animal distinction between the sexes and ought to be used only in speaking of the

22. Others have noted the racism that permeated the nineteenth-century woman's rights movement. See Kerr on Anthony and Stanton's relationship with George Train (127–39). See also Russo and Kramarac, who write that some of the women used racist sentiments to argue for their rights that were grounded in racial and class biases (7).

lower animals. Citizens, thus, ought to "wipe out that purely animal distinction from the national constitution" (*Revolution* Jan. 21, 1869).

In the late 1860s Rose wrote a number of letters for Stanton and Anthony's *Revolution* on such varied topics as her early activities for woman's rights and her disdain when confronted with Dr. Joseph Thompson's stereotypes of women. In the paper, which devoted itself to the concept of "educated suffrage," the women found only one cause that seemed to unify everyone, the *Hester Vaughn* case, an incident that created so much public sentiment that a protest meeting was held in Cooper Union, where Horace Greeley presided and both Stanton and Rose spoke. The case concerned a young woman who had come to America from England and, upon arriving, found the husband she was joining to have taken another wife. She then became a servant, only to be seduced and then abandoned by her employer when he discovered her pregnancy. In a story that parallels the fictional *Charlotte Temple*, Hester gives birth alone in a garret in the middle of winter. When she is found, incoherent and freezing, her baby is dead. Accused of murdering her child, Hester was tried, found guilty, by an all-male jury, of course, and sentenced to be hanged. To Rose, the Vaughn case was a perfect example of a woman not being tried by a jury of her peers. Thanks to the women's action, the governor of Pennsylvania pardoned Hester and she returned to England. It was one of the few concrete victories that Rose and her colleagues who were pushing for universal suffrage would win in the late 1860s.

Perhaps Ernestine Rose just got tired of the internecine warfare. Perhaps she despaired when her closest colleagues resorted to racism to buttress their arguments. Perhaps she just lost her patience with everyone who could not see the logic of her point of view: that in a republic based on freedom, women *and* black men should both be fully recognized as human beings. Perhaps the anti-Semitism and anti-immigrationist sentiments that were always lurking beneath the surface of many woman's rights arguments finally demoralized her. For whatever reason, by the late spring of 1869 Rose had had enough.

The May 1869 American Equal Rights Association meeting in New York City was Rose's last. In this, the final meeting that Rose would attend while still living in the United States, the woman's rights activists were at war.[23] Most of the activists were there: on the platform with Rose were Stanton (serving as president in the absence of Lucretia Mott), Anthony, Lucy Stone, Antoinette Brown Blackwell, Frederick Douglass, and even Madam Anneke (from the 1853 New York City convention) and Jenny d'Hericourt, who was now living in Chicago. The convention was rife with stress caused by, among other things, the racist language in Stanton and Anthony's *Revolution* and by their efforts to doom the ratification of the Fifteenth Amendment. Douglass, who said he had come to the convention more as a listener than as a speaker, objected to Stanton's use of certain names like "Sambo." Douglass added: "I must say that I do not see how any one can pretend that there is the same urgency in giving the ballot to woman as to the negro. With us, the matter is a question of life and death, at least, in fifteen States of the Union" (*HWS* 2: 382).

Many of the women arguing for emancipation for both women and blacks continued to resort to racist language and imagery to fight for woman's suffrage. Anthony argued that, despite the "old anti-slavery school" telling women to "stand back and wait," she urged giving suffrage to "the most intelligent first" (*HWS* 2: 383). Stanton said that she did not believe in allowing "ignorant negroes and foreigners to make laws for her to obey" (*HWS* 2: 391). Paulina Wright Davis argued that black women were more intelligent than black men because the women "have learned something from their [white] mistresses" (*HWS* 2: 391).

23. For information on the convention see *HWS* 2: 378–98 and, even more important, the more complete versions of the convention in the May 13–15, 1869, New York *Times* and *Tribune*.

And if the disagreements about the ratification of the Fifteenth Amendment were not enough, the group also struggled with its bête noire: free love. Although no one spoke in favor of free love, one of the convention issues was whether the group should pass a resolution that they were not free lovers. Rose argued that the resolution should never have been brought up: "when a man comes to me and tries to convince me that he is not a thief, then I take care of my coppers" (*HWS* 2: 389). As Rose had explained previously, the issue was a red herring that the press latched upon to distract attention from the real issues.[24]

In her final speech at her final woman's rights convention, Rose tries to explain everything rationally, but her anger and impatience at the obtuseness of Congress comes through as well. It is anger that has built up for a decade. "Why can't women be treated equally with men?" she asks. "Why has Congress enacted laws to give the negro the right to vote when they don't at the same time protect the negro woman? If Congress really means to protect the negro race," she says, "they should acknowledge woman just as much as man [for] the only way to protect her is the ballot" (*HWS* 2: 396). Rose assures her audience that it is not with individual men that "we war . . . we war with bad principles" (396). Angry that when some men such as Horace Greeley were asked what they meant by "impartial suffrage," they answered that "of course" they meant "men," "the man and the brother," Rose asks if Congress will give voting rights to babies—"the male babies"— before giving the rights to women (*Tribune* May 14, 1869). At this convention, Rose resorts to the most racist imagery she would ever employ: "we might commence by calling the Chinaman a man and a brother, or the Hottentot, or the Calmuck, or the Indian, the idiot or the criminal, but where shall we stop? They will bring in all these before us, and then they will bring in the

---

24. Rose herself called free love "Free Lust" and disapproved of its "animalism" that was a blasphemy to the sacred name of "love." See the Nov. 17, 1869, *Boston Investigator* for a letter from "Montgarnier," who explained that when he and Rose in the mid-1850s had visited Josiah Warren's experimental community, Modern Times, that some labeled a free love community, they had gone away disgusted.

babies—the *male* babies" (*HWS* 2: 397). Then Rose insists, "I will not be construed into a man and a brother. I ask for the same rights for women that are extended to men—the right to life, liberty, and the pursuit of happiness; and every pursuit in life must be as free and open to me as any man in the land" (397). To Rose, then and always, the logic of universal suffrage was obvious. Frustrated, she concludes, "Congress does not seem to understand the meaning of the term 'universal' "(*HWS* 2: 396).

The differences of opinions led to outright hostility during this meeting. Stephen Foster, who argued that he, too, supported universal suffrage, spoke against Stanton and Anthony's notions of "educated suffrage," and their "stigmatization" in the *Revolution* of the Fifteenth Amendment as "infamous." He asked "these women"—Stanton and Anthony—to "retire," so that the American Equal Rights Association could nominate officers who had the respect of all: "I can not work with you," Foster said directly to Anthony, accusing her of keeping no books for the organization,[25] adding that neither he nor the Massachusetts abolitionists would cooperate with a group that "ridicule[s] the negro and pronounce[s] the [Fifteenth] Amendment infamous" (*HWS* 2: 382).

Lucy Stone, who had spent much of the previous year arguing for both the ratification of the Fifteenth Amendment and the necessity of a Sixteenth Amendment that granted suffrage to women, nonetheless agreed with Foster and disagreed with Stanton's and Anthony's "educated suffrage" argument that would give the vote to women before black men. To Stone, as to Foster and others deeply involved in the antislavery movement for over two decades, the issue was one of compromise: black men, they feared, if they were to receive the vote at all, would receive it by only the smallest margin. Thus to them, separating the amendments was a way of acknowledging the political reality that would, they believed, surely doom black male suffrage if women's suffrage were linked to it. On this issue Stone and Rose, while both supporting true universal suffrage, seriously disagreed as to tactics.

25. This is one detail that *HWS*: 2 does not include in its summary of the 1869 convention; see the May 13, 1869, New York *Times.*

Rose hated compromise, and she continued to articulate the importance of universal suffrage even after the Fifteenth Amendment had been passed by Congress on February 27, 1869. In any practical terms, it was far too late at the May 1869 meeting to add universal suffrage to the Fifteenth Amendment; yet, Rose continued to argue for just such a revision while Stanton and Anthony argued that the Amendment, as it stood, not be ratified.

In one of her last talks to the convened group, Rose returned to her 1830s British background by proposing a resolution stating that working women receive inadequate pay and recommending the formation of cooperative societies to secure adequate compensation for women's labor. Joined by one other person who read a series of resolutions adopted at a working women's convention in Boston, Rose was opposed by several who thought the subject of working women's rights was "out of place just now" (*Times* May 14, 1869).

At the end of the second day of proceedings, and her last day of attendance, Rose proposed changing the name of their organization to the "Woman's Franchise Association," explaining that though she "by no means meant to throw the black man overboard," she nonetheless wanted the association to have a name that could not be misunderstood (*Times* May 14, 1869). Lucy Stone disagreed, hoping that the group would not change its name until the black man had obtained suffrage. In fact, at the end of the convention, Stanton and Anthony did split off from the American Equal Rights Association to create the National Woman's Suffrage Association. They were joined by Lucretia Mott, Martha Wright, Madam Anneke, and others. Rose's name was also listed as a member of the charter association, but Rose did not attend the meetings to plan the new group nor any of its meetings, as she and William left for Europe almost immediately following the May convention. Lucy Stone, Antoinette Brown Blackwell, and the majority of the abolitionist men including Wendell Phillips, William Lloyd Garrison, and Frederick Douglass remained in the "Equal Rights" association. A few months later they created their own "woman's suffrage" organization, the American Woman Suffrage Association, with Henry Ward Beecher as president. This split in the activists' organizations lasted more than twenty years. It was only when the groups joined forces at the turn of the century that women, once again, mounted a campaign that finally resulted in women's suffrage.

Three weeks following the fateful 1869 convention, Ernestine and William Rose left New York for Europe. Before they left, Ernestine applied for and received United States citizenship. Their trip was clearly intended to be a lengthy one as several groups gave Rose testimonial gifts upon her departure. Mendum and Seaver organized one testimonial gift through the auspices of the *Boston Investigator*. A New York group organized another testimonial that was given to Rose in a basket of flowers. Susan B. Anthony also organized a testimonial for Rose, including a sum of money and a number of presents.[26] Although her Boston friends Seaver and Mendum seemed to believe that Rose was returning as soon as she obtained "renewed health and vigor," Rose was equivocal in a letter to the *Boston Investigator*, writing after being gone for two months that they had "not yet decided where to go from here" (*BI* Sept. 15, 1869).

Rose left the United States at exactly the moment that the woman's rights organization splintered into two warring groups, a split that would limit their influence and postpone woman's enfranchisement for more than half a century. The great momentum of the 1850s was never regained with the late 1860s conventions, as it became only too easy for woman's suffrage foes to capitalize on the internal conflict.

Perhaps one of the greatest casualties of the split in the groups was the loss of Ernestine Rose's voice to the movement. Torn between the racism of Stanton and Anthony and the political compromises of Stone, the Fosters, and others, Rose, I believe,

---

26. Anthony wrote her friends asking for contributions for the gift for Rose. Martha Wright, for one, sent off five dollars the day after she received Anthony's request. See Wright's "Diary" for June 5 and June 6, 1869, GFP.

had nowhere to go but away. She hated compromise; she loved "truth." It was clear to her that universal suffrage for men and women of all races was the only end that the Declaration of Independence pointed toward. Discouraged, Rose distanced herself from the impotence of the splintered groups. Perhaps also Rose's recent disagreement with Seaver over "the Jews" had something to do with her decision—making her realize that the anti-Semitism and other prejudices that permeated American society were simply too deep for her to overcome. Or, perhaps, her impatience just got the best of her, and she could no longer bear making her reasonable, lucid points over and over to deaf ears. The world she had chosen to live in in 1836—one dominated by the principles of the Declaration of Independence—was, in 1869, not much closer to its founding tenets. Although she would continue to "agitate" in England for another 23 years, Rose's American life was in effect over when she sailed for Cherbourg on June 7, 1869.

·····••❦[9]❦••·····

The Final Years

But I have lived.

—Ernestine Rose, London, 1892

In her first year away from the United States, Ernestine Rose took a variety of water cures, beginning in Luxenill, a hot springs town in France, then moving on to Lake Lucerne in Switzerland to get "braced up" by the mountain air. Rose traveled to Nice, to Paris, then to Homburg, Germany, for its famous waters. Everywhere she was "heartened to find that strangers" she met while traveling knew her name and her "heretical proclivities" (*BI* Sept. 15, 1869). With no set itinerary, the Roses ended their year of travels in the spa town of Bath, England.

Modern readers might well be curious about Rose's year of "taking the waters." But middle- and upper-class European-born people were likely to take just such elaborate, time-consuming restorative travels during the 1870s. Lack of home ownership combined with service-oriented spa towns with comfortable rooms and meals allowed many people to partake of traveling and a water cure. What sounds today like an elaborate and expensive vacation, was, in fact for Rose an inexpensive way to gain strength and to meet new people interested in woman's rights and freethought.

During her year of water cures, the year she turned 60, Rose wrote Horace Seaver and Josiah Mendum at the *Boston Investigator* several times, telling them of the places she was visiting and the people she met. As when she and William had traveled in Europe in 1856, Rose commented on how much she loved France and its people. She wrote of meeting some of the "foremost" men and women in different reform movements including M. C. Lemounier in the Peace Congress, Lion Banjoue, who edited a woman's rights paper, and M'me Marie-Champset, the President of the Society for the Emancipation of Woman (*BI* July 20, 1870). After a seven-week stay, though, Rose was ready to leave Paris, because in the city one could "walk yourself almost to death" (*BI* July 20, 1870).

In a series of letters to the *Boston Investigator* Rose commented on how her health was improving despite her rheumatism. The letters also reveal, indirectly, why the Roses ended their journey in England rather than in Paris, which in many ways they both preferred. At Bath, as elsewhere in England, the accommodations were affordable. Rose explains that when one hired an apartment in Bath, the people who owned the house provided meals for no additional money:

> We have two large rooms, well furnished, one story high, in one of the principal streets, in a private house owned by the people who live in it. For the rooms, with fire and gas, and all kinds of service, we pay £1, 5s. per week, and for that we have our rooms taken care of, and our food cooked and served in our room and all we have to do is to provide whatever we wish to have, order how to have it cooked, and when served. Thus we have all the real comfort of housekeeping without the trouble of it, or servants, and our expenses for living, including *everything*, (we get the best, and beef and mutton is very fine here—the finest we have seen anywhere), is £2, 6s. per week, which is a little more than $11. In New York, to live the same way would cost us from $30–$40. This mode of living is peculiar to England only. You cannot live the same way on the Continent, though you can live very reasonable in many places. (*BI* Feb. 8, 1871).

Never interested in making money, perceiving money-hoarding to be "selfishness," the Roses in retirement had to watch their expenses carefully. Although Rose longed to return to New York City, it was too expensive for them. In Bath, the accommodations were inexpensive and the streets cleaner than Broadway and Fifth Avenue, so, settled in, the Roses decided to remain for the rest of the winter, despite having no friends and few acquaintances and with the winter weather "too cold for my comfort" (*BI* Feb. 8, 1871).[1]

Once they decided to remain for the winter, Rose quickly became part of the civic life of the town. Pleased that Bath was beginning "to move with the world," by allowing women who own or hire houses and pay taxes for one year to vote in local elections, Ernestine and William attended a meeting to support two women running for the school board. There, according to the local newspaper, a woman "from the other side of the Atlantic, but judging from her accent of French extraction" spoke (*BI* Mar. 1, 1871). Although the editors were wrong about where the speaker was born, they were right when they said that this was probably not her first public appearance as the advocate of her sex. Asking if she might speak, Rose mounted the platform when the female candidates would not. Rose explained that she was from across "the great pond" and a resident, though not a native, of the United States. She was in Bath because "of her health." Rose revealed that she and William were "woman's rights people" but that no one should be alarmed at the term. "Woman's rights," Rose explained, simply meant "human rights," because "no woman earnest enough to claim those rights would for one moment have them based on the wrongs of any human being" (*BI* Mar. 1, 1871). When Rose sent the local clipping of her speech to the *Boston Investigator* she added with her usual playfulness, that, despite the fact that women who pay taxes can vote in local elections, Bath still "stands on as firm a foundation, in spite even of the Hot Springs, as ever! How far that foundation would be shaken if their votes were extended even to members of Parliament, of course I would not be bold enough to predict" (*BI* Mar. 1, 1871).

At the end of the winter, the Roses moved to London, where they had both friends and acquaintances and where Ernestine

---

1. In a letter dated Dec. 27, 1870, Rose talks hopefully about "our return" to New York, the city that felt like home to her. See the Feb. 8, 1871, *Boston Investigator.*

reentered public life. It was a fitting place for Rose to end her career, as Moncure D. Conway pointed out in a letter to the *National Reformer.* It was in London, some 37 years earlier, that Rose had first been introduced in public by Robert Owen at the opening of his great hall. Now, one hundred years after Robert Owen's birth, Rose was back in London to give a major speech at his centenary birthday (*National Reformer* May 7, 1871). In the meantime, Conway continued, Rose had "since that time become distinguished in America by a clearness and force which few speakers have attained; and that her long acquaintance with Robert Owen, as well as her representative character toward the principles that must always be associated with her name, render it especially fortunate that she is able to be with us on the centenary birthday of that historical man." Rose used the occasion much as she had used the Thomas Paine celebrations, to talk about woman's rights. Owen, said Rose, had been connected with a number of movements, including those that worked to attain woman's rights. She lauded current writers such as John Stuart Mill who were carrying out his principles. Her speech was well received. Both the London *Reformer* and *Reasoner* wrote that Rose gave *the* speech of the evening, the most appropriate and the best delivered to over 1,000 people (*BI* July 5, 1871).

As well as speaking at South Place Chapel on Robert Owen's birthday celebration, Rose also addressed the Woman's Suffrage Conference on April 28 at the Langham Hotel. There she was described by the *National Reformer* as "the good lady, with her white curls, her erect, healthy-looking body, her clear, distinct voice, her occasional quaint phrases, her stern determination, and her real genius as a speaker, [who] won from those present a far more hearty and lengthy tribute of applause than was accorded to any one else" (*National Reformer* May 7, 1871). Even at age 61, Rose was still being characterized by her appearance, her "quaint" phrasing, as well as by her "real genius" as a speaker.

Over the next two years, Ernestine and William lived in London as Ernestine continued speaking out on women's rights and freethought issues. They became friends with a group of former Americans and freethinking Britishers including Moncure D.

Conway, a "rationalist" who had moved to England from America in 1864; George Jacob Holyoake, the editor of the *Reasoner*; and Charles Bradlaugh, the freethinking editor of the *National Reformer*. Rose spoke at a series of woman's rights meetings in London and, in early 1873, in Edinburgh, Scotland.

In Edinburgh in the depths of winter in her sixty-third year, Rose spoke in support of the progressive Member of Parliament Jacob Bright's bill to "remove the electoral disabilities of women" (*BI* Feb. 26, 1873). First, she demolished the arguments against Bright's call for woman's suffrage. One common argument against woman's suffrage was that "women were not logical." Rose countered by saying that was an illogical argument: "the franchise was never given for logic," argued Rose. Had it been based on logic, Rose wondered how many current members of Parliament would still be in their places? Rose pointed out that one group of opponents argued that women should not have the right to vote because they were inferior to men and another group said women were superior to men and that is why they should not have the vote. Rose countered both by saying that if some women were inferior to some men, though she didn't believe it, couldn't woman be superior in other things and thus balance the other? And, if man behaved so badly that it was unsafe for women to go to the ballot boxes with them, was men's misconduct a good reason to deprive woman of her rights? Shouldn't woman have the franchise and teach man how to behave?

Rose continued her talk with familiar rhetoric: she argued that humanity, justice, and morality recognize no sex. Woman ought to claim suffrage on the ground of simple justice. What dignifies man will not degrade woman—because man has been elevated by the franchise, so, too, will woman be elevated. She will not become "unsexed" with the vote. Surely she might become stronger in mind and more intellectual and take a greater and wider view of the duties and responsibilities of life, but that would not change her nature. Rose concluded by urging people to "trust in the right, do rightly, do justly, and leave all the consequences to themselves" (*BI* Feb. 26, 1873).

In August 1873, after four years in Europe and England, the Roses sailed back to New York City.[2] Despite finding many free-thinking friends in England, the Roses still felt that New York City was home. While in New York, Rose became quite ill, so ill that she was not able to travel to Boston for several months.[3] After her health improved, Rose wrote several times to the *Investigator*, sending articles from the London *Times* and extracts from clergy's talks in New York City. Although she was unable to attend, Rose sent a letter of support to the National Woman's Suffrage Association holding its fifth anniversary meeting in Washington, D.C., in January 1874.

But the Roses' stay in New York did not last. Horace Seaver reveals in the *Investigator* why they were returning to England: he writes that although the American friends of Ernestine Rose would prefer them to remain "on this side of the water," the Roses were, indeed, leaving for a permanent residence in London, where they found living so much less expensive than in New York (*BI* Apr. 22, 1874). Thinking on Rose's career, Seaver speculates that it was Rose's atheism that kept her poor and unpopular: "Twenty-five years ago Mrs. Rose was about the best female lecturer in this country—Liberal, able, eloquent, and witty; and if she had only been a *Christian* she would now be rich, popular, and famous. But as she was merely a *heretic*, and lectured in behalf of reason,

---

2. See the July 23, 1873, *Investigator*. Rose sent Josiah Mendum a letter telling him that she was in London and had engaged their passage "home," leaving Liverpool for New York on August 28. They were, she reported, in tolerably good health and had enjoyed a very agreeable city and country residence in England where they had found many friends.

3. See the Nov. 26, 1873, *Investigator*. "We have been expecting a visit from this able and well-known Liberal lecturer, and had hoped to hear her speak again in Boston, where in former days she was very attractive and did good service for Freedom and Reform. But we hear with much regret that she is so seriously ill that she has not been able to leave her room for some weeks, or even to sit up long at a time. We sincerely hope that her sickness may not prove fatal, for she is a lady of superior ability and of high moral worth, and if only a Christian she would be rich and famous."

freedom, humanity, and equal rights, she is neither wealthy nor distinguished among the multitude—yet, as Henry Clay once said, 'it is better to be right than to be popular' " (Apr. 22, 1874).

In her final activity, Rose, appropriately, gave a major speech to a filled Irving Hall at the May 14–15, 1874, National Woman's Suffrage Association Convention, held in New York City. Joined on the stage by old friends, including Susan B. Anthony, the president, Martha Wright, Antoinette Brown Blackwell, and speakers new to the woman's right stage such as Lillie Devereux Blake, Rose could not help but notice the absence of Lucy Stone, now working for the American Suffrage Association.[4] According to the New York *Herald*, a longtime opponent of woman's rights, Rose "made a stirring appeal for fair play to the enslaved sex, and roused the spirits present" (quoted in the May 27, 1874, *BI*). Rose first spoke on the injustice of keeping woman, bound by the same laws of morality as man, from exercising her legal rights. Suffrage was the "true right" of woman and no one could justify refusing woman her rights (*Times* May 15, 1874). On the second day of the convention, Rose, responding to an earlier speaker's lament that women had not accomplished very much, described the changes in public opinion and in the condition of women in the 38 years since she had been speaking for woman's rights. The progress she perceived in close to four decades was "wonderful." Feeling herself part of a crusade once opposed by almost all presses and now at least tolerated, Rose could see at this, her final convention, the fruits of her pioneering work. She had gone from being one of the few women in the country speaking for woman's rights to being part of a large social movement. On this stage Rose said her goodbyes to the country and the movement that had filled her life. As the once-hostile New York *Times* reported, "Mrs. Rose, who has occupied the same platform for over thirty years, then declared that ill health would prevent her from ever again appearing in public, and on retiring, she was loudly applauded" (May 15, 1974).

4. For information on the convention, see *HWS* 2: 545; see also Harper 1: 458; and the New York *Times*, May 15–16, 1874.

Although the Roses wished to remain in New York, their stay was limited to ten months. Fearing they lacked the money to live a retired life in the United States, in May 1874 they returned to London again, where, according to the *Boston Investigator*, they would reside permanently. Charles Bradlaugh, one of their new friends in London, reported meeting them on his trip to the United States. As Bradlaugh writes from New York City in February 1874:

> Amongst those in this city who have welcomed me back from my Western tour, one of the most pleasant greetings came from Mr. and Mrs. Rose. Ernestine L. Rose, who has stood for very nearly forty years prominent in the Free Thought ranks, is now sixty-four years of age. . . . Her pleasant face and clear honest voice still speak for the woman who filled a gap when there were few women to take such a stand. And although broken health and her silvery locks now give warning that the page of life is nearly filled, she is as true and loyal as ever to the good cause. An Atheist by conviction, she has always avowed her opinions boldly, and despite her Atheism has won the admiration of even her foes. Mrs. Rose, so long ago as 1846, had won a respectful hearing in the House of Representatives from the Legislature in Michigan, and had made her voice known in most of the Eastern and many of the Western cities; and although today failing strength stays her tongue, her mind and heart still fresh and young, yearn in sympathy for those who continue to fight the battle. Mr. and Mrs. Rose intend to make England their permanent abode. (*National Reformer* Feb. 15, 1874)

Returning to England, the Roses continued to opt for another version of a water cure, this time by going to Brighton, a "pleasant town" of some 100,000 inhabitants, considered a "very healthy place" and thus a popular resort town. Although Brighton was a "healthy" place with a large aquarium and a high cliff facing the sea opposite fine buildings and stores that gave it the appearance of "London by the Sea," both the Roses found it to be "very dull, very religious, and anti-progressive" (*BI* Dec. 23, 1874). It was class conscious, which bothered them, with two "seasons": one from July to October for "the people" and one from October to Christmas for "the elite." As Rose who always considered herself one of "the people" explains, during the low season excursion trains ran every Sunday from London bringing what local papers called the "rif-raf" to the beach, despite ministers attempting to have the trains stop running. But after the first of October the excursion trains stop running and "all is safe" from "the rif-raf" (*BI* Dec. 23, 1874).

During their first winter in Brighton, the Roses attended a missionary meeting that followed a convention of 2,000 ministers. At the meeting, Rose heard an anti–woman's rights speech, made up of Bible quotations, misrepresentations, and downright falsehoods. For example, the speaker, a minister, said that "during the French Revolution of 1792, the women of Paris cut off the heads and legs of men, and ate the flesh, and all this was owing to Infidelity and Woman's Rights" (*BI* Dec. 23, 1874). Rose wrote that she had never listened to a speech "with such perfect disgust." Needless to say, after it was over she asked to make a few remarks and spoke about fifteen minutes saying that she was "a Woman's Rights woman." The "glory" the minister had been talking about—the glory of a woman being Queen in her husband's house—was, Rose claimed, degradation and slavery instead. Rose was surprised and pleased to find that her brief talk was well received. The minister who had given the outrageous talk assured Rose afterwards that he, too, would vote for woman's rights if he could only get to be a Bishop and go to the House of Lords. Rose found him to be a hypocrite. The "liberal and rational," she wrote, "don't flourish on Brighton's chalky soil" (*BI* Dec. 23, 1874).

They tried other towns known for their healthy climates as well. In the summer of 1876 they went to Elkley, a hilly place in Yorkshire, and then on to Harrowgate, noted for its mineral springs—though the summer they resided there, 1876, the "sulphur water" was closer to poison and William got quite sick drinking it (*BI* Feb. 21, 1877). Money worries and ill health continued to plague them. As Rose wrote, "comfortable places are dear, and food still dearer," and they were often unsettled trying to find an affordable place for their winters. At the same time, Rose was homesick for her friends in the United States: "I sincerely wish I was back again in good old Boston, for to tell the truth I am terribly home-sick and hope to be there yet—and though nearly 70, (you see I am so unfashionable as to tell my age!) I *would* like to lecture a little more" (*BI* Feb. 21, 1877).

Throughout the remainder of the decade, Ernestine Rose continued to write her friends in the United States and they, in turn, began to memorialize her. Horace Seaver and Josiah Mendum helped erect a "Paine Memorial Hall," or "Temple of Freethought" in Boston in 1874, with four pictures on its walls: those of Thomas Paine, Robert Owen, and Ernestine and William Rose.[5] When Susan B. Anthony spoke in the Hall in the winter of 1876, she began her lecture by referring to Ernestine Rose's picture on the wall facing her, saying that she was always glad to be in the same vicinity "with a picture of that noble worker for the cause of woman's rights" (*BI* Dec. 6, 1876).

Rose's letters went primarily to the Mendums, to Susan B. Anthony, and to woman's rights conventions. To celebrate July 4, 1876, Rose wrote to both the *Investigator* and to Anthony about the importance of the Declaration of Independence. To the *Investigator* she wrote that the Declaration was a "glorious event," which inspired the founders with the "indisputable fact that 'all men' (which means all human beings, irrespective of sex) have a right to 'life, liberty, and the pursuit of happiness.' " (*BI* Aug. 2, 1876). To Anthony she wrote the same words, adding that "we must reassert in 1876 what 1776 so gloriously proclaimed, and call upon the law-makers and the law-breakers to carry that declaration to its logical consistency by giving woman the right of representation in the government which she helps to maintain, a voice in the laws by which she is governed, and all the rights and privileges society can bestow, the same as to man" (quoted in *HWS* 3: 50–51). Rose added that she was pleased to see her name among the vice presidents of the National Suffrage Association

5. That the freethinkers put both Ernestine's and William's pictures on their walls suggests how important William was to the freethought movement, despite the fact that no newspapers, except occasionally the *Boston Investigator*, ever mentioned him. We do know from the *Investigator* that he helped organize and was an active participant in many infidel activities, along with Ernestine. Like so many spouses working at home, his behind-the-scene accomplishments were rarely noticed.

and asked her to "keep a warm place for me with the American people." In another letter two years later, Rose urged Anthony to invoke the younger women in the movement to "go on, go on, halt not and rest not." Though Rose believed that she and her colleagues had accomplished quite a bit, she added "the main, the vital thing, has yet to come. The suffrage is the magic key . . . the insignia of citizenship in a republic" (quoted in *HWS* 3: 120).

In England, Rose was not done with speaking out, even though her health was often infirm. In the summer of 1878, Moncure Conway urged Rose to attend a Unitarian convention in London, which she agreed to as long as everyone understood that she "profess[ed] no religion—I have long ago discarded the very term" (*BI* July 31, 1878). At the conference Rose spoke twice on religion as "a superstition," the great stumbling block of man. She commented, as she had many time before, how men and women created gods in their own images, rather than the other way around. She proposed that people unite, not around religion, but as "Friends of Progress," as people interested in working to benefit the arts, sciences, and social reform—especially woman's rights. A writer for the *Unitarian Herald* called Rose's talk "the most extraordinary speech I ever heard from a woman; and coming as it did from a lady of advanced years, and spoken as it was with a really deep earnestness, it could not but touch all who listened sympathetically" (quoted in July 31, 1878, *BI*).

The decade of the 1880s was a period of loss for Ernestine Rose. First, and most important, William died suddenly of a heart attack in January 1882 as he was walking in London on an errand. Without him, Ernestine was to spend the final ten years of her life increasingly isolated and alone. William had been a "quiet and unassuming" man, wrote Horace Seaver in his obituary. He was, to all who knew him, a kind and benevolent person whose actions always counted for more than his few words (*BI* Feb. 22, 1882). For Ernestine, William was her rocklike companion who had quietly dedicated his life to their causes. As Susan B. Anthony said of William: "[he] gladly furnished her the means of making her extensive tours, so that through his sense of justice she was enabled to preach the Gospel of Woman's Rights, Anti-Slavery, and Free Religion without money and without price" (*HWS* 1:98). William had provided Ernestine with more than financial support for her causes; he also gave her a stability that helped sustain her during the many years when her words seemed to fall on deaf ears. Inspired by the same causes as was Ernestine, William had been content to work behind the scenes, organizing and arranging Thomas Paine birthday celebrations, collecting money for freethought causes, and continuing to work as a jeweler to support Ernestine's travels in the many years when she received little or no pay for her lectures.

Ernestine was to live another ten years alone. During the 1880s most of her close friends died: Lucretia Mott died in 1880; Madam Anneke in 1884; Horace Seaver in 1889; Josiah Mendum in 1891. Her last meeting with Elizabeth Cady Stanton and Susan B. Anthony was in 1883, during their visit to London. Upon seeing Anthony, the first thing Rose did was to throw her arms around Susan's neck and tell her that her heart could break now so that "you might close my eyes, dear Susan!" (Harper 2: 554). Visiting her again, Anthony hoped, momentarily, that she might convince Rose to return to America with her in order to "smooth her last days," but to no avail.[6] Perhaps Rose refused to return to the United States because of her often-present fear of running out of money, knowing that living conditions in the States were more dear than in England. Although Rose had inherited £2,347 from William in 1882, when she died in 1892, the estate had been reduced to £1,723.[7]

6. Stanton and Anthony's visit to Rose is described quite differently in the *History of Woman Suffrage* than in Anthony's letter as quoted in Harper, Vol. 2. In *HWS* the report on the women's visit with Rose was much flatter: they (Stanton?) reported seeing Rose, their "noble coadjutor," "pleasantly situated" and "as deeply interested in the struggles of the hour" as ever (*HWS* 3: 940).

7. See the Yuri Suhl Papers at Boston University for information about William's and Ernestine's wills. William left everything to Ernestine. Ten years later Ernestine would leave her gold watch to Ernest Mendum, the Mendum's son who had been named for her, and the bulk of her estate to her three nieces: Jeannette Pulvermacher of Middlesex, England; Ernestine Radjewski of Berlin, who also appears to have been named for her; and Bertha Sigismund of New York City. Rose's will suggests that she did, indeed, keep in touch with her father and his new wife, their daughter, and her children—the three nieces to whom she left the bulk of her inheritance.

On their trip to England Anthony and Stanton had visited Moncure Conway, whose wife had told them that Emerson, Alcott, Frothinghan, George Ripley, and even William Henry Channing, then in London also, were all "wearying of their early theories and theologies and returning to the old faith" (Anthony to her sister, June 7, 1883; quoted in Harper 2: 563). Anthony was disheartened upon hearing this; she hoped the men's yearning for religious faith in old age was "simply the waning intellect returning to childish things" (563).

Unlike Robert Owen or many of the Transcendentalist men, Ernestine Rose did not forsake her beliefs during her last decade of life. Instead, she was determined to prevent any recantations of her life's work should an illness make her mind feeble. She wrote into her will that her executors "shall not permit my body to be taken into any chapel or church but to carry out my funeral in like manner generally as that of my late husband, William E. Rose."[8] William had had a memorial service led by Charles Bradlaugh that had no mention of religion in it. Similarly, she directed her friend Hypatia Bradlaugh Bonner, Charles Bradlaugh's daughter, to be with her during her final illness lest she be "invaded by religious persons who might make her unsay the convictions of her whole life when her brain was weakened by illness and she did not know what she was doing" (*National Reformer* Aug. 14, 1892).

Ernestine Rose did not recant. At Brighton for the fresh air and sea, Rose suffered a stroke on August 1, 1892; within a few hours she was mostly unconscious, dying three days later on August 4. An attendant and doctor looked over her final hours, and she was "untroubled by any thoughts of religion" (*National Reformer* August 14, 1892). She was, according to George Jacob Holyoake, who delivered the oration at her grave side at Highgate Cemetery in London, ready to die and had been for a number of years. "It is no longer necessary for me to live," she had told him; "I can do nothing now," adding "but I have lived!" (*Brighton Herald* Aug. 13, 1892).

8. For a copy of Rose's will see the papers of Yuri Suhl at the Boston University Library.

I imagine her statement to Holyoake as a matter-of-fact one. "It is no longer necessary for me to live" is an unmartyred assertion that seems to fit perfectly with Rose's outward-focused life. Unable to "do anything"—to speak or write or even read with William—Rose was quite ready for death. As she had written in a sympathy letter to the Garrison family in 1877, "a time comes to all of us to submit to the inevitable" (to Francis Garrison, Jan. 22, 1877, GFP). Her final letters suggest that her infirmities had increased but that her spirit remained strong. She wrote, for example, to Josiah Mendum in June 1886 telling him that "for many years I have been a feeble invalid, almost helpless, yet in all that time I have managed to read, with a great deal of pleasure, the good old *Investigator* (*BI* June 30, 1886). Or she wrote to Edward Strickland from Brighton in 1887 that she has been too ill to write much or to return to "dear America," but she is glad he and his wife are interested in reform movements (to E. Strickland, Brighton, Aug. 30, 1877, SAC). Or, she sent a sympathy note to Josiah Mendum upon hearing of Horace Seaver's death, along with $25—a considerable amount of money for her— to create a monument to Seaver and, perhaps, to signal her forgiveness of their harsh argument in the mid-1860s over "the Jews."

I like to focus on Rose's words, "I have lived." Ernestine Rose lived a very public life for a series of interrelated causes to which she was utterly devoted. Although women would not obtain suffrage in the United States until almost 30 years after her death, it was her pioneering work and her ceaseless efforts, year after year, that helped to create and energize the woman's rights movement. Few of us are as brave as she was. Most of us compromise in order to get small reforms enacted. Her refusal to compromise surely cost her many friendships and much comfort, but those friends who stayed close to her understood her great worth. Walt Whitman, who particularly admired Rose, called her "big, rich, gifted, brave, expansive—in body a poor sickly thing . . . but with a head full of brains—the amplitude of a Webster" (quoted in Reynolds 220). At the end of her life, perhaps while sitting in her study where Rose's picture hung on the wall, Susan B. Anthony wrote that Ernestine Rose, the first woman next to Frances Wright to publicly demand equality of rights for women, was the "most eloquent and logical extemporaneous speaker on our platform" (*National Woman Suffrage Association Report, 1884* 117). When she was on the stage, Anthony said, we all felt safe: "those who sat with her on the platform in bygone days, well remember her matchless powers as a speaker . . . and how safe we all felt when she had the floor" (*HWS* 1:100). The new editor at the *Boston Investigator* wrote in his obituary of Rose that she labored "for the human race with noble purpose and unselfish aim . . . such a life as she lived is to be imitated by those who would add to the glory of humanity" (*BI* Aug. 17, 1892).

Such was the life of Ernestine L. Rose. Even though Rose was one of the most important leaders of the movement she helped to generate, she was not appreciated in her own time and has been relatively unknown in ours. Susan Anthony wrote from Baltimore in 1854 that Rose was not appreciated, "nor cannot be . . . because] she is too much in advance." We need to become reacquainted with her sharp tongue, her ready wit, and her passion to the cause of justice. We might even be ready to appreciate her.

References
Index

References

Manuscript Collections

American Antiquarian Society
    Broadside Collections (1836–69)
    Abby Kelley Foster Papers
Beinecke Rare Book and Manuscript Library, Yale University
    A. J. Macdonald MS
Boston Public Library
    Abner Kneeland Lectures
    Garrison Papers
Boston University Library
    Yuri Suhl Papers
Cooperative Union Library, Manchester, England
    The Robert Owen Papers
Cornell University
    Theresa Wolfson Papers
Houghton Library, Harvard University
    Garnett-Pertz Collection
Library of Congress
    Blackwell Family Correspondence
    Susan B. Anthony Collection
    Susan B. Anthony Scrapbooks
    Frances Wright Papers
    National American Woman Suffrage Assocation Papers
Arthur and Elizabeth Schlesinger Library, Radcliffe College
    Strickland Autograph Collection
    William Lloyd Garrison Papers
    Susan B. Anthony Diary
Smith College Library, Sophia Smith Collection
    Garrison Family Papers

Workingmen's Institute, New Harmony, Indiana
    Maclure/Fretageot Correspondence

Newspapers
(with years consulted in parentheses)

Albany Atlas/Argus (1860)
Albany Evening Journal (1861)
Alexandria Gazette (1854)
Beacon (1836–46)
Boston Investigator (1835–93)
Brighton Herald (1892)
Communitist (1844–46)
Correspondent (1829–30)
Crisis (1832–34)
Detroit Free Press (1846)
Detroit Daily Advertiser (1846)
Free Enquirer (1829–35)
Genius of Universal Emancipation (1827)
Hartford Courant (1853)
Herald of Freedom (1843)
Indianapolis Daily State Sentinel (1855)
Indianapolis Journal (1855)
Liberator (1836–65)
Lily (1849–55)
National Reformer (1870–92)
New Moral World (1834–45)
New York Herald (1837–69)
New York Times (1851–69)
New York Tribune (1841–69)
Pioneer (1833–34)
Regenerator (1844–45)
Sibyl (1856–64)
Social Pioneer and Herald of Progress (1844)
Revolution (1868–70)
Una (1853–55)
Washington Globe (1854)
Woman's Journal (1870)
Workingman's Advocate (1844)

Proceedings and Reports
(in chronological order)

Proceedings of the Anti-Slavery Convention of American Women, held in New York City, May 9th, 10th, 11th & 12th, 1837. New York, 1837.

Proceedings of the Anti-Sabbath Convention. Boston, 1848.

Report of the Woman's Rights Convention held at Seneca Falls, N.Y., July 19th & 20th, 1848. Rochester, 1848.

Proceedings of the Woman's Rights Convention held at the Unitarian Church, Rochester, New York, August 2, 1848. New York, 1870.

Proceedings of the Woman's Rights Convention held at Worcester, October 23d & 24th, 1850. Boston, 1851.

Proceedings of the Woman's Rights Convention held at Worcester, October 15th and 16th, 1851. New York, 1852.

Proceedings of the Woman's Rights Convention, held at West Chester [sic]. Westchester, PA., 1852.

Proceedings of the Woman's Rights Convention, held at Syracuse, September 8th, 9th, & 10th, 1852. Syracuse, 1852.

Proceedings of the Whole World's Temperance Convention, held in New York City, September, 1853. New York, 1853.

Proceedings of the Woman's Rights Convention held at the Broadway Tabernacle in the city of New York, on Tuesday and Wednesday, Sept. 6th and 7th, 1853. New York, 1853.

Proceedings of the National Woman's Rights Convention, held at Cleveland, Ohio on Wednesday, Thursday, & Friday, October 5th, 6th, and 7th, 1853. Cleveland, 1854.

Reports from the New York Woman's Rights Convention held at Rochester, New York, November 30th and December 1, 1853. Rochester, 1854.

Proceedings of the Seventh National Woman's Rights Convention, held in New York City, at the Broadway Tabernacle, on Tuesday and Wednesday, Nov. 25th and 26th, 1856. New York, 1856.

Proceedings of the Free Convention held at Rutland, Vt., June 25th, 26th, 27th, 1858. Boston, 1858.

Report of the Woman's Rights Meeting at Mercantile Hall, May 27th, 1859. Boston, 1859.

Proceedings of the Tenth National Woman's Rights Convention, held at the Cooper Institute, New York City, May 10th & 11th, 1860. Boston, 1860.

Proceedings of the Meeting of the Loyal Women of the Republic held in New York, May 14, 1863. New York, 1863.

Proceedings of the Eleventh National Woman's Rights Convention held at the Church of the Puritans, New York, May 10, 1866. New York, 1866.

Proceedings of the First Anniversary of the American Equal Rights Association held at the Church of the Puritans, New York, May 9 and 10, 1867. New York, 1867.

National Woman Suffrage Association Report of the Sixteenth Annual Washington Convention, March 4th, 5th, 6th, and 7th, 1884. Rochester, 1884.

Works Cited

Alonso, Harriet Hyman. *Peace as a Women's Issue: A History of the U.S. Movement for World Peace and Women's Rights.* Syracuse: Syracuse Univ. Press, 1993.

Alpern, Sara, et al., eds. *The Challenge of Feminist Biography.* Urbana: Univ. of Illinois Press, 1992.

Anderson, Bonnie. *Joyous Greetings: The First International Women's Movement, 1832–60.* New York: Harper Collins, forthcoming.

Anthony, Susan B., and Ida Husted Harper, eds. *The History of Woman Suffrage.* Vol. 4. Indianapolis: Hollenbeck Press, 1902.

Ascher, Carol, Louise DeSalvo, and Sara Ruddick, eds. *Between Women.* Boston: Beacon Press, 1984.

Bacon, Margaret Hope. "By Moral Force Alone: The Antislavery Women and Nonresistance." In *The Abolitionist Sisterhood: Women's Political Culture in Antebellum America,* edited by Jean Fagan Yellin and John C. Van Horne, 275–301. Ithaca, N.Y.: Cornell Univ. Press, 1994.

———. *I Speak for My Slave Sister: The Life of Abby Kelley Foster.* New York: Crowell, 1974.

———. *Valiant Friend: The Life of Lucretia Mott.* New York: Walker, 1980.

Banner, Lois. "Biography and Autobiography: Intermixing the Genres." *a/b: Auto/Biography Studies* (Fall 1993): 159–79.

Barnard, L. E. "Mrs. Ernestine L. Rose." *Liberator* (May 16, 1856). Reprint. *Boston Investigator* (July 9, 1856; Feb. 14, 1877). Reprint. *HSW* 1: 95–100.

Barnes, Gilbert H. *The Antislavery Impulse, 1830–1844.* 1933. Reprint. New York: Harcourt, Brace and World, 1964.

Barry, Kathleen. *Susan B. Anthony: A Biography of a Singular Feminist.* New York, New York Univ. Press, 1988.

Basch, Françoise. *Rebelles Americaines: Mariage, Amour Libre et Feminisme.* Paris: Meridiens-Klincksiek, 1990.

Basch, Norma. *In the Eyes of the Law: Women, Marriage, and Property in Nineteenth-Century New York.* Ithaca, N.Y.: Cornell Univ. Press, 1982.

Bassett, T. D. Seymour. "The Secular Utopian Socialists." In *Socialism and American Life*, edited by Donald O. Egbert and Stow Persons. Princeton: Princeton Univ. Press, 1952.

Beecher, Jonathan. *Charles Fourier: The Visionary and His World.* Berkeley: Univ. of California Press, 1986.

Bell, Susan, and Marilyn Yalom, eds. *Revealing Lives.* New York: State Univ. of New York Press, 1990.

Bender, Thomas. *New York Intellect: A History of Intellectual Life in New York City.* New York: Knopf, 1987.

Berg, Barbara J. *The Remembered Gate: Origins of American Feminism.* New York: Oxford Univ. Press, 1978.

Bester, Arthur. *Backwoods Utopias: The Sectarian Origins and the Owenite Phase of Communitarian Socialism in America.* Philadelphia: Univ. of Pennsylvania Press, 1970.

Blackwell, Alice Stone. *Lucy Stone: Pioneer of Woman's Rights.* Boston: Little, Brown, 1930.

Blatt, Martin Henry. *Free Love and Anarchism: The Biography of Ezra Heywood.* Urbana: Univ. of Illinois Press, 1989.

Bogin, Ruth, and Jean Fagan Yellin. "Introduction." In *The Abolitionist Sisterhood: Women's Political Culture in Antebellum America,* edited by Jean Fagan Yellin and John C. Van Horne, 1–19. Ithaca, N.Y.: Cornell Univ. Press, 1994.

Branch, Edward Douglas. *The Sentimental Years: 1836–1860.* New York: Appleton-Century, 1934.

Braude, Ann. *Radical Spirits: Spiritualism and Women's Rights in Nineteenth-Century America.* Boston: Beacon Press, 1989.

Buhle, Mari Joe, and Paul Buhle. *The Concise History of Woman Suffrage.* Urbana: Univ. of Illinois Press, 1978.

Burkett, Nancy. *Abby Kelley Foster and Stephen S. Foster.* Worcester: Worcester Bicentennial Commission, 1976.

Burns, William. *Life in New York*. New York, 1851.

Campbell, Karlyn Kohrs. *Man Cannot Speak for Her*. Vol. 1. New York: Greenwood Press, 1989.

————, ed. *Women Public Speakers in the United States, 1800–1925*. Westport, Conn.: Greenwood Press, 1993.

Cazden, Elizabeth. *Antoinette Brown Blackwell: A Biography*. Old Westbury, N.Y.: Feminist Press, 1983.

Chadwick, John White, ed. *A Life for Liberty: Anti-Slavery and Other Letters of Sallie Holley*. 1899. Reprint. New York: Negro Univ. Press, 1969.

Chambers-Schiller, Lee. " 'A Good work among the People': The Political Culture of the Boston Antislavery Fair." In *The Abolitionist Sisterhood: Women's Political Culture in Antebellum America*, edited by Jean Fagan Yellin and John C. Van Horne, 249–75. Ithaca, N.Y.: Cornell Univ. Press, 1994.

Chevigny, Belle Gale. "Daughters Writing: Toward a Theory of Women's Biography." *Feminist Studies* (Spring 1983): 79–103.

Claeys, Gregory. *Citizens and Saints: Politics and Anti-Politics in Early British Socialism*. Cambridge: Cambridge Univ. Press, 1989.

Clark, Christopher. *The Communitarian Movement: The Radical Challenge of the Northampton Association*. Ithaca, N.Y.: Cornell Univ. Press, 1995.

Clark, Elizabeth. "The Politics of God and the Woman's Vote." Ph.D. diss., Princeton Univ., 1989.

Cockrell, Dale, ed. *Excelsior: Journals of the Hutchinson Family Singers, 1842–1846*. Stuyvesant, N.Y.: Pendragon Press, 1989.

Cole, George D. H. *The Life of Robert Owen*. London: Macmillan, 1960.

Conrad, Charles. "Ernestine Potowski Rose." In *Women Public Speakers in the United States, 1800–1925*, edited by Karlyn Kohrs Campbell, 350–68. New York: Greenwood Press, 1989.

————. "The Transformation of the 'Old Feminist' Movement." *Quarterly Journal of Speech* 67(1981): 284–97.

Conway, Jill. "Women Reformers and American Culture, 1870–1930." *Journal of Social History* (Winter 1971–72): 164–78.

Cott, Nancy. *Bonds of Womanhood*. New Haven, Conn.: Yale Univ. Press, 1977.

————. *Root of Bitterness*. Boston: Little, Brown, 1972.

Cromwell, Otelia. *Lucretia Mott*. New York: Russell and Russell, 1958.

Dare, Philip N. *American Communes to 1860: A Bibliography*. New York: Garland, 1990.

Davis, Paulina Wright. *A History of the National Woman's Rights Movement, for Twenty Years.* New York: Journey-men Printers' Co-operative, 1871.

D'Hericourt, Jenny. "Madame Rose." *La Revue Philosophique et Religieuse.* 1856: 129–39.

——— "Mrs. Ernestine L. Rose." *Boston Investigator* (Dec. 8, 1869).

Douglas, Ann. *The Feminization of American Culture.* New York: Knopf, 1977.

Dubois, Ellen Carol. *Feminism and Suffrage: The Emergence of an Independent Women's Movement in America.* Ithaca, N.Y.: Cornell Univ. Press, 1978.

———, ed. *Elizabeth Cady Stanton, Susan B. Anthony: Correspondence, Writings, Speeches.* New York: Schocken, 1981.

Dumond, Dwight L. *Antislavery: The Crusade for Freedom in America.* Ann Arbor: Univ. of Michigan Press, 1961.

Elkins, Stanley. *Slavery: A Problem in American Institutional and Intellectual Life.* 1959. Chicago: Univ. of Chicago Press, 1976.

Epstein, William H., ed. *Contesting the Subject: Essays in the Postmodern Theory and Practice of Biography and Biographical Criticism.* West Lafayette, Ind.: Purdue Univ. Press, 1991.

Ernst, Robert. *Immigrant Life in New York City, 1825–1863.* New York: Kings Crown Press, 1949.

Evans, Sara M. *Born for Liberty: A History of Women in America.* New York: Free Press, 1989.

Flexner, Eleanor. *Century of Struggle: The Woman's Rights Movement in the United States.* New York: Atheneum, 1973.

French, Roderick. "Liberation from Man and God in Boston: Abner Kneeland's Free-Thought Campaign." *American Quarterly* 32 (1980): 202–21.

Friedman, Lawrence Jacob. *Gregarious Saints: Self and Community in American Abolitionism, 1830–70.* New York: Cambridge Univ. Press, 1982.

Frothingham, Octavius Brooks. *Gerrit Smith, A Biography.* New York: G. P. Putman's Sons, 1878.

Garnett, Ronald George. *Co-operation and the Owenite Socialist Communities in Britain, 1825–45.* Manchester, Eng.: Manchester Univ. Press, 1972.

Garrison, Dee. "Two Roads Taken: Writing the Biography of Mary Heaton Vorse." In *The Challenge of Feminist Biography*, edited by Sara Alpern et al., 65–79. Urbana: Univ. of Illinois Press, 1992.

Garrison, William Lloyd. *Letters.* Ed. Walter Merrill. 6 Vols. Cambridge: Belknap Press of Harvard, 1971–81.

Ginzberg, Lori D. *Women and the Work of Benevolence: Morality, Politics, and Class in the Nineteenth-Century United States.* New Haven: Yale Univ. Press, 1990.

Glückel of Hameln. *Memoirs of Glückel of Hameln.* Trans. Marvin Lowenthal. New York: Schocken Books, 1977.

Greeley, Horace. *Recollections of a Busy Life.* New York: J. B. Ford, 1868.

Griffith, Elisabeth. *In Her Own Right: The Life of Elizabeth Cady Stanton.* New York: Oxford Univ. Press, 1984.

Grimké, Angelina. *Appeal to the Christian Women of the South.* New York: American Anti-Slavery Society, 1836.

Grimké, Sarah. *Letters on the Equality of the Sexes and the Condition of Woman.* Boston: I. Knapp, 1838.

Guarneri, Carl J. *The Utopian Alternative: Fourierism in Nineteenth-Century America.* Ithaca, N.Y.: Cornell Univ. Press, 1984.

Gurko, Miriam. *The Ladies of Seneca Falls.* New York: Schocken Books, 1976.

Hallowell, Anna Davis, ed. *James and Lucretia Mott: Life and Letters.* Boston: Houghton Mifflin, 1884.

Hamm, Thomas D. *God's Government Begun: The Society for Universal Inquiry and Reform, 1842–46.* Bloomington: Indiana Univ. Press, 1995.

Harper, Ida Husted. *The Life and Work of Susan B. Anthony.* 3 vols. Indianapolis: Bowen-Merrill, 1889–99; 1908.

Harrison, J.F.C. *Quest for the New Moral World: Robert Owen and the Owenites in Britain and America.* New York: Scribner's, 1969.

Harvey, Roland Hill. *Robert Owen, Social Idealist.* Berkeley and Los Angeles: Univ. of California Press, 1949.

Herttell, Thomas. *Remarks Comprising in Substance Judge Herttell's Argument.* 1839. Boston: J. P. Mendum, 1867.

Hewitt, Nancy. "On Their Own Terms: A Historiographical Essay." In *The Abolitionist Sisterhood: Women's Political Culture in Antebellum America,* edited by Jean Fagan Yellin and John C. Van Horne, 23–31. Ithaca, N.Y.: Cornell Univ. Press, 1994.

———. *Women's Activism and Social Change: Rochester, New York, 1822–1872.* Ithaca, N.Y.: Cornell Univ. Press, 1984.

Heyrick, Elizabeth. *Immediate not Gradual Abolition of Slavery.* London, 1842.

Homberger, Eric, and John Charmley, eds. *The Troubled Face of Biography.* New York: St. Martin's, 1988.

Irwin, Inez Haynes. *Angels and Amazons: A Hundred Years of American Women.* New York: Doubleday, 1934.

Johnson, Linck C. "Reforming the Reformers: Emerson, Thoreau, and the Sunday Lectures at Amory Hall, Boston." *ESQ* (1991): 235–89.

Kaplan, Marion A. *The Making of the Jewish Middle Class: Women, Family, and Identity, in Imperial Germany.* New York: Oxford Univ. Press, 1991.

Karcher, Carolyn. *The First Woman in the Republic: A Cultural Biography of Lydia Maria Child.* Durham, N.C.: Duke Univ. Press, 1994.

Kerr, Andrea Moore. *Lucy Stone: Speaking Out for Equality.* New Jersey: Rutgers Univ. Press, 1992.

Kolmerten, Carol. *Women in Utopia: The Ideology of Gender in the American Owenite Communities.* Bloomington: Indiana Univ. Press, 1990.

Kraditor, Aileen. *Means and Ends in American Abolitionism.* New York: Pantheon Books, 1969.

———. *Up from the Pedestal.* Chicago: Quadrangle Books, 1968.

Lasser, Carol, and Marlene Deahl Merrill, eds. *Friends and Sisters: Letters Between Lucy Stone and Antoinette Brown Blackwell, 1846–93.* Urbana: Univ. of Illinois Press.

Leopold, Richard William. *Robert Dale Owen, A Biography.* Cambridge, Mass.: Harvard Univ. Press, 1940.

Lerner, Elinor. "Jewish Involvement in the New York City Woman Suffrage Movement." *American Jewish History* (1981): 442–61.

Lerner, Gerda. *The Grimké Sisters from South Carolina.* Boston: Houghton, 1967.

———. *Women and History.* New York: Oxford Univ. Press, 1986.

Leslie, Edmund. *Skaneateles.* New York, 1902.

Levy, Leonard. *Blasphemy in Massachusetts: Freedom of Conscience and the Abner Kneeland Case.* New York: DeCapo Press, 1973.

Lewis, Henry. "Ernestine Rose: First Jewish Advocate of Women's Rights." *Forward* June 19, 1927.

Lutz, Alma. *Crusade for Freedom: Women of the Antislavery Movement.* Boston: Beacon Press, 1968.

———. *Susan B. Anthony.* Boston: Beacon Press, 1960.

Macdonald, George E. *Fifty Years of Freethought.* 2 vols. New York: Arno Press, 1972.

Malmgreen, Gail. *Neither Bread nor Roses: Utopian Feminists and the English Working Class, 1800–1850.* Brighton, Eng.: Noyce, 1978.

May, Samuel J. *Memoir of Samuel Joseph May.* Boston, 1873.

———. "The Rights and Condition of Women." Syracuse, 1846.

M'Knight, James. "A Discourse Exposing Robert Owen's System as Practiced by the Franklin Community at Haverstraw." New York, 1826.

Melder, Keith E. "Abby Kelley and the Process of Liberation." In *The Abolitionist Sisterhood: Women's Political Culture in Antebellum America,* edited by Jean Fagan Yellin and John C. Van Horne, 231–49. Ithaca, N.Y.: Cornell Univ. Press, 1994.

———. *Beginnings of Sisterhood: The American Woman's Rights Movement, 1800–1850.* New York: Schocken Books, 1977.

———. "The Beginnings of the Women's Rights Movement." Ph.D. diss., Yale Univ., 1965.

Mill, Harriet Taylor. "Enfranchisement of Women." *Westminster and Foreign Quarterly Review* 55, no. 2 (1850): 289–311.

Miller, Sally M. *The Radical Immigrant.* New York: Twayne, 1974.

Mott, Lucretia. *Discourse on Women.* Philadelphia, 1850.

Neidle, Cecyle. *America's Immigrant Women.* Boston: Twain, 1974.

O'Brien, Sharon. "Feminist Theory and Literary Biography." In *Contesting the Subject: Essays in the Postmodern Theory and Practice of Biography and Biographical Criticism,* edited by William H. Epstein, 123–33. West Lafayette, Ind.: Purdue Univ. Press, 1991.

O'Connor, Lillian. *Pioneer Women Orators: Rhetoric in the Antebellum Reform Movement.* New York: Columbia Univ. Press, 1954.

O'Neill, William L. *Everyone Was Brave: A History of Feminism in America.* Chicago: Quadrangle Books, 1969.

Owen, Robert. *The Life of Robert Owen, by Himself.* New York: Knopf, 1920.

Owen, Robert Dale. *Treading My Way.* New York, 1874.

Palmer, Elihu. *Principles of Nature.* London, 1819.

Pease, Jane H., and William H. Pease. *Bound with Them in Chains: A Biographical History of the Antislavery Movement.* Westport, Conn.: Greenwood Press, 1972.

Perry, Lewis. *Radical Abolitionism: Anarchy and the Government of God in Antislavery Thought.* Ithaca, N.Y.: Cornell Univ. Press, 1973.

Podmore, Frank. *Robert Owen, A Biography.* New York: D. Appleton, 1924.

Post, Albert. *Popular Freethought in America, 1825–1850.* New York: Columbia Univ. Press, 1943.

Pugh, Sarah. *Memorial of Sarah Pugh.* Philadelphia, 1888.

Putnam, Samuel P. *Four Hundred Years of Freethought.* New York: The TruthSeeker Company, 1894.

Reps, John W. *Washington on View: The Nation's Capital since 1790.* Chapel Hill: Univ. of North Carolina Press, 1991.

Reynolds, David S. *Walt Whitman's America: A Cultural Biography.* New York: Alfred A. Knopf, 1995.

Roberts, Mary L. "Ernestine L. Rose and Frances Wright: Free Thinkers and Feminists." M.A. thesis, Sarah Lawrence College, 1980.

Rose, Ernestine L. "A Defense of Atheism, being a lecture delivered at Mercantile Hall, Boston, April 10, 1861." Boston, 1889.

————. "An Address on Woman's Rights, delivered before the People's sunday Meeting in Cochituate Hall . . . October 19, 1851." Boston, 1851.

————. "Review of Horace Mann's Two Lectures, delivered in New York, February 17th and 29th, 1852." Boston, 1852

————. "A Speech of Mrs. Rose, a Polish Lady, at the Anniversary Paine Celebration in New York, January 29, 1850." New York, 1850.

————. "Two Addresses delivered by Ernestine L. Rose at the Bible Convention, held in Hartford, Conn in June, 1854." Boston, 1888.

Rudnick, Lois. "The Male Identified Woman and Other Anxieties: The Life of Mabel Dodge Luhan." In *The Challenge of Feminist Biography,* edited by Sara Alpern et al., 116–39. Urbana: Univ. of Illinois Press, 1992.

Ryan, Mary P. *Women in Public: Between Banners and Ballots, 1825–1880.* Baltimore: Johns Hopkins Univ. Press, 1990.

Russo, Ann, and Cheris Kramarac. *The Radical Women's Press of the 1850s.* New York: Routledge, 1991.

Sargant, William. *Robert Owen and His Social Philosophy.* 1860. New York: AMS Press, 1971.

Schappes, Morris. "Ernestine Rose: Her Address on the Anniversary of West Indian Emancipation." *Journal of Negro History* (July, 1949): 344–55.

————. "Ernestine Rose, Queen of the Platform." *Jewish Life* (March, 1949): 7–10.

Scott, Joan Wallach. *Only Paradoxes to Offer: French Feminists and the Rights of Man.* Cambridge, Mass.: Harvard Univ. Press, 1996.

Seller, Maxine Schwartz, ed. *Immigrant Women.* Philadelphia: Temple Univ. Press, 1981.

Sharistanian, Janet. "Introduction: Feminism, Biography, Theory." *a/b: Auto/Biography Studies.* (Fall, 1993): 155–58.

Sherr, Lynn. *Failure Is Impossible: Susan B. Anthony in Her Own Words.* New York: Random House, 1995.

Sklar, Kathryn Kish. "Coming to Terms with Florence Kelley: The Tale of the Reluctant Biographer." In *The Challenge of Feminist Biography,* edited by Sara Alpern et al., 17–34. Urbana: Univ. of Illinois Press, 1992.

———. *Florence Kelley and the Nation's Work: The Rise of Women's Political Culture, 1830–1900.* New Haven: Yale Univ. Press, 1995.

———. "Women Who Speak for an Entire Nation: American and British Women at the World-Slavery Convention, London, 1840." In *The Abolitionist Sisterhood: Women's Political Culture in Antebellum America,* edited by Jean Fagan Yellin and John C. Van Horne, 301–35. Ithaca, N.Y.: Cornell Univ. Press, 1994.

Smith, Page. *Daughters of the Promised Land.* Boston: Little, Brown, 1970.

Smith-Rosenberg, Carroll. "The Female World of Love and Ritual: Relations Between Women in Nineteenth-Century America." *Signs* 1(1975): 1–29.

Sorin, Gerald. *The New York Abolitionists: A Case Study of Political Radicalism.* Westport, Conn.: Greenwood, 1971.

Spann, Edward K. *Brotherly Tomorrows: Movements for a Cooperative Society in America, 1820–1920.* New York: Columbia Univ. Press, 1989.

Speicher, Anna. " 'Faith Which Worketh By Love': The Religious World of Female Antislavery Lecturers." Ph.D. diss., George Washington Univ., 1996.

Stansell, Christine. *City of Women: Sex and Class in New York, 1789–1860.* Urbana: Univ. of Illinois Press, 1986.

Stanton, Elizabeth Cady. "An Address of Mrs. Elizabeth Cady Stanton, delivered at Seneca Falls and Rochester, New York, July 19th & August 2d, 1848." New York, 1870.

———. *Eighty Years and More.* New York: European Publishing Co., 1898.

Stanton, Elizabeth Cady, Susan B. Anthony, and Matilda Joslyn Gage, eds. *The History of Woman Suffrage.* 3 vols. New York: Fowler and Wells, 1881–86.

Sterling, Dorothy. *Ahead of Her Time: Abby Kelley and the Politics of Anti-Slavery.* New York: Norton, 1991.

Suhl, Yuri. *Ernestine L. Rose: Women's Rights Pioneer.* 1959 (as *Ernestine L. Rose and the Battle for Human Rights.* New York: Biblio Press, 1990.

Swerdlow, Amy. "Abolition's Conservative Sisters: The Ladies' New York City Anti-Slavery Societies, 1834–1840." In *The Abolitionist Sisterhood: Women's Political Culture in Antebellum America,* edited by Jean Fagan Yellin and John C. Van Horne, 31–45. Ithaca, N.Y.: Cornell Univ. Press, 1994.

Taylor, Barbara. *Eve and the New Jerusalem: Socialism and Feminism in the Nineteenth Century.* New York: Pantheon Books, 1983.

Thompson, William. *An Inquiry into the Principles of the Distribution of Wealth.* 1824. New York: Burt Franklin, 1968.

Turner, James. *Without God, Without Creed: The Origins of Unbelief in America.* Baltimore: Johns Hopkins Univ. Press, 1985.

Tyler, Anbinder. *Nativism and Slavery: The Northern Know Nothings and the Politics of the 1850s.* New York: Oxford Univ. Press, 1992.

Underwood, Sara. *The Heroines of Free Thought.* New York: Charles Somerby. 1876.

Van Broekhoven, Deborah Bingham. "Let Your Names Be Enrolled: Method and Ideology in Women's Antislavery Petitioning." In *The Abolitionist Sisterhood: Women's Political Culture in Antebellum America,* edited by Jean Fagan Yellin and John C. Van Horne, 159–201. Ithaca, N.Y.: Cornell Univ. Press, 1994.

Walker, Cheryl. "Feminist Literary Criticism and the Author." *Critical Inquiry* 16 (1990): 551–71.

Walters, Ronald G. *American Reformers, 1815–1860.* New York: Hill and Wang, 1978.

Ward, Susan Hayes. *The History of the Broadway Tabernacle Church.* New York, 1901.

Warren, Sidney. *American Freethought, 1860–1914.* New York: Gordian Press, 1966.

Wheeler, Marjorie Spruill. *One Woman, One Vote: Rediscovering the Woman Suffrage Movement.* Troutdale, Ore.: NewSage Press, 1995.

Whitman, Walt. "Notes and Fragments." In *Complete Prose Works,* edited by Richard M. Bucke. New York: G. P. Putnam's Sons, 1902.

Wilentz, Sean. *Chants Democratic: New York City and the Rise of the American Working Class, 1788–1850.* New York: Oxford Univ. Press, 1984.

Williams, Carolyn. "The Female Antislavery Movement: Fighting Against Racial Prejudice and Promoting Women's Rights in Antebellum

America." In *The Abolitionist Sisterhood: Women's Political Culture in Antebellum America,* edited by Jean Fagan Yellin and John C. Van Horne, 159–79. Ithaca, N.Y.: Cornell Univ. Press, 1994.

Wollstonecraft, Mary. *Thoughts on the Education of Daughters with Reflections on Female Conduct in the More Important Duties of Life.* London, 1787.

Yellin, Jean Fagan and John C. Van Horne, eds. *The Abolitionist Sisterhood: Women's Political Culture in Antebellum America.* Ithaca, N.Y.: Cornell Univ. Press, 1994.

———. *Women and Sisters: The Antislavery Feminists in American Culture.* New Haven: Yale Univ. Press, 1989.

Index

References to frequently cited sources, such as other biographers of Rose or newspapers in which Rose's speeches were printed, are cited in the index only when they are discussed.

—*Reactions to Rose*, xvii, xxiii, 35–
36, 50–51, 66–67, 81, 84, 87,
100–101, 109, 119, 125, 126,
129, 132, 136–37, 138–39,
143–45, 151, 154, 158–59,
163–64, 165–67, 169, 172,
178, 184n. 2, 211, 215, 221–
22, 225, 244n. 17, 258, 268
—*Rose's opinions on*: abolitionism,
58, 65–66, 170; atheism, 228–
31; belief, 107; Bible, 65, 96,
106, 229; capitalism, 34, 48,
54, 132n. 1, 147; Civil War,
231–32; community, 47, 98n.
25, 151; conventions, 192, 199,
202, 216–17; Declaration of
Independence, xxviii, 55, 65, 70,
86, 110, 162, 165, 167, 246,
267; divorce, 121–23, 176,
200–201, 219–21; education,
79, 89, 162n. 7, 168, 171–72,
176, 196, 210; Emancipation
Proclamation, 236; England,
186–87, 194–95; equality, 2, 19,
24, 39, 43–44, 54–55, 58, 69–
70, 98n. 25, 109, 111, 120,
162, 170, 187; France, 188–89,
195; free love, 253, 253n. 24;
God, 229–30; government, 48,
56; human rights, 104, 109,
111, 162, 203, 234–35;
individualism, 132; Jews, 238–41
passim; laws, 66, 85, 93, 116–
18, 123–25, 131, 146–47, 168,
168–69, 170, 194, 197; marriage,
79, 85, 108, 196, 206–7, 218;
married women's property rights,
33, 37, 54n. 13, 116, 165, 197,
217; men, 79, 121, 145, 174,
186; national organizations, 99;
politics, 194; private property,
50, 52; professions, 132, 146,
150; prostitution, 122–23, 172;
reason, 24, 86, 91; reform,

250–51; religion, 41–43, 49, 78,
95, 96–97, 106, 150, 170, 174–
75, 212, 223–24, 230, 268,
270; slavery, 110–11, 145, 212,
228, 232, 236; socialism, 34,
54, 54n. 13, 122, 132n. 1;
spiritualism, 154–56, 186, 209,
223; truth, 79, 80, 91; universal
suffrage, 235, 245–46, 247,
252–54, 262; woman's nature,
80, 85–86, 91–92, 93, 97–99,
168, 174; woman's rights
movement, 264; woman's
sphere, xxiii, 49, 80, 85–86, 93,
95–96, 98, 101, 120, 196;
women's rights, 47, 49–50, 70,
81, 84–87, 93, 101, 111, 120,
122, 145, 150, 167, 235
Rose, William, 9, 19, 39, 39n. 3,
41, 51, 55; death, 268; importance to freethought movement,
267n. 5; occupation, 3; support
for Ernestine, xxiv, 33, 153–54,
173–74, 206–7, 208, 228, 256
Rousseau, Jean Jacques, 10
Royal, Anna, 148
Ruddick, Sara, xxin. 4
Rudnick, Lois, xxvii
Russo, Ann, 250n. 22
Ryan, Mary P., 21n. 26, 36
Rynders, Captain, 66–67

Sargent, William, 10n. 13
Say, Lucy Sistaire, 30n. 34
Schappes, Morris, xviii, 110n. 5
Scott, Joan Wallach, xxin. 4, 84n.
14
Seaver, Horace, 55, 163, 178, 201,
204, 207, 211, 231, 256, 263,
267, 269, 271; debate with
Rose, 238–41. *See also* Rose,
Ernestine
Second Great Awakening, 25, 73

Secular reform, 24n. 30
Sedgwick, Catharine, 76
Seneca Falls. *See* Woman's rights
　conventions
Seward, William, 225, 225n. 8
Shaker communities, 44
Skaneateles community, 44, 46–47,
　51–55, 98n. 25
Sklar, Kathryn Kish, xx, 58n. 16,
　59n. 18, 63n. 21, 65n. 24
Smith, Adam, 11, 132n. 1
Smith, Ann, 147
Smith, Elizabeth Oakes, 88
Smith, Gerrit, 94, 96, 147
Smith, Page, xviii
Smith-Rosenberg, Carroll, 134
Social Reform Convention (Boston
　1844), 48, 53n. 12
Social Reform Societies. *See*
　Owenism
Socialism, 15, 43, 53n. 12, 54. *See
　also* Rose, Ernestine
Socialland community, 19
Society for Moral Philanthropists,
　2, 26, 32
Spann, Edward K., 44n. 4
Speicher, Anna, 78, 90n. 17
Spiritualism, 53n. 12, 142, 154–56,
　204, 205–6. *See also* Rose,
　Ernestine
Stansell, Christine, 22n. 27, 95,
　123
Stanton, Elizabeth Cady, xviiin. 3,
　xxii, 24, 39n. 2, 63, 74, 77, 79,
　83n. 12, 84, 96n. 24, 121n. 15,
　128n. 19, 135–36, 160, 210,
　216, 218n. 5, 227, 243, 251;
　American Equal Rights Associa-
　tion, 246–47, 248, 252; and
　Susan B. Anthony, 133; on
　divorce, 217–19, 219–23 *passim*,
　221n. 6; Fifteenth Amendment,
　242, 250; *History of Woman*

Suffrage, 75–76, 87, 269n. 6;
　National Woman's Suffrage
　Association, 255–56; racial
　arguments for women's suffrage,
　246–48, 249–50, 254–55; and
　Ernestine Rose, 133–34, 269,
　269n. 6; Woman's National
　Loyal League, 232, 233, 237.
　See also Rose, Ernestine
Stanton, Henry, 63, 216, 218n. 5
Sterling, Dorothy, 46n. 7, 64n. 23,
　68, 90n. 17
Stevens, Thaddeus, 242
Stone, Lucy, xxii, 39n. 2, 64, 64n.
　23, 65, 72, 75–76, 77, 78, 78n.
　7, 79, 83n. 12, 84, 94–95, 95n.
　22, 95n. 23, 104, 118, 118n.
　13, 119, 120, 121n. 15, 124n.
　16, 152, 160, 161, 162, 163,
　165, 171, 175–76, 182, 191,
　192, 198, 221, 245, 254–55,
　255; American Equal Rights
　Association, 248, 252; American
　Woman Suffrage Association,
　264; Woman's National Loyal
　League, 233
Stowe, Harriet Beecher, 148; *Uncle
　Tom's Cabin*, 69, 96n. 24, 163;
　"Uncle Tom's Cabin," 112
Suffrage, 214–56 *passim*; Negro,
　212; universal, 31, 84, 242,
　244–48 *passim*; women's and
　female, 77, 81, 99, 165, 245
Suhl, Isabelle, xxv
Suhl, Yuri, xviiin. 3, xxv–xxvii,

Tammany Hall, 30, 32, 34, 41
Tappan, Arthur, 23, 62, 148
Tappan, Juliana, 23
Tappan, Lewis, 23, 62, 63
Taylor, Barbara, 18n. 18
Taylor, George, 53n. 12